Britain Faces Europe

BRITAIN
FACES
EUROPE

Robert L. Pfaltzgraff, Jr.

University of Pennsylvania Press
Philadelphia, 19104

To my parents

A Foreign Policy Research Institute book

INTRODUCTION

Since World War II British thought on foreign policy has undergone a drastic transformation. During the first decade after the war British policymakers and non-governmental elites sought to pare Britain's international commitments, but without abandoning their conception of Britain as a power with interests in many parts of the world. In the decade between 1957 and 1967, however, Englishmen questioned and, in many cases, rejected earlier conceptions of Britain's foreign policy. In place of once widely shared beliefs about the importance of worldwide interests in the Commonwealth and a special relationship with the United States, a broadly-based "European" consensus emerged in Britain. The development of such a consensus in Britain, an object of examination in this volume, represents the substitution of regional European interests for the global perspective which once guided British foreign policy.

How does a people, especially one with a history of worldwide interests and commitments, reconcile itself to such drastically altered circumstances as those to which the British since World War II have had to adapt? How does a people which historically has viewed with disfavor, and even hostility, the unification of continental Europe, reformulate its foreign priorities so as to assign a place of primary importance to participation in the European integration movement? The study of the development of a European consensus in Britain is an examination of both the shift in British foreign policy and the process by which governmental leaders and other relevant elites decided to join the European Economic Community (EEC).[1] Undoubtedly, however, there are many kinds of circumstances in which a people choose to join

---

[1] In this study the term "elite" is used to mean (a) groups whose views the government regularly solicits on issues of major importance, including the Confederation of British Industry, the National Farmers Union, and the Trades Union Congress; and (b) groups whose views are widely and regularly disseminated both in official and public circles, including the press, and the statements of the leaders of major political groups and their principal members.

a political or economic unit larger than that in which they have held membership.[2] In Britain, support for the Common Market was based largely upon a series of expectations of gain or, stated negatively, expectations of loss from non-participation. Decision-makers as well as the leaders of interest groups, political parties, and other elites may choose or reject membership in a political or economic unit beyond the nation-state in accordance with the specific gains or losses they envisage from such a course of action. In this study, integration is viewed as a process in which the government, together with groups in the private sector, accepts membership in an institution beyond the nation-state. Membership in such an institution, as in the case of the European Community, places the following kinds of constraints on the national unit: (1) the abandonment or adjustment of national policies to conform with policies of the unit beyond the nation-state; (2) restrictions on the authority of the member-state in relationships with non-member states; (3) participation in a decision-making unit in which weighted-majority voting, rather than unanimity, prevails, at least on certain categories of issues; and (4) development of policies by the unit beyond the nation-state in specified sectors of activity, such as agriculture and transport in the economic sector.

The focal point of this study is the response of the British government to changing international and domestic environments, including demands by domestic elite groups. Statements of expectations in written and oral pronouncements both at the governmental and private levels provide one focal point for studying the integrative process. In fact, in Britain the absence of opposition from elites, interest groups, and a majority of the general public was one necessary pre-condition for a successful governmental policy for Common Market membership. At the time of the Brussels negotiations, after the first British application, divisions within Britain reduced the flexibility of the government and portrayed to the Common Market Six the image of a divided country. By the time of the second British Common Market application, the policy of the Wilson government reflected a far more broadly based consensus in favor of EEC membership. By 1967 the problems facing Britain's Common Market candidacy stemmed from factors other than

---

[2] Among the studies of political integration, see, for example, Karl W. Deutsch, *et al., Political Community and the North Atlantic Area.* Amitai Etzioni, *Political Unification.* Ernst B. Haas, *Beyond the Nation-State: Functionalism and International Organization.* Philip E. Jacob and James V. Toscano (eds.), *The Integration of Political Communities.*

domestic opposition to EEC membership, such as the structural weakness of the British economy, the commitment to international economic policies which were more appropriate to the Britain of an earlier period, and the opposition of France to the admission of Britain to the European Community.

However important the development of broadly based domestic support for Common Market entry, the policies adopted by successive British governments in the period under examination were, of course, crucial in affecting the prospects for EEC membership. Decisions taken at the time of the formulation of the Rome Treaties placed constraints on the maneuverability of British policymakers in later years. The effort of the British government to reconcile its Commonwealth and European Free Trade Area (EFTA) commitments and interests with Common Market membership, together with Britain's special relationship with the United States, affected the range of policy options available to decision-makers. As its assessment of Britain's international political, strategic, economic, and technological position changed, the British government altered its foreign policy priorities. Thus in this study attention is focused on factors in the international environment to which British decision-makers responded in framing their policy toward Common Market membership.

Although the student of British political problems has available sources of data which are lacking in, for example, studies of developing countries, there are serious gaps in information even in the study of "developed" political systems such as that of Britain. Much relevant data on communications within the British government, or on relations between the official sector and key interest groups, are not available. In the absence of access to official memoranda which might shed light upon the decision-making process but remain classified, the student of politics must often rely upon less than perfect information, together with whatever professional judgment he is able to bring to bear upon problems of such importance as the reorientation of British policy from a global to a European framework. Despite such limitations, it may be possible, by means of a study such as this, to add to knowledge not only about the nature and growth of support for, and opposition to, integration at the international level, but also to shed light upon the domestic and international forces in response to which Britain altered her policy in the decade between 1957 and 1967.

The author is indebted to the Penfield Fund, University of Pennsylvania, for a grant which enabled him to spend several months in

Britain during the academic year 1962–63. For research conducted in Britain in 1965 and 1966 and in the preparation of this manuscript, the author received assistance from the Foreign Policy Research Institute, whose studies in European-Atlantic relationships have been generously supported by a grant from the A. W. Mellon Educational and Charitable Trust.

Although the author alone is responsible for judgments expressed in this study, he benefited from the valuable insights provided by the following persons whom he interviewed: Richard Bailey, then Director, Political and Economic Planning, London; Paul Bareau, Editor, The *Statist;* R. Colin Beever, Secretary, Labour Committee for Europe; Miss Nora Beloff, The *Observer;* Miss Ursula Branston, Conservative Research Centre; Alastair Buchan, then Director, Institute for Strategic Studies; Mrs. Miriam Camps, Political and Economic Planning; John Cockcroft, Guest, Keen and Nettleford (GKN) Industries; Mrs. Elma Dangerfield, Executive Editor, *European-Atlantic Review;* Sir Geoffry de Freitas, M.P.; W. de Hoghton, Confederation of British Industry; François Duchène, The *Economist;* David Ennals, M.P.; J. Felgate, Confederation of British Industry; J. Forsyth, British Iron and Steel Federation; Murray Forsyth, Political and Economic Planning; Richard Fry, City Editor, The *Guardian;* Arthur Gaitskell; Robert Garlick, Secretary, Britain in Europe; Lionel Gelber; Peter Goldman, then Director, Conservative Political Centre; John Harris, then Director of Publicity, Labour Party; Ralph Harris, Director, Institute of Economic Affairs; J. Hills, Research Department, Trades Union Congress; David Howell, Conservative Party Headquarters, London; R. J. Jarrett, Executive Secretary, Common Market Campaign; D. Walwin Jones, Director General, United Kingdom Council of the European Movement; Uwe Kitzinger, Nuffield College, Oxford University; Christopher Layton, then Liberal Party Headquarters; Kenneth Lindsay, former Member of Parliament; S. Mukherjee, Assistant, Research and Economics Department, Trades Union Congress; John Pinder, then Director of International Operations, Economist Intelligence Unit; Roy Pryce, then Director, European Communities Office, London; Samuel Silkin, M.P.; Asher Winegarten, Chief Economist, National Farmers' Union; Frederick W. Mulley, M.P., Minister of State, Foreign Office; Albert Murray, M.P.; Peter Ramsbotham, British Embassy, Paris; P. Rotherham, Research Director, Associated Rediffusion; Andrew Shonfield, Director of Studies, Royal Institute of International Affairs; Peter Shore, Research Secretary, Labour Party; Samuel Silkin, M.P.;

Oliver Smedley, Cheap Food League; Peter Watts, Executive Secretary, Federal Union, London; Mrs. Shirley Williams, M.P., Parliamentary Secretary, Ministry of Labour.

For research assistance, the author is indebted to Miss Carol-Lee Hurley and Chander T. Rajaratnam. Mrs. Margaret Capotrio, Assistant Editor, and Robert C. Herber, Managing Editor of ORBIS, furnished editorial assistance in the preparation of the manuscript. In the typing of the manuscript Miss Lynne Koch provided invaluable help.

The author is grateful to Professor Edward G. Janosik, Chairman, Department of Political Science, State University College, Geneseo, New York, for comments and critiques, especially in the initial stages of this research. Finally, for their continuing support and encouragement, the author is indebted to Dr. Robert Strausz-Hupé and Dr. William R. Kintner, Director and Deputy Director, respectively, of the Foreign Policy Research Institute, in whose book series this volume is included.

Philadelphia, Pa.   Robert L. Pfaltzgraff, Jr.
February 1969

 # Table of Contents

Chapter 1

BRITISH FOREIGN POLICY AND EUROPEAN INTEGRATION, 1957–1961

At the end of World War II, few Englishmen questioned the place of their country in world politics. In 1945, Britain had large armies and held under her sway not only a vast empire, but huge tracts of captured territory. She was a world power without whose contributions victory might have been denied the Allies.

In less than two decades, however, Britain's international position had profoundly changed. No longer was a worldwide empire of hundreds of millions governed from Whitehall. The once vast military power became miniscule compared with that of the United States and the Soviet Union. With the advent of new military technologies, the gap between Britain and the superpowers widened, even though Britain attempted until the Suez crisis of 1956 to develop and maintain a military capability based on nuclear weapons as well as counterinsurgency and conventional forces.[1] Without rival in western Europe in 1945, Britain faced a decade later a group of Continental neighbors whose rates of economic growth surpassed her own. Certain in 1945 about Britain's place in world affairs, a decade later Englishmen had begun to question their country's national purpose, as well as the assumptions which guided British foreign policy.[2]

Seldom, if ever, do people living at a given moment in history perceive accurately the forces shaping their future. Only in retrospect does it seem possible to identify the major trends in the life of a nation at a particular time. So it was in Britain in the aftermath of World War II. Like many peoples elsewhere, the British saw their country's place in world politics in terms of their understanding of the recent and remote past. Little in history bespoke the need for British participation

---

[1] See R. N. Rosecrance, *Defense of the Realm: British Strategy in the Nuclear Epoch*, especially Ch. 7.
[2] See, for example, Arthur Koestler (ed.), *Suicide of a Nation?*, Anthony Hartley, *A State of England;* John Mander, *Great Britain or Little England?*

in the European integration movement. From the Elizabethan Age to the twentieth century, England turned primarily to the world beyond the seas for trade and expansion. Historically, the interest in the building of an overseas empire, together with the isolation from European neighbors provided by the Channel, molded to a large extent contemporary British thought about Europe. As a result, even in the mid-twentieth century, the British found it difficult to consider themselves fully "European."

Two World Wars tested and reinforced Britain's links with the rest of the English-speaking world. Her emergence from World War II, weakened but victorious, strengthened an insular pride and gave Englishmen an added confidence in the adaptability of their parliamentary institutions and in the durability of the "island race." In the decade and a half after World War II, the task of passing the legacy of British institutions and political practices to a host of dependent peoples around the world preoccupied Britain. In the Commonwealth, Britain saw herself as the leader of a worldwide association of heterogeneous peoples. The existence of the Commonwealth masked the disintegration of the British Empire and the withdrawal of Britain from regions in which she once had major commitments. Even though Commonwealth countries were no longer governed from Whitehall, British leadership of the Commonwealth, which contained hundreds of millions of people and embraced nearly one-fourth of the total territory of the world, gave to Britain at least the illusion of Great-Power status. For generations the primary objective of British foreign policy had been to safeguard the links between the Mother Country and her colonies, to oppose the unification of Europe under a hostile power, and to maintain toward her European neighbors, her principal challengers, a position of strength. Hence membership in European integrative institutions would conflict with Britain's foreign policy objectives and interests.

The destruction wrought by World War II, combined with the emergence of superpowers to the east and west, spurred continental Europeans to integrative efforts after 1945. Among those nations which had suffered widespread wartime destruction and defeat, namely, the Common Market Six, the impetus was greatest. In such nations, the need for economic and political units beyond the nation-state seemed urgent to important segments of the population. In contrast, Englishmen, their country having emerged, nominally at least, a victor in World War II, did not see the need for their government to alter its foreign policy and to assume a role of leadership in European integration. Britain's great contribution to the Allied cause had obscured the weakened position in which she emerged from World War II. Even though Britain found it necessary to cut overseas commitments to correspond with reduced capabilities, she sought to retain her position as a nation entitled to participate in the councils of the superpowers.

In the late 1960's it was fashionable to criticize postwar British foreign policy for having failed to give priority to European integration and for having attempted to do too much with too little. Although from the perspective of the 1960's the case for British entry into the Common Market appeared ever more convincing, Britain's international role of the 1945–1956 period resembled more that of a superpower than that of her continental European neighbors. In contrast to other major European powers, all of which had experienced defeat in World War II, Britain strove to maintain a worldwide presence, if on a reduced scale. Despite periodic balance of payments crises and demands in the domestic sector upon limited funds, successive governments, Labour and Conservative, devoted to defense a greater percentage of the gross national product than other West European governments. Britain fought to a successful conclusion a counterinsurgency war in Malaya. Until the Suez crisis of 1956, Britain not only maintained her special relationship with the United States, but enjoyed a considerable measure of diplomatic independence. The British took the initiative in the formation of a joint European response to the United States' offer of Marshall Plan aid. Foreign Secretary Ernest Bevin played a major role in the diplomacy leading to the Brussels Pact, which the British saw as a forerunner of The North Atlantic Treaty Organization (NATO). In the early 1950's, despite the special relationship, British policy did not always accord with that of the United States. In contrast to U.S. policy, Britain extended diplomatic recognition to Communist China and attempted, during the Korean conflict, to exert a restraining influence on the United States. In 1954 the British advised the United States against intervening militarily in the Indochina war and played a major role in the Geneva Conference. Although the failure of the European Defense Community (EDC) in 1954 is attributable in part to the unwillingness of Britain to join and thus to quiet French fears about German rearmament, the British government took the lead in proposing and negotiating an alternative. Anthony Eden revived and modified the Brussels Pact so that Germany could be rearmed and admitted to NATO without French opposition. Sir Winston Churchill and Eden were instrumental in arranging the Geneva Summit Conference of 1955.

For more than a decade after World War II, British foreign policy was based on the existence, as Churchill suggested in a speech at the 1948 Conservative Annual Conference, of three interlinked circles:

> The first circle for us is naturally the British Commonwealth and Empire, with all that that comprises. Then there is also the English-speaking world in which we, Canada, and the other British Dominions and the United States play so important a part. And finally there is United Europe.[3]

According to prevailing sentiment, British foreign policy should retain for London the freedom to maneuver in each of the three imaginary circles without becoming fully linked to any one of them, especially not to western Europe, which Churchill ranked third in his list of major British foreign policy interests. Indicative of Churchill's conception of the priorities of foreign policy was his famous statement to Charles de Gaulle during the war which the French President recounts in his wartime memoirs: "There is something you ought to know; each time we must choose between Europe and the open sea, we shall always choose the open sea. Each time I must choose between you and Roosevelt, I shall always choose Roosevelt." [4]

One reason for British opposition to full participation in the European integration movement was the notion of the inherent instability of Continental political systems as compared with Britain, with her long tradition of representative government. In addition, the idea seemed incompatible with Britain's global responsibilities and worldwide interests and relationships. Because of Britain's links with a widely dispersed Commonwealth and her special relationship with the United States, British policymakers were not prepared politically, or perhaps even psychologically, to give priority to European integration. Instead, Britain was bound to friends and interests in several parts of the world, from whom and from which she could not disassociate herself.

This was the thinking which influenced British policy toward European integration for almost a generation after World War II. Leaders of both major political parties carefully restricted the part they envisioned for Britain in European integration. Even Churchill, a leading proponent of a rapprochement between Germany and France as the

---

[3] Winston S. Churchill, *Europe Unite: Speeches, 1947 and 1948*, 417–418.
[4] Charles de Gaulle, *Unity: 1942–1944*, p. 227.

cornerstone for the integration of the Continental powers in western Europe, did not foresee Britain's participation on equal terms with France and Germany. Britain was to stand instead on a level with the United States and the Soviet Union as a power separate from an integrated Europe. Similarly, Bevin thought of European integration as a goal to be approached only gradually, rather than as an objective for whose attainment Britain should join institutions with complex procedures for decision-making.

To be sure, the British view of Europe was not so restrictive as to prevent membership in certain regional organizations, so long as participation did not conflict with obligations elsewhere in the world.[5] However, the British were not prepared to join as full members in the formation of the European Coal and Steel Community (ECSC), although the Conservative party, then in opposition, urged the British government to participate in the negotiations for its formation. Official British opposition to ECSC was based upon the Labour government's dislike, as Prime Minister Attlee put it, of the "supranational principles underlying the French proposal."[6] Labour was not prepared to permit decisions affecting Britain's welfare state to be taken outside Whitehall. The Conservative position differed essentially in tactics. The Conservatives would have participated in the negotiations for the formation of ECSC in order to ensure that the Community conformed to British needs and interests. As Churchill suggested, in a summarization of the Conservative position during the course of a parliamentary debate: "I would add, to make my answer quite clear to the right honorable and learned Gentlemen, that if he asked me: 'Would you agree to a supranational authority which has the power to tell Great Britain not to cut any more coal or make any more steel, but to grow tomatoes instead'? I should say, without hesitation, the answer is 'No.' But why not be there to give the answer"?[7]

Despite differences in tactics, British opposition to membership in European integrative institutions rested upon a consensus which included both major parties. As in the case of the European Coal and Steel Community, the Labour and Conservative leaderships did not

---

[5] Britain accepted membership, for example, in the following organizations: Council of Europe, European Payments Union, Organization for European Economic Cooperation, and Western European Union.

[6] Great Britain, *Parliamentary Debates* (Commons), Vol. 476 (June 13, 1950), cols. 35–37.

[7] Great Britain, *Parliamentary Debates* (Commons), Vol. 476 (June 27, 1950), cols. 2147–48.

differ greatly on the question of British membership in the proposed European Defense Community. In August 1950, Churchill, speaking in the Consultative Assembly of the Council of Europe, urged the Assembly to "make a gesture of practical and constructive guidance by declaring ourselves in favour of the immediate creation of a European Army under unified command, and in which we should all bear a worthy and honorable part." [8] But the part Churchill, not unlike the Labour government, envisaged for Britain, bore greater similarity to the part to be played by the United States than it did the place to be accorded France. Only the military forces of continental West European countries, not those of Britain, would be merged in a European army. Undoubtedly, Britain's unwillingness to join EDC contributed to the collapse of efforts to form a European army. In marked contrast to their position a decade later, the French were not prepared in 1954 to participate in a European political-military unit in which the other major member would be Germany.

As in the case of other European integrative institutions, Britain's outlook on foreign affairs precluded membership in the European Economic Community (EEC) during its early formative years. At that time, Britain could have played a major role in structuring the Common Market to take account of major British and Commonwealth interests. If Britain had chosen to join in the formation of the EEC, given existing British interests outside Europe and her apprehensions about European integration, the Common Market might have assumed a far different form. For Britain to have joined the Common Market in the form it took in the Rome Treaty would have presupposed a fundamental change in British foreign policy priorities. In fact, the Messina Conference of June 1–2, 1955, in which the foreign ministers of the Six met to discuss the formation of a customs union, attracted little attention in Britain. On June 7, the Six invited Britain to send a representative to attend the conference to draft the Rome Treaty. In their reply to the invitation of the Six, the British expressed reservations about further efforts toward European economic integration and wished, so they stated, to avoid the creation of new institutions which might overshadow the Organization for European Economic Cooperation (OEEC). [9] Nevertheless, Britain participated until November 1955

[8] Council of Europe, Consultative Assembly, *Reports*, Part I, 228.
[9] The British reply contained the following passage: "Her Majesty's Government are naturally anxious to ensure that due account should be taken of the function of existing organizations such as OEEC and that their work should not be

in the deliberations in Brussels on the formation of the Common Market. At that time the British, unwilling to proceed with the Six in the drafting of the Rome Treaty, withdrew from the negotiations. The departure of her representatives marked a turning point in Britain's relations with the Six, for the planners of the EEC proceeded in their work without her. Britain forfeited the opportunity to participate as a founder nation and thus to influence the EEC during its developmental stage.

Until 1961 Britain held that she could not join the Common Market because membership was incompatible with other more important commitments. One reason for holding this position was Commonwealth relationships, including in particular the preservation of preferential tariff arrangements for Commonwealth trade. As Chancellor of the Exchequer Harold Macmillan suggested on November 26, 1956, in a House of Commons debate on European trade policy: "If the United Kingdom were to join such a customs union (as the European Economic Community), the United Kingdom tariff would be swept aside and would be replaced by this single common tariff . . . We could not expect the countries of the Commonwealth to continue to give preferential treatment to our exports to them if we had to charge them full duty on their exports to us." [10] The Commonwealth mystique—the idea of Britain as the leader of a worldwide, multiracial association—lived on even after the Commonwealth no longer accepted British leadership or supported Britain in major crises such as the Suez affair of 1956.

Macmillan's statement of British policy regarding Common Market membership echoed the pronouncements of spokesmen for the Labour government several years earlier. Britain was unwilling to participate in an integrative scheme which embodied the institutional arrangements of the EEC. Britain was not prepared to adapt her social, economic, and agricultural policies to those envisaged by the Six. However, like other European colonial powers earlier in the postwar period, Britain was engaged in a reorientation of historic significance in

---

unnecessarily duplicated. They also hope that the views of different countries affected may be heard. On this understanding Her Majesty's Government will be glad to appoint a representative to take part in these studies and have noted that they are intended to begin in Brussels on July 9 next. There are, as you are no doubt aware, special difficulties for this country in any proposal for 'a European common market.' Quoted in Hans Joachim Heiser, *British Policy with Regard to the Unification Efforts on the European Continent*, 97.
[10] Great Britain, *Parliamentary Debates* (Commons), Vol. 561 (November 26, 1956), col. 37.

her foreign policy—from a preoccupation with overseas commitments and responsibilities to a concern primarily, and perhaps ultimately exclusively, with European affairs.

Participation in institutions at the international level is partly the result of expectations of gain.[11] In the decade following World War II, few Englishmen could see the advantage of participation in the European integration movement. By 1957, however, many had become convinced that Britain should take part in plans for the eventual elimination of trade barriers in western Europe.[12] Such interest was not incompatible with British support, nearly a decade earlier, for OEEC, under whose auspices West European governments undertook to lower barriers to intra-European trade. Although Britain could not commit herself fully to EEC membership, she could not ignore the potential for economic gain to be found in the growing markets of continental Europe.[13] If not prepared to join the Common Market by 1957, Englishmen in all political parties as well as in industry, the trade union movement, and the press, saw the need for steps designed to assure continued access to Continental markets. Thus the policy proposals the British government put forward were based upon a consensus which included members of both major political parties as well as the press, the trade union movement, and industry. Far from moving boldly at this time to "give the country a lead," to use a British cliché, the British government developed a policy which reflected, but also strengthened, a consensus already firmly based upon major elites. Moreover, the policy the British government put forward was hardly a major departure from previous postwar policies. Again the British sought to reconcile a growing interest in the dynamic markets of western Europe with interests and commitments with other Commonwealth countries and the United States.

During preparations for an OEEC Council meeting in Paris in July 1956, the British proposed the establishment of a free trade area to link the EEC with other OEEC countries. On July 21, the OEEC Council set up "Working Party No. 17" to study possible ways of freeing trade between the Six and the rest of OEEC.[14]

---

[11] See Ernst Haas, *The Uniting of Europe*, especially Chapter 1.
[12] See Chapter 2 for an examination of the rise of support in Britain for British participation in a European free trade area.
[13] For an examination of the growth of British trade with continental western Europe in this period, see Chapter 3.
[14] According to Chancellor of the Exchequer Macmillan's report to the House

By the end of 1956, Britain had decided to give priority to a free trade area embracing the Six, as well as European countries outside the Common Market, including Britain. A January 31, 1957 memorandum submitted to the OEEC Council called for the formation of a free trade area limited to industrial goods and excluding agriculture.[15] While giving her industrialists access, without tariff barriers, to the booming markets of continental Europe, this proposal would have enabled Britain to retain the freedom to continue the preferential arrangements which apply to imports of foodstuffs from the Commonwealth. The exclusion of agriculture was deemed necessary in order to preserve the markets of colonial and Commonwealth countries, for many of which Britain was the principal source of income. Moreover, agriculture was left out because Britain was not prepared at this time to jeopardize the position of its own farmers by exposing them to competition from the Six. Had the proposal for a free trade area been accepted, it would have enabled Britain to reconcile her growing interest in European markets with her commitments in other parts of the world.

By their proposal the British sought to preserve the freedom to fix tariffs toward countries outside the free trade area, retaining for Britain and the rest of the Commonwealth the lower tariffs provided by the Imperial Preference system. In addition to voicing their fear of elaborate institutional arrangements as embodied in EEC, in the free trade proposals the British were unwilling to see European economic integration as anything more than a "concept related primarily to the removal of restrictions on trade such as tariffs and quotas."[15] In contrast, in the Common Market Six, and especially among the proponents of the EEC, there was the expectation that the Common Market was

---

of Commons on July 24, 1956: "The study group which we set up . . . is to take into account the possibility of creating a free trade area, to include the customs union itself and other members of the Organization (OEEC)." Great Britain, *Parliamentary Debates* (Commons), Vol. 557 (July 24, 1956) col. 211.

[15] Great Britain, *A European Free Trade Area: The United Kingdom Memorandum to the Organization for European Economic Cooperation.* Cmnd. 72. (February 1957). The Memorandum stated: "The United Kingdom and most other European countries protect their home agriculture by one means or another for well-known reasons, and will wish to continue to do so. The United Kingdom would not in the foreseeable future be prepared to remove protection in this field and to permit the free entry of foodstuffs as is intended for other products; nor would Her Majesty's Government expect other countries to take such action. . . ."

[16] *Ibid.*, p. 5.

part of an integrative process from which might come eventually a politically united Europe.[17]

Differing perspectives about the goals, as well as the form, of European integration separated Britain from her Continental neighbors, and contributed to the failure of the negotiations for a European free trade area. The Six, and especially France, saw the proposed free trade area for what it was: a device whereby Britain would gain for herself the best of two worlds—preservation of her privileged position in Commonwealth markets together with access to the rapidly growing markets of western Europe. The French were apprehensive about "deflections of trade, or the problem of the definition of origin, in the proposed free trade area." [18] Moreover, French officials suggested that it might not be practical for members of the projected free trade area to retain independent trade policies. Unless the countries of the free trade area were prepared to undertake obligations similar to those to be assumed by the Common Market members, the advantages accruing to these nations should remain more limited than those to be enjoyed by states which joined the EEC. According to this reasoning, Britain, for example, should not be given access to a huge European market without concessions on behalf of European integration similar to those which France was about to make.

For more than a year, negotiations for the formation of a free trade area dragged on before they broke down in November 1958. On November 14, Minister of Information Jacques Soustelle announced that France had decided that "it is not possible to create the free trade area as wished by the British, that is, with free trade between the

---

[17] See, for example, Altiero Spinelli, *The Eurocrats: Conflict and Crisis in the European Community*, especially Chapter 1; and Walter Hallstein, *United Europe: Challenge and Opportunity*, especially Chapter 3.

[18] The Inter-Governmental Committee on the Establishment of a European free trade area, in its Memorandum on January 31, 1958, entitled "Definition of Origin of Goods in the Free Trade Area," offered the following definition of the term "deflections of trade": "In a free trade area, trade from third countries may tend to circumvent the higher national tariffs on basic materials and on semi-manufactures and components; materials or components may be brought into the area countries with lower tariffs, may be processed there sufficiently to qualify under the origin rules, and then be re-exported in processed form to the countries with higher tariffs. The same problem could arise from differences other than tariffs in protection against non-area countries." *Negotiations for a European Free Trade Area: Documents Relating to the Negotiations from July 1956 to December 1958.* Cmnd. 64, 105. See also G. D. N. Worswick, "European Economic Community and the Free Trade Area Negotiations, 1956–1958." In G. D. N. Worswick (ed.), *The Free Trade Area Proposals*, pp. 97–99.

Common Market and the rest of the OEEC, without a single external tariff barrier around the seventeen countries, and without harmonization in the economic and social spheres." [19]

When the negotiations were suspended, agreement had been reached on several issues. These included the methods by which tariffs and quotas might gradually be eliminated, the rules for freeing movements of capital and permitting international exchanges in services, rules regarding the right of firms in one country to establish operations in another country, and rules about restrictive business practices and state aid to industries. Some progress had been made in reconciling national positions on such problems as agricultural policy and the movement of workers. However, agreement eluded the negotiators on the fundamental issues.

Before the collapse of the negotiations, it had not been possible to reach accord on external tariffs and commercial policy toward nations which were not members of the projected free trade area. For example, the negotiators had been unable to resolve their differences on the definition of origin of goods and relations between the free trade area and the Commonwealth, with its preferential trading system. Without a solution to the Commonwealth problem, Britain was not prepared to accede to a free trade area in Europe. Finally, the negotiators had yet to agree on procedures for the "harmonization and co-ordination" of their internal economic and social policies. Nor had they decided on the institutional system and voting rules for the free trade area.[20]

The collapse of the free trade area negotiations reflected Britain's inability to reconcile her European and non-European interests. But the negotiations provided as well an indication of the growing cohesiveness of the Six on economic policy. In their relations with outside powers, even by 1958 the EEC had developed a degree of unity on commercial policy. According to Reginald Maudling, who had represented Britain, "the Six countries of the Common Market, as a matter of principle, always spoke with a single voice during the free trade area negotiations." Maudling contended that solidarity manifested by the Six had led to two consequences: "first, that before any of them could speak they had to agree on their point of view, which often took a

[19] *Financial Times* (London), November 15, 1958, p. 1.
[20] OEEC, *Report to the Chairman of the Council* (By the Chairman of the Inter-Governmental Committee on the Establishment of a European Free Trade Area). *Negotiations for a European Free Trade Area: Documents Relating to the Negotiations from July 1956 to December 1958.* Cmnd. 641.

very long time; and secondly, once they had agreed on their point of view, by mutual concession and negotiation, their negotiating position was frozen and they could not make an concessions very early in negotiations. . . ." [21] Subsequently, in the British bid for Common Market entry, and in the Kennedy Round negotiations for the expansion of international trade, outside countries including Britain and the United States faced a similar problem in negotiating with the EEC. Having reached a delicate compromise among themselves only after protracted discussion and sometimes at the expense of third countries, the Six were not prepared to jeopardize the newly formed Common Market consensus in order to build a more broadly based consensus. Even in the free trade negotiations of 1958 Britain was not able to benefit from differences among the Six in order to obtain concessions. Whatever their disagreements, the EEC countries, as they would in the future in the Kennedy Round negotiations with the United States, negotiated with Britain as a unit.

Having failed in her bid for the creation of a free trade area which would have included the EEC, Britain attempted to devise another policy to assure access to Continental markets. Once again, the British sought to reconcile Commonwealth and European interests. During the first half of 1959 there was much discussion in Britain about the course of action the government should adopt vis-à-vis European integration.[22] Early in 1959, the Swedish and Swiss governments proposed the formation of a free trade area embracing certain European countries which were not members of the Common Market. Although Britain's "ultimate goal," according to her Chancellor of the Exchequer, remained "the association of the Six with the other countries of the OEEC," the British government was prepared to "examine all possible steps (including a European free trade area which does not include EEC countries) which might help towards this end." [23] After preliminary negotiations during the early months of 1959, Sweden, on May 27, invited Austria, Denmark, Norway, Portugal, Switzerland, and the United Kingdom to send delegations to Stockholm to work out plans for a free trade area.

---

[21] Great Britain, *Parliamentary Debates* (Commons), Vol. 599 (February 12, 1959), col. 1381.

[22] However, Britain's relationship with the EEC or other European integrative institutions did not evoke a debate of such proportions as to become an issue in the General Election of 1959. D. E. Butler and Richard Rose, *The British General Election of 1959*, p. 72.

[23] Great Britain, *Parliamentary Debates* (Commons), Vol. 605 (May 14, 1959), col. 1404.

On July 21, a ministerial meeting in Stockholm recommended that a European Free Trade Association (EFTA) be established.

The Stockholm Convention, signed in January 1960, included a commitment to a simple schedule of tariff reductions and quota liberalization, escape clauses, a "rules of origin" system to prevent trade deflection, a general prohibition in principle against official or private policies which discriminated against or restricted trade in order to offset concessions granted in the treaty, and provision for the establishment of minimal administrative machinery.[24] It also provided for free trade in industrial goods, although by special arrangements certain foodstuffs, such as fish, fish oils, and fish meals, were to be admitted to the United Kingdom from other member countries. Moreover, in an Agreement on Agriculture, the British agreed to reduce tariffs on Danish exports of certain types of meats and dairy products. The "Little Free Trade Area" also provided for the gradual abolition of tariffs among the Seven over a transitional period to end in 1970. Tariffs would be reduced by 20 percent on July 1, 1960, and by 10 percent each year thereafter until 1970, on a timetable virtually the same as that of the EEC. EFTA permitted each member to retain its tariff levels toward third countries and hence did not affect materially other British trade relations, including Commonwealth preference. EFTA provided a device for avoiding, for the moment, a decision between the Commonwealth and Europe, for the British hoped that it might furnish a "bridge" to at least a portion of Europe, while leaving intact traditional economic links.

In the months following the formation of EFTA, Britain reassessed her policy toward European integration. In the spring of 1960, the British government had decided to explore the possibility of Common Market membership and to give serious and detailed thought to the implications of such a course for the Commonwealth and domestic British interests. The shift in attitude toward integration became apparent when the Minister of State, John Profumo, addressed the Political Committee of the Western European Union (WEU) Assembly. He announced that Britain was prepared to consider the possibility of becoming a full member of ECSC and the European Atomic Energy Community (EURATOM),[25] the European Atomic Energy Com-

---

[24] Great Britain, *Convention Establishing the European Free Trade Association.* Cmnd. 1026.

[25] In response to a question in the House of Commons on policy toward EEC, Prime Minister Macmillan had hinted that his government was "working out our

mission. The announcement, however, was not a request for membership; it was an expression of Britain's willingness to consider an invitation from the Six.[26] In a speech to the Commons on July 25, Foreign Secretary Selwyn Lloyd hinted that Britain was considering Common Market membership. Lloyd suggested that EFTA might prove inadequate in the attainment of the major objective which Britain had set for it, namely, the building of a bridge between the Common Market Six and those West European countries, chiefly Britain, which remained on the periphery of the EEC. He invited the Six to propose solutions for the three basic problems confronting Britain in her relations with the Six: domestic agriculture, Commonwealth trade, and safeguards for other EFTA members.[27]

Prime Minister Macmillan took another step which prepared the way for an eventual British bid for EEC membership. On July 27, 1960, Macmillan made several changes in his cabinet. Selwyn Lloyd was shifted from the Foreign Office to become Chancellor of the Exchequer. Lord Home succeeded Lloyd as Britain's foreign secretary; and the chief whip, Edward Heath, was given the title of Lord Privy Seal, together with special responsibilities for European relations. Because of Lord Home's peerage, Heath became the government's chief spokesman on foreign affairs in the House of Commons.[28] Duncan Sandys took the post of Secretary for Commonwealth Relations, while Peter Thorneycroft returned to the cabinet as Minister of Aviation. Heath, Sandys, and Thorneycroft had each taken an interest in European integration during the previous decade. Whatever the reason for these cabinet changes, they enabled the British government to press forward its exploration of the problems of Common Market membership.

During the year before Britain first applied for Common Market membership, British officials held informal discussions with the leaders of EEC countries. At this time, the British made an effort to develop an

approach" to the Six. "We have the very encouraging fact that the Six have now said that they would like to negotiate. We hope they will soon be making specific proposals upon which negotiations between the two bodies could be made." Great Britain, *Parliamentary Debates* (Commons), 624 (May 26, 1960), col. 678.

[26] Western European Union, *Debates*, Sixth Ordinary Session, First Part (June 1960), 137. See also *Times* (London), June 3, 1960, p. 11.

[27] Great Britain, *Parliamentary Debates* (Commons), Vol. 627 (July 25, 1960), col. 1105.

[28] In his maiden speech in the House of Commons after his election in 1950, Heath had called for British membership in the ECSC. Great Britain, *Parliamentary Debates* (Commons), Vol. 476 (June 26, 1950), cols. 1959–1964.

understanding of the detailed problems to be resolved and the concessions which EEC countries might be prepared to make in order to accommodate Britain if she decided to enter the Common Market. In addition to more detailed discussion at lower levels, British leaders met with their Continental counterparts. For example, Prime Minister Macmillan, in August 1960, visited Bonn for talks with Chancellor Adenauer.[29] In November, Macmillan and Foreign Secretary Home went to Rome for consultations with Italian leaders. Subsequently, ministerial spokesmen revealed on various occasions that discussions between Britain and members of the Six were continuing.[30]

Finally, in the early months of 1960 an interdepartmental committee of senior civil servants in the Economic Steering Committee, concerned with economic policy, undertook to evaluate the courses of action open to Britain in her relations with the Six.[31] This committee had as its chairman Sir Frank Lee, who by 1960 had become Permanent Secretary at the Treasury and a proponent of British Common Market membership.[32] Both the Foreign Office and the Treasury contained groups of permanent civil servants who were essentially pro-European in outlook. In the year before Britain made application, the Foreign Office as well was engaged in a study of the implications of EEC membership. Studies undertaken in the Treasury and Foreign Office yielded evidence that the problems of adjustment to the Common Market, although formidable, were not insurmountable. The Commonwealth, it was realized, consisted essentially of a series of bilateral relationships, for the most part economic in nature, between Britain and former colonial countries. In many cases, it would be possible to preserve such links; in others, adjustments could be made to reconcile them with Common Market membership.

Especially in the year preceding July 1961, British spokesmen stressed the need for Britain to find a way somehow to prevent the

---

[29] In a joint communiqué after their discussions, they declared that "it is essential in the interest of European unity that a solution should be found to the problems arising from the existence of two economic groups in Europe." Quoted in Sydney H. Zebel, "Britain and West European Integration." *Current History*, Vol. 40, No. 233 (January 1961), 45.

[30] For example, on February 22, 1961, Edward Heath declared that Britain was engaged in "exploratory talks" with West Germany and Italy concerning British entry into the Common Market. He announced that discussions with the French government were about to begin. Great Britain, *Parliamentary Debates* (Commons), Vol. 635 (February 22, 1961), col. 492.

[31] Miriam Camps, *Britain and the European Community, 1955–1963*, p. 280.

[32] See Anthony Sampson, *Anatomy of Britain*, p. 290.

deepening of the division of western Europe into the trading blocs represented by EEC and EFTA. They were optimistic about eventually resolving major differences between Britain and the Six. It was suggested, for example, that the French concept of a *Europe des patries* accorded with British views about European integration. By February 1961, Britain had announced her willingness to accept in principle a common external tariff and had hinted that she might be willing to participate in the institutions of the Six.[33] As Macmillan suggested in the Commons on April 26, 1961, the key problem confronting Britain was whether Common Market membership could be reconciled with other British commitments, especially to the Commonwealth and EFTA.[34]

Official British statements during the early months of 1961 reveal the cautious movement of British policy toward a decision to apply for Common Market membership. At a meeting of the WEU Council of Ministers in February 1961, Edward Heath suggested that if the Six "can meet our Commonwealth and agricultural difficulties, the United Kingdom can then consider a system based on a common or harmonized tariff on raw materials and manufactured goods imported from countries other than the Seven or the Commonwealth." [35] Clearly, Britain was ready to accept, in principle, a common external tariff and thus join a customs union which might discriminate against imports from Commonwealth countries.

When Macmillan addressed the WEU Assembly, which met for the first time in London on May 29, 1961, he expressed Britain's desire to explore the possibility of Common Market membership, and declared that Britain was "determined to press forward with the consolidation of western Europe." [36] The Assembly responded with a recommendation that the WEU Council, which consisted of the representatives of Britain and the Six, should begin general discussions among delegates from member-states and between representatives of WEU members and the Commission of the EEC "with a view to preparing an agreement providing for the accession of the United Kingdom to the EEC

---

[33] *Times* (London), February 28, 1961, p. 12.
[34] Great Britain, *Parliamentary Debates* (Commons), Vol. 639 (April 26, 1961), col. 233.
[35] *Times* (London), February 28, 1961, 12.
[36] Western European Union, Assembly, *Proceedings Seventh Ordinary Session*, First Part (June 1961), Vol. 1, 57.

without weakening the political content of the Treaty of Rome." [37]

In the months before applying for EEC membership, the British government had held discussions with EFTA countries. At the meeting of the EFTA Ministerial Council in Geneva in February 1961, Britain and her partners agreed to make tariff reductions in July which had been scheduled for the end of the year. This step brought tariff cuts in EFTA into harmony with those of the Six. The Ministerial Council also discussed the problem of associate membership for Finland, which subsequently became associated with EFTA after the signing of an agreement in Helsinki on March 27, 1961. Finally, the Ministerial Council heard Heath's report on British talks with German and Italian officials, as well as recent developments in Britain's relations with the Six.

Between June 27 and 29, 1961 the EFTA Ministerial Council held a meeting in London which was to have important consequences for Britain in the Brussels negotiations. The delegates from EFTA countries undoubtedly returned from London in the belief that a British application for Common Market membership was imminent. It soon became evident that other EFTA governments, in anticipation of the British EEC application, had made their own preparations to adapt their policies in the light of Britain's EEC decision. Both Denmark and Norway announced their intention to apply for Common Market membership. Moreover, the government of Ireland had followed closely and responded quickly to the shift in British policy toward European integration. Heavily dependent on trade with Britain, Ireland announced her application for Common Market membership at the same time as Britain. Thus some of Britain's closest trading partners, even in advance of the announcement of the British decision, took steps to assure that their trading interests would be safeguarded in an enlarged European Community.

At the EFTA Ministerial Meeting of June 27–29, the British informed their EFTA partners that they intended to seek Common Market membership, but not to join until they had achieved tariff reductions over the whole of western Europe—between the Six and Seven. As in the case of the Commonwealth, however, the British sought to avoid a situation in which EFTA countries would be granted a veto over the terms for Common Market membership. In order to

---

[37] *Ibid.*, p. 90.

safeguard the principal economic interests of her EFTA partners, Britain agreed, in the communiqué issued after the meeting, not to join the Common Market until suitable arrangements had been made for member countries.[38] Far from providing a bridge to the Six as British leaders had expected, EFTA burdened Britain with still other problems to be resolved before joining the Common Market. Contrary to British expectations, EFTA did not strengthen, and may even have weakened, Britain's negotiating position. At the very least the British commitment to find mutually satisfactory solutions to major EFTA problems would have lengthened the Brussels negotiations and thus delayed British entry into the EEC.[39]

In the weeks before the announcement of Britain's first decision to apply for Common Market membership, British official attention was turned to the potential implications of such a course of action for the Commonwealth. On June 13, Macmillan declared that although the government had made no decision to apply for EEC membership, senior ministers from his cabinet would visit Commonwealth countries.[40] The purpose of the visits was to consult on possible arrangements by which Britain, if she chose to enter the Common Market, could safeguard vital Commonwealth interests.

The statements issued following consultations in Commonwealth countries stressed, for the most part, the potentially disruptive effects which British membership in the EEC might have upon markets in Britain for Commonwealth goods.[41] New Zealand, whose livelihood depended on trade with Britain to a far greater extent than other Commonwealth countries, said it was willing "to examine alternative methods for protecting New Zealand interests in the course of the (forthcoming Brussels) negotiations." However, New Zealand officials

---

[38] *EFTA Bulletin* (July 1961), p. 8. According to the communiqué issued at the close of the EFTA meeting: ". . . Ministers resolved that the European Free Trade Association, the obligation created by the Convention between the Members, and the momentum towards integration within the Association would be maintained at least until satisfactory arrangements have been worked out in negotiations to meet the various legitimate interests of all Members of EFTA, and thus enable them all to participate from the same date in an integrated European market."

[39] The Brussels negotiations, however, collapsed before major EFTA problems had been considered.

[40] Great Britain, *Parliamentary Debates* (Commons), Vol. 642 (June 13, 1961), col. 204.

[41] Great Britain, *Commonwealth Consultations on Britain's Relations with the European Economic Community,* Cmnd. 1339.

declared they did not see "any way of protecting New Zealand's vital interests other than by the maintenance of unrestricted duty-free entry" into Britain. In a somewhat stiffer attitude than that of New Zealand, Australia declared that the market for much of her export trade might be jeopardized in the event that Britain joined the EEC. Australian Prime Minister Menzies argued that British participation in European integration might have the effect of weakening the Commonwealth. The Anglo-Canadian communiqué, issued after consultations in Ottawa, noted "the grave concern of the Canadian government about the implications of possible negotiations between Britain and the European Economic Community, and about the political and economic effects which British membership in the European Economic Community would have on Canada and on the Commonwealth as a whole." The Anglo-Indian joint statement referred to the "serious damage which was likely to be caused to India's export trade if the United Kingdom were to join the Community without securing agreement on special measures necessary to adequately safeguard it." Malayan officials saw little danger to their exports of rubber and tin, neither of which were subject to the EEC external tariff; nor did the government of Pakistan raise strenuous objections. However, Britain encountered stiff opposition to her proposed EEC bid from Ghanaian and Nigerian officials, who saw the Common Market as a device for the perpetuation of the economic links which were vestiges of the colonial period.

In the Commonwealth consultations British officials received a foretaste of the objections which Commonwealth members would raise during the Brussels negotiations. The visits by British officials to Commonwealth countries do not seem to have influenced greatly the British decision to apply for Common Market membership, for the Macmillan cabinet must have anticipated many of the criticisms which were raised. With its survey of Commonwealth opinion completed by mid-July, the government prepared for the announcement of its Common Market decision and pressed forward with plans for the detailed negotiations which followed the Prime Minister's announcement.

Amid a discussion in the press about the respective merits of Britain's joining the Common Market, Macmillan on July 31 announced the government's decision to the House of Commons.[42] He informed the House that after nine months of "useful and frank discussions" with

---

[42] Among Britain's "prestige papers," there was general support for Common Market membership. See Chapter 2.

the Six, "we have now reached the stage where we cannot make further progress without entering into formal negotiations. . . . Therefore, after long and earnest consideration, Her Majesty's Government have come to the conclusion that it would be right for Britain to make a formal application under Article 237 of the Treaty (of Rome) for negotiations with a view to joining the European Economic Community. . . ." [43]

In the period between 1957 and 1961 British policy had undergone a major change. The willingness of Britain to enter negotiations for membership in the EEC, even at the risk of weakening cherished historic ties, meant, in effect, that the Macmillan cabinet recognized increasingly the limitations of British power—economic, political, and military—in the world of the 1960's.[44] By 1961 the British had come to doubt the durability of the base which sustained Britain's relatively high living standards and pretentions to power in world politics. Participation in the European Community, Englishmen in growing numbers believed, might offer a potential solution to the dilemma facing them as a nation: how to maximize British political influence and invigorate Britain's domestic economy in a world in which increasingly she lagged behind the two superpowers as well as the leading members of the Common Market.

In announcing its decision to apply for EEC membership, the government adopted a policy which had considerable support among British elites. However, the Common Market initiative was not based upon as broad a consensus as the earlier free trade area initiatives. In contrast with previous British efforts to reconcile European and Com-

---

[43] Great Britain, *Parliamentary Debates* (Commons), Vol. 645 (July 31, 1961), col. 930. The government motion on the application for Great Britain's entry into the EEC stated: "This House supports the decision of Her Majesty's Government to make formal application under Article 237 of the Treaty of Rome in order to initiate negotiations to see if satisfactory arrangements can be made to meet the special interests of the United Kingdom, of the Commonwealth, and of the European Free Trade Association, and further accepts the undertaking of Her Majesty's Government that no agreement affecting these special interests or involving British sovereignty will be entered into until it has been approved by this House after full consultation with other Commonwealth countries, by whatever procedure they may generally agree." On August 3, the House of Commons, by a vote of 313 to 5, gave formal approval to the Macmillan Cabinet's decision to apply for Common Market membership. One Conservative and four left-wing Labour members voted against the Government motion. Twenty-five Conservatives and all but five Labour members abstained.
[44] See Chapter 3 for an examination of the considerations which appear to have led the British government to apply for Common Market membership.

monwealth interests, the British government faced opposition within both major parties and within other important groups in Britain. Although the Macmillan cabinet sought to build a broadly based European consensus which might strengthen and revitalize the Conservative party, the immediate effect of the Common Market decision, as subsequent chapters will show, was to produce new cleavages in British politics. To a far greater extent than in its earlier policies which, like the Common Market decision, were designed to reconcile Commonwealth and European interests, the British government now found itself in advance of public opinion, and in some cases in opposition to elite opinion. Given the long-standing British commitment to the Commonwealth and the U.S. special relationship, this opposition is understandable. For unlike previous policies, the Common Market decision represented a decision to give greater importance to British relations with continental Europe, rather than the Commonwealth.[45]

---

[45] In 1961, however, British spokesmen still stressed the importance of the Commonwealth. For example, Duncan Sandys, Commonwealth Secretary and a leading "European" in the Macmillan Cabinet declared: "I believe that my European friends will understand me if I say that if I were forced to make this cruel choice I would unquestionably choose the Commonwealth. Happily, we are not confronted with this dilemma." Great Britain, *Parliamentary Debates* (Commons), Vol. 645 (August 3, 1961), col. 1775.

 Chapter 2

THE "EUROPEAN" CONSENSUS, 1957–1961

In the period before Britain's first application for Common Market membership, Englishmen in increasing numbers, outside official circles as well as within the government, focused their attention upon the European Community movement. Within British industry, the press, the trade union movement, and in the political parties were to be found persons who favored first British membership in the proposed free trade area and later EEC entry. In the period between 1956 and 1961, support for Common Market membership became most pronounced among persons of higher education who were comparatively young. The most ardent supporters were persons under the age of forty. For the most part, they were the activists in the Europe-oriented organizations, the writers of pro-European editorials in the press, and the organizers of factions in the political parties and the trade union movement.[1]

---

[1] According to an elite survey of British opinion on the Common Market, based on selected names contained in *Who's Who*, "Compared with those expressing negative views, those strongly in favor of Britain's membership in the Common Market were younger, were more likely to have attended one of the private schools, contained a higher proportion of Oxford and Cambridge graduates, were more likely to be members of clubs (especially the military and political clubs), were more attached to the *Times* as their daily newspaper, and were more likely to be earning their livings as university professors, company directors, and bishops." Mark Abrams, "British Elite Attitudes and the European Common Market." *Public Opinion Quarterly*, Vol. XXIX, No. 2 (Summer 1965), p. 224. A poll taken by Social Surveys, Ltd. (Gallup Poll), in June 1961 yielded similar findings. The age group between sixteen and twenty-four years registered 45 percent in favor of Britain's joining the EEC. Similarly, groups between twenty-five and thirty-four, and between thirty-five and forty-four years of age, had percentages of fifty-one and fifty-three, respectively, in favor of British EEC membership. Moreover, members of upper and upper-middle, as well as the middle-class, were in favor—60 and 55 percent respectively—of Britain's acceding to the Rome Treaty. Those with higher education tended to support Common Market membership, while the reverse was the case with those who had left school at an early age. Professional groups, office workers, and those in managerial positions had a greater percentage of Common Market advocates than did factory,

The 1961 British application for EEC membership was preceded by the rise of expectations of gain, primarily economic—but also political and military—which might accrue from participation, in one form or another, in the European integration movement. By July 1961 the Macmillan cabinet enjoyed considerable, but by no means full, support among British elites for its Common Market policy. Although there remained a great gulf between the government and much of British opinion both at the elite and mass levels, there was a base of support, greater than ever before, for the British application for Common Market membership.

OPINION AND THE FREE TRADE AREA PROPOSALS

Despite the primary orientation of British thought and foreign policy toward the Commonwealth and the special relationship with the United States, there existed in Britain in the postwar period a variety of "European" groups whose members had sought to promote European integration. Such groups as the United Kingdom Council of the European Movement [2] and an organization known as Federal Union dedicated to the creation of a world government based on federalist principles, disseminated information to parliamentarians, business leaders and other opinion molders.[3] The United Kingdom Council sponsored meetings designed to increase awareness of, and support for, the proposed free trade area. Several of its members were active in the European-Atlantic Group, an organization closely related to the Coun-

shop or farm labor groups. Finally, of all regions of the United Kingdom, the south of England registered the highest percentage of persons in favor of Britain's joining the EEC. Social Surveys Ltd. (Gallup Poll), *Britain and the European Common Market.* A Gallup Enquiry conducted for the *Daily Telegraph,* pp. 18–19.

[2] The United Kingdom Council of the European Movement was founded in 1948 following the Hague Conference on European Unity held that year. At the Hague Conference Sir Winston Churchill had delivered a major address in support of European integration. In addition to Churchill, the United Kingdom Council included Members of Parliament, industrialists, and military leaders. Rather than enrolling a mass membership, the Council chose instead to encourage leading Englishmen to support European integration and to limit its membership to persons who had contributed in one way or another to this cause. The Council was the British counterpart of similar organizations established in other West European countries after the Hague Conference.

[3] Founded in 1938, Federal Union had as its objective to "develop a conscious public opinion in favour of democratic federalism." See *Federal Union* (Pamphlet setting forth the principles and objectives of the organization), published by Federal Union.

cil which attempted through public meetings and publications to build support for European integration.[4]

In the development of support in Britain for Common Market membership, Federal Union played a role of considerable importance. One of the earliest proponents of British membership in the Common Market, Federal Union, in the spring of 1956, advocated that Britain join ECSC, Euratom, and the EEC. The leaders of Federal Union saw European integration as an important step toward a global federal organization.[5] Because regional integration appeared more easily attainable than the more remote goal of world government, Federal Union devoted a substantial portion of its efforts toward the development of British support for European integration. In several ways, members of Federal Union influenced British opinion on the Common Market, especially at the elite level. In the period between 1956 and 1961, a group of "European" Federal Union members met regularly in order to discuss the potential implications of Common Market membership, and to formulate for their organization a policy on British participation in the European integration movement. In such meetings Federal Union members, as well as non-members who were sympathetic to the idea of British participation in European integration, sharpened their views and broadened their knowledge of European integration. Those in attendance at such meetings included journalists, Members of Parliament, and trade unionists, most of whom were under the age of forty. These meetings, together with literature published and distributed by Federal Union, enabled the idea of Common Market membership to be

---

[4] The European-Atlantic Group published a journal called the *European-Atlantic Review* which in 1963 became the European *Review*. The Publicity Director of the United Kingdom Council served also as Joint Executive Editor of the *European-Atlantic Review* with the Director-General of the Council. The *Review's* editorial board included Sir Edward Beddington-Behrens, who was also Chairman of the United Kingdom Council's Executive Committee.
[5] For a critical view of the activities of Federal Union, as well as the United Kingdom Council of the European Movement, See R. Hugh Corbet, "The Federalist Pressures in Britain," in *Britain, Not Europe*, edited by R. Hugh Corbet, for the Anti-Common Market League, p. 20. "Imbued with notions of world government, federalists for over two decades have been promoting the United Europe idea in Britain. Sophisticated propagandists all, their public utterances today are chiefly economic. This is especially true of those whose motives and careers depend on constituency votes. Baldly stated, federalist motives would render little endearment to British people, both in this country and abroad. Party policies have in the past involved Commonwealth development. People may, therefore, be excused for inattention to the 'European' advocates. Nevertheless, there are now in Britain several federalist pressure groups operating under various guises."

spread among newspaper editorial writers, Members of Parliament, and other persons capable, in turn, of influencing a broader segment of British opinion.

Literature published under the auspices of Federal Union stressed the importance of Common Market membership to Britain's future. Britain could not hope to achieve the full benefits of European integration if she confined her participation to a free trade area as outlined by the government in its White Paper of January 1957. The literature of Federal Union expressed several expectations of gain from Common Market membership. A United States of Europe, based on federalist principles, with an elected parliament and centrally controlled armed forces, would make another war in Europe impossible. Such a federation would "build up a prosperous and stable European economy, based on a great common market which would raise standards of living in Europe and also provide the means of giving greater aid to less developed countries." [6] According to a statement of policy, a United States of Europe would exercise a magnetic attraction upon the "oppressed peoples of Eastern Europe." Therefore, in 1957, Federal Union urged the British government to "participate as a full member of the proposed European Common Market and Euratom on terms which would further British interests more effectively than merely by joining the free trade area."

Federal Union members undertook a variety of other activities in order to disseminate their views about European integration. In particular, Federal Union conducted the first major study of the potential effects of British membership in a European free trade area. [7] To finance the study, its backers set up the Britain in Europe Fund in order to attract support which Federal Union, because of its avowedly world government orientation, might not be able to obtain. British companies, trade associations and labor unions were solicited for financial contributions. [8] The study was published by the Economist Intelligence Unit, a research organization which included among its staff persons who were also members of Federal Union.

Because it was the first comprehensive survey of the potential impact of the freeing of European trade upon British commerce and industry,

---

[6] Federal Union, "Policy Statement," *World Affairs*, No. 237, 16.
[7] Economist Intelligence Unit. *Britain and Europe*.
[8] Twenty-five British companies, fourteen trade associations and nineteen trade unions contributed financially to the study. Economist Intelligence Unit. *Britain and Europe*, vii–viii.

the study marked an important step in the development of support in Britain, first for the idea of a free trade area, and later for the Common Market. After assessing the likely impact of a free trade area upon individual British industries, the authors concluded that on balance, manufacturing industry in Britain would "gain appreciably" in a European free trade area. If it did not have access to the Common Market on terms equal to those of its continental competitors, British industry would be placed "at a very serious disadvantage in competing with German industry not only in the EEC, but in the rest of Europe and in the world at large." [9] Moreover, from the standpoint of consumers' interests as well, Britain stood to gain. In sum, the study indicated that Britain faced a clear-cut choice between growth and influence, on the one hand, and stagnation and impotence on the other.

Federal Union used its resources to spawn other "front organizations" which might generate support for European integration in a manner in which the parent organization itself could not. In 1958, for example, Federal Union, as a result of the growing interest among business leaders in European markets, established an organization called Britain in Europe, whose goal was to help members keep abreast of developments in the European Communities by means of lectures and printed materials.[10]

Having surveyed the potential impact of the Common Market and the proposed free trade area upon British industry, members of Federal Union undertook in 1958 another extensive study, focused this time upon major Commonwealth problems which might confront Britain

---

[9] The Economist Intelligence Unit classified industries in five categories: (a) Industries gaining, listed in order of the estimated annual increase in output that would be secured in 1970 if there was a free trade area: motor vehicles, chemicals, wool, electrical engineering, general engineering, rubber manufactures, steel, hosiery, clothing. . . . The relative gain was estimated to vary widely: from 10 to 20 percent of total output in 1970 for the first two, between 5 and 10 percent for the next four, and 5 percent or less for the remaining three. (b) Industries which might benefit as much from free trade as those listed above, but for which no estimate of production in 1970 had been made: non-ferrous metals, metal manufactures, aircraft, shipbuilding, oil refining, building materials, glass, scientific instruments, etc., sporting goods. . . . (c) Industries losing, where production and/or employment was likely to be lower if there were a free trade area: cotton, rayon, paper, leather, watches and clocks. (d) Industries which might lose as much in a free trade area as those listed above, but where the balance of gain and loss remains doubtful: china, footwear, and toys. (e) Industries least affected: railway engineering, jute manufacturers, furniture.
[10] Economist Intelligence Unit, *Britain and Europe*, pp. 36–37.

either as a member of a free trade area or the Common Market.[11] The authors of this study, the first major study of its kind, examined the pattern of Commonwealth trade, together with the categories of commodities which might be affected by British membership either in a free trade area or the Common Market. Although EFTA would have little impact upon Commonwealth trade, the authors of the study concluded that British membership in the Common Market would lead to a substantial reorientation of British trading patterns. The crux of the problem, it was acknowledged, was whether the conditions for British entry into the Common Market which might be damaging to the Commonwealth could be compensated by gains in the EEC from greater economic growth or from more liberal trading policies. To an extent not possible if she remained outside, as an EEC member Britain could encourage Common Market countries to adopt economic arrangements favorable to the Commonwealth. A substantial portion of trade between Britain and the Commonwealth, consisting of raw materials upon which neither Britain nor other Commonwealth countries imposed tariffs, would not be affected by British entry into the Common Market.[12] In sum, the problems which would confront Britain if she applied for Common Market membership, while formidable in some cases, did not pose insuperable obstacles to EEC entry.

At this time, few other Englishmen shared the enthusiasm of Federal Union for EEC membership. Before 1961, neither major political party gave official endorsement to full British participation in European integrative institutions. With few exceptions, members of both parties accepted the major assumptions as well as the principal foreign policies which issued from such assumptions. Yet in 1956 a small group of Members of Parliament had ventured to suggest that Britain participate in negotiations then under way among the Six for the establishment of the Common Market. A resolution expressing this sentiment was introduced in the House of Commons in July 1956 with the support of nearly sixty Conservative MP's as well as some Liberals.[13] This motion stated the signers' agreement in principle with the creation by stages of

---

[11] Economist Intelligence Unit, *The Commonwealth and Europe;* Economist Intelligence Unit, *Britain, the Commonwealth and European Free Trade*, p. 38.
[12] Economist Intelligence Unit, *The Commonwealth and Europe*, pp. 463–476.
[13] *Times* (London), July 12, 1956, p. 8. The following members were listed as sponsors: Robert Mathew, Geoffrey Rippon, Sir Keith Joseph, Arthur Holt, John Rodgers, and Harold Steward.

a customs union in Europe, and suggested that Britain take part in the negotiations "with a view to ensuring that if, or when, any treaty is signed the way will be open for British participation in the Common Market on an acceptable basis and in accordance with the interests of the Commonwealth and Empire." [14] Subsequently, forty-six Labour MP's tabled a similar motion, proposing that the British government "endeavor to negotiate arrangements which would make it possible for the United Kingdom to participate in the advance towards a Common Market without detriment to the interests of the Commonwealth." [15] In December 1956, a group of Conservatives introduced in the House of Commons a motion urging their leaders to call a conference of European powers to consider "further practical steps towards European unity." [16] The motion stated that "the best interests of the United Kingdom and the rest of the Commonwealth lie in the closer association of the United Kingdom with western Europe in conditions which safeguard existing Commonwealth relationships." This motion, because it did not call specifically for membership in the Common Market, attracted the support of more than 100 Conservative MP's.

It was the Liberal party, however, which was the first to call officially for Common Market membership. Historically a party of free trade, the Liberals not only supported British participation in the proposed free trade area, but even adopted at their annual meeting in 1956 a resolution which stated that the "economic integration of western Europe, and particularly the establishment of a Common Market, should receive the active participation of Britain as essential both to the peaceful future of Europe and the economic prosperity of our own country...." [17]

---

[14] *Times* (London), July 19, 1956, p. 6.

[15] *Ibid.*

[16] *Times* (London), December 13, 1956, p. 10. Signers included Geoffrey Rippon, who tabled the motion, Martin Maddan, Sir Patrick Spens, Colonel Stoddart-Scott, Bernard Braine, and John Rodgers.

[17] *Liberal Assembly 1956: Policy Resolutions Adopted at Folkestone on 27–29 September.* London, Liberal Party, 1956. See also *Liberal Assembly 1957: Resolutions Adopted at Southport on 19–21 September.* London, Liberal Party, 1957. The following year, after the British government had announced its proposal for a European free trade area, the Liberal party, in a resolution adopted at its 1957 annual conference, urged "the British government to take the initiative in European affairs, in particular by giving a positive lead in the negotiations for a European Free Trade Area and by close association with the proposed European Nuclear Energy Pool." Liberal Assembly 1957: Resolutions adopted at Southport on 19–21 of September.

At this time, the proponents of Common Market membership were neither representative of prevailing sentiment in their respective parties nor in the country at large.[18] Although the government's free trade area proposal was based upon a consensus which included a majority of members of both major parliamentary parties, only a minority of MP's was prepared to call for Common Market entry. The proposed free trade area was appealing for several reasons. In parliamentary debates held between 1956 and 1958 the following themes were present: Britain might forestall German economic predominance in western Europe. Commonwealth preferences were declining in importance as Commonwealth countries developed their own industries and placed restrictions on imports from Britain. A tariff around the Common Market, together with the reduction and eventual abolition of trade barriers within the EEC, might exclude Britain from the expanding markets of western Europe. Numerous backbenchers expressed the view that Britain and the other nations of Europe could survive only as members of a larger grouping. The nation-states of western Europe were, as one MP suggested, "too small and too insecure, both politically and economically, to pursue their own policies entirely alone." [19] Therefore, Britain must come to terms with the European integration movement.

By the middle of 1956, the proposal for the Common Market and the idea of a broader free trade area had become the topic of editorials in numerous journals and newspapers. According to the leading British newspapers, participation in the projected free trade area would enable Britain to achieve the advantages of economies of scale, including greater markets and lower unit costs, while providing the additional

---

[18] In addition to the above-mentioned motions, two Members of Parliament ventured to suggest that Britain should consider Common Market membership. During the course of a major Commons debate on European trade policy, held on November 26, 1956, Frederick W. Mulley (Labour, Sheffield Park), who in 1965–66 was Minister of Aviation in the Wilson government and subsequently became a Secretary of State in the Foreign Office in the co-ordination of policy for the second British EEC application, declared that Britain could not really separate the political from the economic considerations of European integration. By joining the Common Market, Britain's manufacturers would improve their "competitive position by having a home market, or at least a market without tariff restriction, of greater size than that of the United States." This point of view had the support of Martin Maddan (Conservative, Hitchen) who held membership in Federal Union. Great Britain, *Parliamentary Debates* (Commons), Vol. 561 (November 26, 1956), especially cols. 75–78; 124–127.
[19] Great Britain, *Parliamentary Debates* (Commons), Vol. 561 (November 26, 1956), col. 84.

capital needed to assist developing Commonwealth countries.[20] If Britain remained aloof from European economic unity, however, European competition, especially from German industry, would create an economic challenge of the first magnitude to Britain's industrial future.

The Suez crisis, which occurred at precisely the time when the British were formulating their proposal for a European free trade area, contributed to a rise of support within the British press. The Suez crisis, editorial writers held, had strengthened the prospects for the creation of a Common Market and made more urgent Britain's participation in a free trade area if Europe was to regain greater freedom of action.[21] A theme which grew in intensity in the 1960's found expression: in European integration lay the alternative to excessive economic, military, and political dependence upon the United States.[22]

The inability of the negotiators to make substantial progress in 1958 toward the creation of a free trade area led to a discussion in the press of the implications for Britain of the failure of the negotiations. The government was criticized for the slowness with which Britain was adopting policies designed to create a free trade area.[23] It was suggested that in the absence of a free trade area embracing the EEC and other European countries, western Europe would be divided into two competing trading blocs. As a result, NATO might be weakened. If Britain and Germany held membership in different trading blocs, Britain might be hard pressed to earn the foreign exchange needed to maintain military forces in the Federal Republic. Hence Britain, for political as well as economic reasons, should seek, as a matter of urgency, to reach agreement on a free trade area.[24]

The idea of free trade in Europe had evoked the interest of business leaders in Britain as early as 1955. Like most other Englishman, industrialists initially favored British membership in a free trade area and only later supported EEC entry. In both cases they viewed British participation primarily as a means to assure economic gains for their

---

[20] See, for example, the *Financial Times* (London), June 26, 1956, p. 6; *Times* (London), September 21, 1956, p. 11.

[21] See, for example, the *Manchester Guardian*, January 2, 1957, p. 6; *Daily Mail* (London), January 19, 1957, p. 1.

[22] See Chapter VII for an examination of such sentiment in the 1960's.

[23] See, for example, the *Daily Mail* (London), February 8, 1957, p. 1; *Time and Tide* Vol. 38, No. 9 (March 2, 1957), 235.

[24] See, for example, the *Financial Times* (London), March 3, and 20, 1958; the *Daily Telegraph* (London), July 9, 1958; the *Daily Mail* (London), January 3, 1958; the *Times* (London), July 9, 1958, November 18, 1958; the *Manchester Guardian*, November 18, 1958; the *Yorkshire Post* (Leeds), December 16, 1958.

particular firm or, more broadly, for their industry or the British economy.

It is the practice of the British government to solicit the views of interest groups, such as the Federation of British Industries (FBI), the Trades Union Congress (TUC), and the National Farmers Union (NFU) on issues of vital concern to such organizations, before making decisions or carrying out policies already adopted. In fact, such interest groups have been accorded the right to consult the British government on all policies of major importance to them.[25] They maintain liaison with ministries in Whitehall as well as with Members of Parliament. However, because the locus of political power in Britain lies with the executive to a far greater degree than in the United States, interest groups concentrate their efforts upon cultivating relationships with cabinet ministers and civil servants. In an interactive process, interest groups received reports about official policy from Whitehall and provided information which helped keep the government informed of business and trade union attitudes on the projected free trade area, and later, the Common Market.

In 1955, the FBI had begun to study the implications of European free trade for British industry. After the Messina Conference, the FBI had set up the so-called Panel of the Overseas Trade Policy Committee, which was charged with the task of considering alternative forms of association between the Six and Britain.[26] In September 1956, after

---

[25] For an examination of the role of interest groups in the British political system see, for example: J. D. Stewart, *British Pressure Groups: Their Role in Relation to the House of Commons;* J. W. Grove, *Government and Industry in Britain;* Allen Potter, *Organized Groups in British National Politics.*

[26] At this time the FBI was the leading representative of British industry. Its membership consisted of nearly 300 trade associations, themselves representing some 40,000 firms, and more than 7,700 individual firms engaged in production in Britain. About 40 percent of its member firms had less than 100 employees. The FBI, with its membership of large and small firms, was a spokesman for large and small companies. Each member company, regardless of size, had an equal vote in the election of representatives to the Grand Council, the governing body of the FBI. The Grand Council had a membership of 400, of whom two-thirds represented trade associations and one-third individual member companies. The Grand Council met monthly and was elected for a term of three years. Moreover, the FBI had ten Regional Councils which gave consideration to policy matters. The Regional Councils sent representatives to the Grand Council and provided information about members' views on questions such as that of EEC membership which the FBI as a whole might have under examination at a given time. See *FBI: What it is and What it Does,* revised edition, pp. 1–2. In 1965, the FBI merged with several other industrial interest groups to form the Confederation of British Industry. See Chapter 8.

studying the report issued by the Spaak Committee regarding the formation of the Common Market, the Committee submitted its findings and recommendations to the FBI Grand Council. The Committee rejected the idea of British membership in the proposed Common Market, since to join the EEC would mean "forfeiture of the preferences at present enjoyed by Commonwealth countries on their exports to the U.K." [27] The Committee held that although "the aggregate benefits still accruing to British industry as a whole from the imperial preference system were probably not substantial," and might be reduced even further in the years ahead, they were, nevertheless, still important to some industries. Therefore, concluded the report, Britain should seek some other device than Common Market membership as a means of "warding off the detrimental effects of the collective action which the Six countries were at present taking." Not unlike the general British reaction to the problems posed by the formation of the Common Market, the solution which appealed to the FBI Committee was membership in a free trade area.

In November 1956, the FBI forwarded to the government the findings of a survey just completed on the question of European free trade.[28] In response to a request from the President of the Board of Trade, the FBI had undertaken a survey of industrial opinion which revealed considerable interest in a free trade area among British industrialists.[29] Although some businessmen were apprehensive that British membership was likely to mean the loss of trade preferences in the Commonwealth, there was a broad consensus in support of British participation in a European free trade area.[30] Some respondents expressed certain reservations, including the need for anti-dumping legislation to prevent unfair competition to British industry from other free

---

[27] Federation of British Industries, *The FBI and European Integration*, p. 2.

[28] According to the FBI, "Not only the 287 member trade associations and the ten Regional Councils but also all the 7,500 individual firms of the FBI were given the opportunity of expressing their views, and many hundreds of letters and memoranda were received, tabulated and summarized." *FBI Review*, No. 81 (December 1956), 18.

[29] *Times* (London), October 3, 1956, p. 6.

[30] *FBI Review, Loc. cit.,* p. 51. (Italics in original). ". . . The opinions of the trade associations indicate that the weight of British industrial opinion is in favour of negotiations for the setting up of a European Free Trade Area, *provided that* the rate at which such erosion of the Imperial Preference system as has occurred is not accelerated and that adequate safeguards are devised to ensure that, if we are asked to compete with our European rivals in our home market as well as in theirs, we do so on equal terms."

trade area members.[31] After the completion of this survey, the President of the FBI, in a statement announcing support, termed the proposed free trade area a challenge to British industry, which "in this country has not known the full force of European competition in the home market for a quarter of a century." [32]

The FBI next established a small working party to follow closely the negotiations between Britain and her prospective free trade area partners, and to "make representations to the government on matters of general policy involving a wide range of industry." [33] The Federation also undertook to provide information to its members about the general nature of the free trade area as well as the progress of the negotiations. In April 1957, the FBI prepared and distributed a booklet entitled *A Survey for Industrialists*. This publication provided information about the Treaty of Rome, and dealt with the safeguards and conditions considered by the FBI to be necessary to minimize the dangers of a free trade area to British industry.[34]

The membership of another major industrial interest group, the National Union of Manufacturers, however, was less enthusiastic about British participation in a European free trade area. The President of the NUM feared that Britain's smaller firms and lighter industries might suffer losses in a free trade area.[35] Thus the responses from some business leaders to the government's proposal for a free trade area indicated that not all of British industry shared the view of greater prosperity through European free trade.

In the autumn of 1957 the FBI, together with the Association of British Chambers of Commerce (ABCC) and NUM, issued a detailed

---

[31] *Times* (London), November 2, 1956, p. 3.

[32] *FBI Review*, No. 82 (January, 1957), 18.

[33] *Ibid.*, p. 51.

[34] See the *Times* (London), April 18, 1957, p. 6. The study was notable as the first document published in Britain giving a detailed description of the Treaty of Rome, of which no English translation was available at that time. *FBI Review*, No. 86 (May 1957), p. 33.

[35] The president of the NUM had issued a statement on April 3, 1957, expressing concern for the future of British industry in a free trade area: "It may be true that, in the long run and for the country as a whole, the establishment of free trade in Europe is desirable, and if the evidence supports this view the Government is no doubt justified in changing long-established policies to attain that end. But if, as I believe can be maintained with equal force, this change of policy may result in the grave weakening or total destruction of a number of industries in this country, then the Government must take all possible steps to protect, as far as possible, those individuals, both owners and work-people, who will suffer directly from it." *Times* (London), April 4, 1957, p. 6.

statement reiterating basic requirements for British industry in a European free trade area. The statement urged the government not to give up Britain's "right to maintain its own tariff policy vis-à-vis the outside world and not to join a common external tariff with the EEC." [36] According to the statement, the industrialists agreed with the "government's declared policy that food, feeding stuffs, drink, and tobacco should not be included in the European free trade arrangements."

In contrast to certain other major groups in Britain, the trade union movement did not give great support to the proposal for British participation in a European free trade area. In the British labor movement only the TUC General Council, its principal policymaking body, gave systematic thought, in the period between 1956 and 1961, to the impact of a European free trade area and the EEC upon British workers.[37] Its affiliated unions allowed the General Council to take the lead in formulating trade union policy on European economic integration.[38] In October 1956, the General Council had begun to study proposals for a free trade area between Britain and other countries in western Europe.[39] In that month several members of the General Council issued a statement urging the government to take part in negotiations for a European free trade area.[40] In November 1956, the General Council issued its first major statement on European free trade, a document which was sent to the government and all affiliated unions.[41] The TUC suggested that Britain might face "serious disadvantages both economic and political," should she decline to participate in

---

[36] "The proposed free trade area in Europe, if the U.K. is to enter it, would not be incompatible with the maintenance of the existing structure of Imperial Preference and the Convention establishing the EFTA should be so shaped that Imperial Preference is not jeopardized." Association of British Chambers of Commerce, Federation of British Industries, and National Union of Manufacturers, *A Joint Report on the European Free Trade Area.* (1957)

[37] With more than 8 million members, the TUC represents the vast majority of the British labor movement. Craft, industrial and general unions have affiliations with the TUC. Member unions range in size from the Transport and General Workers' Union, with its 1,250,000 members, to labor organizations with less than 100 on their rolls. For a discussion of the organization and activities of the TUC, see "The Trades Union Congress," *Encyclopaedia Britannica*, Vol. 22, pp. 151–152, Trades Union Congress, *ABC of the TUC* (London, 1962); and Martin Harrison, *Trade Unions and the Labor Party Since 1945*, 1968 ed.

[38] Political and Economic Planning, *Trade Unions and the Common Market*, 4–75.

[39] George Woodcock, "The TUC and Europe," *Spectator*, No. 6765 (February 21, 1958), p. 224.

[40] *Times* (London), October 11, 1956, p. 5.

[41] Trades Union Congress, *Economic Association with Europe* (London, November 1956).

the European integration movement.[42] It was noted that in a European free trade area, inevitably some industries would gain, while others would lose. The Council called upon both management and workers to "play their full part" to become more competitive in order to take "full advantage of the wider European markets" which might be opened to British industry.

The TUC saw the need for plans, including unemployment pay, retraining schemes, and relocation assistance to help workers displaced as a result of industrial change in a free trade area—and in a Common Market—to adjust to new conditions. The leadership of the TUC, like others, especially in the Labour party, contended that the British government should reserve for itself control over economic and social policies, including the right to take unilateral action to restrict imports during balance of payments crises. Also of great concern to the TUC was the question of full employment both in a free trade area and the Common Market.[43]

Although recognizing the need for British participation in a European free trade area, the TUC was never among the more enthusiastic proponents of European integration. Officially, the British trade union movement remained more cautious than its Continental counterparts toward the idea of a European free trade area. In the period when the formation of a free trade area was under discussion and later, when attention was turned to EFTA and Common Market membership, the TUC broadened its contacts with Continental labor organizations. In meetings between British and other European trade union groups, especially in the European Regional Organization of the International Confederation of Free Trade Unions (ICFTU),[44] the question of

---

[42] "Our trade with Western Europe would suffer if a Customs Union with which the United Kingdom was not in any way associated was to be formed: our goods would meet tariff barriers where competing goods from countries in the Customs Union would enter free, and the tariffs of some of the present low-tariff countries in Europe might be raised substantially for our goods. Moreover, if Britain had no association with the Common Market, and if in time the Common Market did succeed in raising the economic efficiency of its members, while at the same time Britain's relative prosperity and competitiveness suffered through exclusion, then clearly this would affect our influence and standing in the world." See also TUC, *Report 1957*, 268–269.

[43] According to the General Council: "It is important that the (free trade) agreement should embody, in specific terms, an action which member countries intend to take, individually and in concert, to achieve and maintain full employment." *Ibid.*, p. 270.

[44] The ICFTU is composed of trade unions which left the communist-controlled World Federation of Trade Unions to establish their own organization. European

European integration was considered. Such contacts undoubtedly served to increase British trade unionists' knowledge of labor conditions on the Continent.[45] Nevertheless, the TUC, while in advance of the rank and file of the British labor movement in recognizing the need for European free trade, accepted only with considerable reservation the idea of British participation in a free trade area. To a greater extent than in the case of other major groups, the British government was in advance of the trade union movement in its advocacy of British participation in a European free trade area. In general, however, the free trade area policy the British government evolved in this period was the product of interaction between public officials and the private sector. In this process of interaction, the government reflected and helped to mold a consensus broadly based among major British elites in favor of participation in a free trade area.

THE EFTA AND COMMON MARKET CONSENSUS

By the end of 1958 the idea of membership in a European free trade area had attracted considerable support in Britain. The formation of the Common Market had contributed to a growing interest in European integration. The failure of the free trade area negotiations led

---

Christian trade unions, together with the TUC and Scandinavian labor groups, were among the founders of the ICFTU. Since 1949, the ICFTU and the WFTU have engaged in a contest to organize unions in less developed areas of the world, with the ICFTU especially active in India and West Africa. *Encyclopaedia Britannica*, Vol. 22, 385.

[45] According to Charles Geddes (later Lord Geddes), a former president of the TUC and representative of the Executive Committee of the European Regional Organization (ERO), of the International Confederation of Free Trade Unions (ICFTU):

The majority of the continental trade union movements are committed to the idea of European political, social, and economic integration. Through the ERO they have tried to change the view of the TUC. Now that Britain is favourably considering a free trade area, pressure upon the TUC to go even further into an integrated Europe will be more vigorously applied.

The British TUC's attitude to all this has been sceptical tolerance. Despite the creation of the Council of Europe and the formation of the European Coal and Steel Community, their general idea is that this was all right for those who wanted it; they did not mind watching the wagon go by so long as they were not committed to ride on it. My personal task as the TUC's representative on the ERO economic committee was to ensure that the wording of the reports and recommendations was in such terms as they could be swallowed without too much mental indigestion. The general council was prepared to accept the terms 'adaptation and harmonization' in place of 'integration and cooperation,' an almost classic example of turning the blind eye to an unwelcome development. Charles Geddes, "Wages and the Common Market," *The Listener*, Vol. LVII, No. 1462 (April 4, 1957), p. 539.

Englishmen to think anew about Britain's relationship with the European Community. In fact, the failure of British efforts to evolve a new relationship with the European Community was followed by still further efforts, subsequent to which Britain was prepared to make concessions previously considered unthinkable. Having developed expectations of gain from participation in the projected free trade area, Englishmen began, early in 1959, to search for some alternative scheme to benefit from European integration.

Within British political parties, interest in EFTA, and to a lesser extent, Common Market membership, gained new adherents as well as continuing support from those who earlier had urged Britain to seek EEC entry. At this time, however, the idea of a "Little Free Trade Area" found favor with most, but not all, MP's.[46] To many in Britain, EFTA appeared to provide only a short-term solution to the problem of European trade. Even in 1959, while expressing expectations of gain from EFTA membership, the Conservative party in its publications acknowledged—as did industrialists, trade unionists, and the writers of press editorials—that the Outer Seven was but a temporary expedient before the creation of a larger trading unit in Europe.[47] Although the form which a larger trading unit would assume was not specified,

---

[46] For example, in a parliamentary debate on February 12, 1959, Mark Bonham Carter (Liberal, Torrington) declared that the government "should state that they are willing to consider joining the Common Market and that, with that end in view, they are initiating conversations with the Commonwealth and with other OEEC countries." On the same day, the parliamentary Liberal party, in an amendment introduced on the Commons Order Paper, urged the government to "start negotiations with a view to the entry of the United Kingdom into the European Economic Community." Several Labour members, in agreement with this Liberal position, urged Britain to apply for membership in the Common Market. Great Britain, *Parliamentary Debates* (Commons), Vol. 599, (February 12, 1959), cols. 1430–1431. Liberal Party Research and Information Department, *Current Topics*, Vol. 1, No. 4, p. 1.

[47] "The removal of tariff and the barriers to trade between the Seven would be valuable in itself. The Seven represent not only a large market for engineering and iron and steel products, motor cars and consumer goods of all kinds, but one of the most rapidly expanding markets. A free trade area of the Seven would of itself avoid the danger that the Six Common Market Powers would be able to forge ahead in a unified economy free from tariff barriers, while the rest of Europe remained isolated in small units separated by tariff barriers and less attractive to U.S. investment. Above all, it would make easier an approach to European economic cooperation. The tariff reductions of the Seven would be phased to keep in step with those of the Six. Negotiations could be conducted between the two groups instead of between the many individual countries. The free trade area of the Seven would therefore provide a bridge to a wider association of Europe, which is both economically and politically the only long-term solution." Conservative Political Center, "Towards a Free Trade Area," *Two Way Topics*, No. 28 (August-September 1959), 1.

Englishmen for the most part favored the abolition of tariff barriers between the Six and Seven. If EFTA was formed largely to enable Britain to reduce trade barriers between the EEC and other West European countries, the apparent inability of Britain to utilize EFTA, in the months after its formation, to achieve this objective contributed to a rise in support for Common Market membership.

Within the parliamentary Conservative and Labour parties, for example, support for EEC entry increased as MP's became fearful of the potentially adverse effects of an economic division in Europe. On May 26, 1960 a group of twenty-five Labour MP's, led by Roy Jenkins, a leading "European" in his party, tabled a motion proposing that the British government "repair some of the damage to British relations with Europe by a new initiative towards the Six involving willingness to join Euratom, the acceptance of the principle of a customs union, and some sacrifice of British sovereignty if this is necessary to promote closer political unity." [48]

On the same day, Liberal members tabled a similar motion calling upon the government to consult with the Commonwealth and EFTA, "with a view to negotiating membership for the United Kingdom and such other countries as are willing to join the European Economic Community, and the association with it of the remaining members of the European Free Trade Association." [49] At its annual conference in Eastbourne from September 29 to October 1, the Liberal party adopted a similar resolution. However, the Liberals stressed also that the Common Market represented "a step toward the political integration" of Europe. Therefore, the party urged the government "to take the lead in establishing common political institutions for western Europe of which she is a part." [50]

A few Conservative party members pressed the government to apply immediately for Common Market membership. On June 24, 1960, a Conservative motion was published in the Commons Order Paper urging the government forthwith to formulate "firm proposals" for negotiations with the Common Market.[51] The motion had as sponsors

---

[48] *Times* (London), May 27, 1960, p. 8. The Labour Motion included as sponsors Frederick Mulley, George Strauss, Charles Pannell, Ernest Thornton, and John Hynd.
[49] *Ibid.*
[50] The Liberal Party Organization, *Liberal Assembly 1960: Resolutions Adopted at Eastbourne, 29th–30th September–October 1.* London, 1960, p. 4.
[51] *Times* (London), June 25, 1960, p. 5.

all officers of the Conservative backbenchers' committee on foreign affairs.

Just a month later, on July 25, a group of forty-two prominent persons, including MP's from all parties and industrialists, issued a statement calling on the government to re-examine its policy and to begin negotiations for EEC entry. The signatories suggested that British Common Market membership would contribute to the unity of the free world,[52] and would not endanger the Commonwealth. "Indeed, it would seem to be in the Commonwealth's interests that Britain should share in the greater opportunities for prosperity created by a wider European economic area, and the Commonwealth should have direct links with the European market, for the system of imperial preference is insufficient for the needs of most expanding Commonwealth countries." [53]

In the six months before the announcement of the British EEC decision, Members of Parliament in favor of such a course of action engaged in a variety of activities in support of Common Market membership. For example, during the foreign affairs debate in the Commons on May 17 and 18, Liberal MP's tabled an amendment in which they expressed regret about the alleged "misjudgment and hesitation" in British policy toward the Common Market. Instead, the government should apply for EEC membership and undertake to negotiate amendments "to meet the special circumstances of Britain, other members of the European Free Trade Association, and the Commonwealth." [54]

In contrast to many members of other parties, Liberals envisaged gains for British farmers from Common Market membership. It was pointed out that British farms were larger, on the average, than their counterparts in the Six. British yields per acre were among the highest in western Europe, and Britain's agriculture was more highly mechanized than that of Common Market countries. As a member, Britain could have a voice in determining target prices for foodstuffs in the Community. By accepting the EEC agricultural policy, moreover, Britain could save millions of pounds each year in farming subsidies.

---

[52] *Times* (London), July 25, 1960, p. 7.
[53] The statement has as sponsors Jo Grimond, leader of the Liberal Party, Roy Jenkins, for the Labour Party, Peter Kirk, Conservative, and Lawrence Robson, an industrialist and former Liberal candidate.
[54] Liberal Party Research and Information Department, *Current Topics,* Vol. 1, No. 2 (June 1961), 2.

This saving could be used to reduce indirect taxes on consumer goods in Britain. Finally, according to Liberals, the cost of living would rise only slightly if Britain adopted the Common Market agricultural policy.

As a means of rallying domestic support for a Common Market application, the Conservative and Unionist Central Office issued a leaflet on June 10, 1961 setting forth several gains which might come from British EEC membership. According to this publication, "The future relationship between Britain, western Europe and the Commonwealth has become one of the outstanding issues of the day." [55] On the unity of western Europe depended the whole outcome of the East-West struggle. European integration would increase the strength of the West. The Conservative party suggested that "Britain's integration with the European Economic Community, provided this has the endorsement of the Commonwealth and takes full account of the position of her EFTA partners, could bring great political and economic benefits." Thus, while the government remained officially uncommitted to Common Market membership, the Conservative party had already embarked upon an effort to increase public support for such action.

In leaflets published under its imprimatur in the weeks before the announcement of the 1961 Common Market decision, the Labour party examined the basic provisions of the Rome Treaty and set forth considerations which, it was held, should influence Britain's decision to apply for membership. British policy should be based upon an assessment of the potential effects of EEC entry upon the Commonwealth, British trade, industry, agriculture, and Britain's ability to plan her economy. [56] While not opposing a Common Market bid at this time, the Labour party suggested that regardless of whether or not Britain became a member, she must take steps to assure greater growth rates and competitive vigor in industry: "There is no reason for supposing that a blast of competitive fresh air from the Continent would in itself suddenly improve the sleepy standards of British industry." British membership would have "far-reaching effects" on the Commonwealth, since Britain "would be entering into a closer economic and political relationship with the Six than it now has with the Commonwealth." Moreover, the precise gains and losses from Common Market membership could not be assessed until the terms of entry became clear, a

---

[55] Conservative and Unionist Central Office, *Weekend Talking Point*, No. 349, (week ending June 10, 1961), 1.
[56] Labour Party, *Talking Points*, No. 11 (July 19, 1961), 1.

position to which Labour party leaders were to adhere until the autumn of 1962, when the party leadership placed itself on record in opposition to EEC membership on the terms being negotiated in Brussels.[57]

Although in the summer of 1961 all British political parties contained proponents of Common Market membership, there were many who remained skeptical, if not hostile, to such a bid. For example, Sir Anthony Eden, speaking at a rally of Yorkshire Young Conservatives, stressed the importance of Britain's ties with other Commonwealth countries, although he did not rule out a British EEC bid.[58] On June 20, 1961, seven Conservative backbenchers, in an amendment to a motion, stressed the dangers of Common Market membership. Commonwealth relationships might be placed in jeopardy if Britain joined the EEC.[59] Perhaps anticipating the government's impending decision, two Conservative backbench MP's tabled a motion on July 26 opposing Common Market membership if such a course of action led to "any national derogation of British sovereignty." [60] This motion gave warnings to the government not to sacrifice Commonwealth interests and British agriculture in negotiations with the Six. Its sponsors included Mr. Robin Turton (Thirsk and Malton) and Sir Derek Walker-Smith (Hertford East), both of whom were former Ministers of Health. Especially in the period between July 1961 and January 1963, both became vocal critics of British Common Market policy. Their motion had the support of at least thirty other Conservative Members of Parliament.

At this time, moreover, there were sizable forces in the Labour party in opposition to Common Market membership. On July 27, 1961 the Labour party had published an agenda containing a list of resolutions submitted to the party's annual conference scheduled to begin on October 2 in Blackpool. Of the twenty-two resolutions on the Common Market, the authors of half were opposed categorically to British EEC membership. Only two of the resolutions expressed unequivocal support for Common Market entry.[61] Loyalties to the Common-

---

[57] For an examination of Labour party policy at the time of the Brussels negotiations, see Chapter 4.

[58] According to Eden: "No British Government can enter into engagements which do not fully honour its obligations to those who have stood by us in good times and bad with a loyalty beyond compare in the history of the world." *Guardian* (Manchester and London), June 12, 1961, p. 3.

[59] *Times* (London), June 21, 1961, p. 4.

[60] See the *Times* (London), July 27, 1961, and the *Daily Telegraph* (London), July 27, 1961.

[61] See the *Financial Times* (London), July 27, 1961.

wealth made it difficult, if not impossible, for certain MP's to support a British EEC bid. Britain, it was feared, might participate in the European Community only to find that she had weakened or broken cherished bonds with former overseas possessions.

Divisions of opinion within the parliamentary parties reflected divergent views held by Conservative and Labour voters in Britain. In the summer of 1961, many voters remained unconvinced that Britain should apply for Common Market membership. According to a poll conducted just a month before the announcement of the British EEC decision, a majority of those voters questioned in each party thought that British entry might be either a "bad thing" for them or made "no difference" to them. Although Conservative voters registered a higher percentage than Labour in support of a British Common Market bid, a higher percentage of Conservatives ranked themselves as opponents of EEC entry.

TABLE 1

EFFECT OF BRITAIN JOINING THE EUROPEAN COMMON MARKET
(Percentages)

Question: As far as you, yourself, and your family are concerned, do you think it will be a good thing or a bad thing if Britain decides to join the European Common Market, or won't it make any difference to you one way or the other?

| | | Voting in 1959 | | |
	Total	*Cons.*	*Lab.*	*Rest*
Good Thing	28	33	24	27
Bad Thing	19	25	21	11
No Difference	53	42	55	62

Dates of fieldwork: June 29–July 3, 1961.
Source: Social Surveys (Gallup Poll) Limited. *Britain and the ECM: A Gallup Poll Conducted for the Daily Telegraph.* (London), 1961, p. 34.

Given the state of public opinion, it would have been unusual if Britain's parliamentary parties on the eve of the government's announcement of July 31 had a vocal majority in favor of Common Market membership. Thus, in deciding to apply for EEC entry, the British government chose a course of action which did not have as broad a base of support among major elites as had been the case with its earlier free trade area policies.

Within the press, however, there was a general consensus, which included the vast majority of leading newspapers, in favor of Common Market membership. After the failure of the free trade area negotiations, some British journals for the first time began to consider favorably the idea of EEC entry.[62] For example, in a series of editorials in November and December 1958, the *Economist*, the first major British journal to advocate EEC membership, suggested that, in the short-run, the Common Market was not likely to affect adversely Britain's exports to the Six. However, the existence of the EEC might have serious long-range implications for British trade. At the end of December, the *Economist* published an editorial, signed "By a Good European," proposing Common Market membership.[63] Such a policy, it was suggested, would prevent discrimination against British exports and contribute to a general reduction in European trade barriers. In negotiations with the Six, Britain might minimize losses in Commonwealth trade by achieving for the Commonwealth compensation in the form of new markets in western Europe in exchange for anticipated losses of Commonwealth markets in Britain. But the British faced yet another formidable problem, namely, to convince continental Europeans that Britain "is no longer interested in dividing Europe," and "in claiming a special relationship with the United States which leaves France out of the great power club and works against France's interests." [64]

In many cases, the British press viewed the Outer Seven as a useful device for eventually bringing West European countries into one trading group.[65] EFTA might provide a "bridge" between the two emerging blocs, although it was to be regretted that "paradoxically Britain, in joining EFTA, must draw farther from the Six in order eventually to get closer to the EEC." [66] In their editorials, however, not a few journals questioned the utility of EFTA. Because it did not compare in economic strength with the Common Market, EFTA could bring little pressure upon the Six for agreement with Britain. More-

---

[62] See, for example, the *Economist*, Vol. CXC, No. 6024 (February 7, 1959), 471.

[63] This article, entitled "Join the Common Market?" was prepared by a young editorial writer, Mr. Christopher Layton, who was a member also of Federal Union and active in work on behalf of the Liberal party. According to Layton, he and some other members of the editorial staff of the *Economist* viewed this article as a "trial balloon" designed to gauge the reaction of the journal's readers to a somewhat "radical" proposal. See the *Economist*, Vol. CLXXXIX, No. 6018 (December 27, 1958), 1138.

[64] *Economist*, Vol. CXCI, No. 6034 (April 18, 1959), 207.

[65] See, for example, the *Times* (London), May 20, 1959, p. 11; the *Daily Telegraph* (London), September 7, 1959, p. 10; the *Scotsman* (Edinburgh), May 27, 1959, p. 8; the *Manchester Guardian*, May 28, 1959, p. 8; *Time and Tide*, Vol. 40, No. 23 (June 6, 1959), 639.

[66] *Daily Mail* (London), November 24, 1959, p. 1; see also the *Financial Times* (London), July 20, 1959, p. 6.

over, EFTA membership had saddled Britain with the problems of European neutrals, of which three—Austria, Sweden and Switzerland —were her partners in the Outer Seven.[67]

In the latter months of 1959, many British journals published editorials calling upon Britain to make a greater political commitment to Europe. For example, it was suggested that negotiations on Britain's political and economic relations with Europe should "embrace the whole range of European interests, including the vital problems of defense, of nuclear weapons, of the Commonwealth and underdeveloped countries in general, and of political consultation and alignment." [68] Thus, a changed British outlook about foreign policy priorities which attached new importance to European integration must precede new approaches by Britain to the Six. Therefore, the British government should make a concerted effort to "destroy the impression that we are cold-shouldering Europe" by abandoning "every vestige of aloofness" toward the Common Market.[69]

In the case of at least one newspaper, the call for a new British political commitment to European integration even included the pooling of Britain's nuclear capability with that of her Continental neighbors. The *Guardian* saw in the placing of Britain's nuclear force under European control a means for breaking the economic deadlock between the Six and Seven. Such a decision might have other implications: It would reduce the burden of a costly nuclear force, whose utility was considered to be dubious. If Britain's nuclear weapons provided only a marginal increment to Western strength, at great cost to the British taxpayer, they might prove of greater value as a deterrent if they were merged with a "European" atomic force. Of more immediate consequence, however, editorial writers shrewdly pointed out, Britain's nuclear weapons might provide a bargaining device for Common Market membership.[70] Although such a proposal, of course, was not popular in Britain in this period, its acceptance would have heightened French interest in British entry, but at the risk of widening the gap between supporters and opponents of Common Market member-

---

[67] See, for example, the *Economist*, Vol. CXCIV, No. 6083 (March 26, 1960), 1195; the *Guardian* (Manchester and London), December 1, 1959, p. 8. On August 24, 1959, the *Manchester Guardian* changed its name to the *Guardian*. Since 1959 the *Guardian* has been published both in London and Manchester.

[68] See, for example, the *Financial Times* (London), November 19, 1959, p. 10.

[69] *Daily Mail* (London), November 17, 1959, p. 10. See also the *Guardian* (Manchester and London), November 14, 1959, p. 8.

[70] *Guardian* (Manchester and London), May 2, 1960, p. 8.

ship. By 1959, and even by 1963, Englishmen, by and large, were not prepared to accept a political commitment to Europe which included the sharing of nuclear weapons.

During the year before the announcement of Britain's first Common Market decision, leading British journals for the most part adopted editorial policies in support of EEC entry.[71] It was generally acknowledged that the longer Britain delayed in applying for EEC membership, the more difficult would her entry become.[72] If, however, Britain joined the Common Market, she might experience several important gains: access to the rapidly growing markets of the Six; rising rates of economic growth; and the strengthening of her economy by the injection of greater competition. In European economic integration lay "the great counterpoise to Communist economic strength." EEC entry was not incompatible with Commonwealth interests. In fact, it was asserted, the "economic interests of the Commonwealth as a whole are undoubtedly on the side of our association with the most promising growth market in the world." [73] As a member of the EEC, Britain would be able to "act as a sort of liberal stabilizer" in encouraging the development of political stability and representative government on the Continent.[74] In general, the British press held a view common among other proponents of EEC entry: as a member of the Common Market, Britain might assume the leadership of an integrated Europe—a role which, incidentally, de Gaulle coveted for France. If Britain remained outside the Common Market, according to British editorial opinion, the leadership of an integrated Europe might fall to Germany, rather than France. However appealing the role of leader of an integrated Europe might be to those in Britain who sought for their country a new place in world affairs in the post-colonial period, it undoubtedly influenced

[71] *Daily Telegraph* (London), July 25, 1960, p. 10. See also the *Times* (London), September 8, 1960, p. 13; the *Spectator*, No. 6936 (June 2, 1961), p. 783; the *Daily Herald* (London), July 2, 1960, p. 1; the *Observer* (London), July 3, 1960, p. 8; the *Spectator*, No. 6893, p. 6; the *Statist*, Vol. CLXXI, No. 4306 (September 17, 1960), p. 396; the *Guardian* (Manchester and London), December 20, 1960, p. 8. (See the same newspaper, December 16, 1960, p. 10 for another expression of this view); *Time and Tide*, Vol. 42, No. 1 (January 6, 1961), 4. See also the *Yorkshire Post* (Leeds), January 25, 1961, p. 6.
[72] *Financial Times* (London), February 19, 1961, p. 8; see also the *Scotsman* (Edinburgh), February 17, 1961, p. 10; *Yorkshire Post* (Leeds) April 14, 1961, p. 8; the *Guardian* (Manchester and London), February 17, 1961, p. 10; the *Statist*, Vol. CLXXIII, No. 4329 (February 25, 1961), 303.
[73] *Sunday Times* (London), June 18, 1961, p. 10.
[74] *Time and Tide*, Vol. 42, No. 25 (June 22, 1961), 1004.

de Gaulle's outlook toward British Common Market membership. The discussion in Britain on Common Market entry had at least two audiences—domestic and foreign. What appealed to one might not necessarily find favor with the other. The problem of satisfying widely diverse "constituencies" contributed to the difficulties facing the British government in its Common Market bid.

In some British periodicals editorial writers questioned the validity of one of Britain's basic reservations about European integration; namely that Britain, because of her obligations to the Commonwealth, could not join wholeheartedly in the European integration movement. In fact, the press was among the first of the major British elites to question, and reject, the widely held assumption that Britain's primary foreign policy objective lay in the preservation and strengthening of the Commonwealth, and that Commonwealth interests precluded a more active British role in the European integration movement. Contrary to the prevailing British belief, the Commonwealth did not afford great potential for the expansion of exports. In recent years, Commonwealth preferences had lessened, and in the long run Commonwealth countries might even benefit from British Common Market membership. The growth of British trade with the Commonwealth had not kept pace with the growth of Commonwealth trade as a whole. Britain's trade with western Europe was rising at a more rapid rate than her trade with the Commonwealth. There was relatively little opportunity for further reductions in the barriers to intra-Commonwealth trade, since other Commonwealth countries, for the most part, were not prepared to open their markets to British exports which competed with their own industries. Only by strengthening her own economy through Common Market membership could Britain hope in the long run to retain influence in the Commonwealth. Politically, as well, the Commonwealth offered few opportunities for Britain to enhance her international position vis-à-vis the United States and the Soviet Union. Increasingly, the Commonwealth resembled the United Nations in size and in discord. No longer was the Commonwealth an organization with clear-cut criteria for membership (except in the case of South Africa, which left in 1961 because of pressure by the non-white majority of newer members, against the wishes of Britain). In brief, the government was the object of criticism for having given undue deference to the Commonwealth in the formulation of British foreign policy.[75]

---

[75] *Daily Herald* (London), July 13, 1961, p. 6. See also the *Spectator*, No. 6917 (January 20, 1961), 63; the *Observer* (London), March 12, 1961, p. 10; the *Daily*

Not without justification, British editorial writers concluded that the United States, especially since the inauguration of the Kennedy Administration, had reappraised its policy toward the Six and Seven. Although successive U.S. administrations had seen European integration as compatible with U.S. foreign policy, the United States now clearly expressed its preference for the more tightly-knit EEC over the less cohesive EFTA. Macmillan, it was suggested, had returned from his talks in Washington in April 1961 with the knowledge that the United States clearly favored British membership in the Common Market and had even urged such a course of action upon the Prime Minister. Allegedly, President Kennedy made it clear that the United States favored British entry into the Common Market because it accorded with the "grand design" for an Atlantic Partnership which would have included an integrated Europe, with Britain as a member.[76] The U.S. preference for the Six over the Seven made even more imperative a British decision to join the Common Market.[77] Only as a leading member of an enlarged European Community could Britain hope to retain a special relationship with the United States. Henceforth the United States would look to an integrated Europe, rather than Britain, as the ally with which to establish a special relationship.[78] Thus, by the summer of 1961, the British government's Common Market policy not only enjoyed widespread support within the British press; in some cases, editorial opinion was considerably in advance of the government in calling for a British political, and even military, commitment to an integrated Europe.

As in the case of the press, the collapse of the free trade area talks had led British industrial organizations to give thought to alternative courses of action. Initially, the idea of a "little free trade area" had appealed to business leaders as a temporary expedient designed both to achieve for British industry some of the benefits of wider markets and as a device for eventually bringing together all OEEC members into one trading organization.

Most British industrialists had welcomed the formation of EFTA. If

---

Telegraph (London) July 28, 1961, p. 10; the *Economist*, Vol. CXCVLLL, No. 6132 (March 4, 1961), 826; *Time and Tide*, Vol. 41, No. 24 (June 11, 1960), 655; the *Guardian* (Manchester and London), March 8, 1961, p. 10.

[76] For a more detailed examination of the changing British estimate of the special relationship see Chapter 3.

[77] See, for example, the *Guardian* (Manchester and London), April 26, 1961, p. 10.

[78] See, for example, the *Guardian* (Manchester and London), May 29, 1961, p. 10; the *Daily Mail* (London), April 27, 1961, p. 1; the *Economist*, Vol. CXCIX, No. 6140 (April 29, 1961), 421; the *Times* (London), June 7, 1961, p. 13.

they could not gain immediate access to the greater and more dynamic markets of the EEC, they might at least expand in a more limited fashion what they saw as their domestic market by joining a smaller trading organization. However, a review of the annual reports of British manufacturers of such varied products as machine tools, bicycles, chocolates, woolen goods, linen thread, and automobiles from the end of 1958 until the announcement of the Common Market decision, reveals as a dominant theme a preoccupation with the need for a bridge between the Six and Seven. Even by 1958, the apparent inability of the Six and Seven to form a larger free trade area had given impetus to efforts by British industrialists to acquire production facilities on the Continent. Before 1959, however, British industrialists had generally confined their European investment to the acquisition of existing firms rather than the construction of new production facilities in Continental western Europe.[79]

As British trade and expectations of gain from greater access to the dynamic markets of the Six increased, British direct investment in the EEC rose. In 1961, a year in which Britain's total direct investment abroad fell by 13 percent, British industrialists had increased by about 25 percent their direct investment in the Six. As recently as 1958, British direct investment abroad had totalled some £144 million, of which the EEC countries had received only £8.4 million. By 1961, however, British direct investment abroad had increased by about 50 percent over its 1958 level and Britain's stake in Common Market countries had grown threefold, from £8.4 million to £25.3 million. In France and West Germany, the most important increases were registered. During this same period British direct investment in other EFTA countries had increased from less than £3 million in 1958 to £8 million in 1961.[80] Thus it can be seen that British investment in the Common Market rose at the same time as interest in EEC membership.

There was another reason for the growing interest among British industrialists in markets in Europe. The attention the free trade area proposal had focused on western Europe had awakened many businessmen in Britain to the existence of a large market just across the Channel. Having observed the phenomenal growth of West European economies, they saw the possibility of a larger share in these burgeoning markets for British exports. In considerable numbers British busi-

---

[79] *Times* (London), September 15, 1959, p. 17.
[80] *Times* (London), November 28, 1962, p. 15.

nessmen, in some cases for the first time, ventured with success into West European markets.[81] Such success generated even greater optimism about the opportunities for exports and, in turn, gave rise to support for Common Market membership.

By 1959 there was support among British industrialists for EEC membership. One reason for the changing British outlook was the growing interest of U.S. businessmen in the Common Market. Industrialists in Britain increasingly took the view that "big American firms will pour capital into the Common Market if they see that the scheme is succeeding. Then we shall have to compete with American plants and American know-how working out on a base with Continental costs." [82] Moreover, British industrialists were fearful of cartels which they believed Continental Europeans might form in the Common Market, both to monopolize sales there and to enable manufacturers to cut prices in world markets.

In the months after its formation, industrial leaders in Britain had come to doubt the utility of EFTA as a device for bringing together the Six and Seven. As such doubts increased, industrialists turned to Common Market membership as the only long-term solution to the division of western Europe into two economic blocs. An examination of the 1960 annual reports of British companies, as compared with previous years, reveals a marked increase in support for Common Market membership.

In 1960, British industrialists found another reason to reassess Britain's relationship with the Common Market. The so-called Hallstein Plan for accelerating the rate at which the EEC fulfilled its objectives might pose new problems for exports from Britain to the Six.[83] More-

---

[81] "Trade on the Ebb Tide," *The Annual Report of the Manchester Guardian Staff on Industrial Conditions, Problems and Views* (Manchester 1958), p. 17.

[82] Statement by Financial Editor, *Manchester Guardian*. Quoted in the *New York Times*, March 15, 1959, p. 30.

[83] The Hallstein Plan had several principal features: (1) Tariff reductions within the Common Market, scheduled to take place on July 1, 1960, and December 31, 1961, would be 20 percent instead of 10 percent. Allowing for the 10 percent reduction made on January 1, 1959, tariffs would be reduced by a total of 50 percent, instead of 30 percent by December 31, 1961. The Commission would be willing to extend these tariff reductions to outside countries, provided that they did not go below the EEC common external tariff; (2) the first step toward the EEC common external tariff would take effect on July 1, 1960, instead of December 31, 1961. The common external tariff would be fixed provisionally at a level 20 percent below the arithmetical mean between the tariffs of the six members. "A lower external tariff would help to reconcile the low-tariff Benelux countries to the idea of raising their tariffs earlier than they had bargained for.

over, so long as the government's policy remained obscure, businessmen could not make investment and marketing decisions about the
EEC. In the belief that Britain might be on the verge of joining the
Common Market, buyers in the Six had postponed purchases of British
goods at the prospect of lower tariffs and, hence, lower prices.

In the period before Britain's first Common Market application,
bankers became particularly strong proponents of EEC entry. Such
expectations as those which other business leaders held also found favor
with bankers: Britain's exclusion from the EEC would result in a
further decline in British trade; Britain's economic interest lay in
bridging the gap between the Six and Seven; outside the Common
Market, Britain would receive from the United States less investment
capital and the know-how which frequently accompanies it. But proponents of Common Market membership in the City, the financial dis-
trict of London, saw other potential benefits: by signing the Rome
Treaty Britain would gain "a powerful new prop for sterling," since
presumably the Common Market countries would reach agreement
eventually on a scheme for pooling their currency reserves. Britain's
membership in the Common Market would enhance her ability to
provide capital to the developing countries of the Commonwealth.[84]
Among merchant bankers, it was widely held that the City of London
would offer the EEC facilities for banking and insurance second to
none. London might emerge as the leading financial center of an enlarged Common Market, since the British for centuries had developed
a knowledge of the needs of exporters selling in every world market.[85]

The creation, in November 1960, of the Export Council for Europe
pointed up the growing interest among industrialists in trade with
Europe. Although formed as a result of the initiative of the President
of the Board of Trade, the Export Council for Europe had as members
thirty-one prominent figures in British industry and commerce, in

---

The 20 percent would become permanent if countries outside the Common
Market agreed to reduce their tariffs in the same proportion. . . . The proposed 20
percent reduction of the common tariff would mean that in most cases France and
Italy would have to lower their tariffs more drastically and the Benelux countries
would have to raise theirs less drastically than is now envisaged." *Times* (London), March 4, 1960, p. 10.
[84] See, for example, "Commonwealth and Common Market." The *Banker*, Vol.
CXV, No. 426 (July 1961), 532; "Report of Westminster Bank Limited," *Economist*, Vol. CXCVIII, No. 6127 (January 28, 1961), 392.
[85] See, for example, the *Financial Times* (London), November 15, 1961, and
Jeremy Raisman, "The Open Secret Weapon of the Banking World," *European-
Atlantic Review*, Vol. XI, No. 3 (July–August 1961), 15–18.

addition to representatives from the Treasury, Foreign Office, and Board of Trade. Moreover, the Council had as sponsoring organizations the ABCC, FBI, and NUM, as well as the Trades Union Congress and banking interests in the City of London. The Export Council for Europe had as its objective "to explore, promote, and publicize existing trade opportunities in Europe, to seek new openings for the sale there of British products, and to ensure that every advantage is taken of them." [86] During its first year, the Council dispatched missions to European countries to assess the future prospects for British trade.[87] It published its findings in reports, of which some 90,000 copies were distributed. In general, the Council expressed optimism about the prospects for British exports to Continental western Europe, provided Britain's industrialists made a greater effort to market their products abroad.

By the spring of 1961, the quest for an end to the economic division in Europe had strengthened the consensus among industrialists that Britain should apply for Common Market membership. A former president of the FBI, Sir William McFadzean, at that time chairman of the Export Council for Europe, declared in Berlin on May 4, 1961, that business leaders in Britain were "very much in favor of the United Kingdom joining the EEC." [88] At approximately the same time the official journal of the Institute of Directors, another leading organization of British businessmen, expressed support for a British application for Common Market membership.[89]

At a conference in London in June 1961 the ABCC pledged its conditional support for Common Market membership,[90] and urged the adoption of a decimal currency to correspond with the monetary systems of Britain's prospective EEC partners. Moreover, at the time of the government's announcement of July 31, the President of the NUM expressed his organization's approval of the decision. To the question, "Do you consider that the United Kingdom should join the Common

---

[86] Export Council of Europe, *Trading Opportunities in Europe*, Part One, London, (1961), 4.
[87] "Their primary task was to establish contacts and ascertain facts including not only where the British export effort was failing so that faults could be remedied, but even more where it was succeeding so that success could be emulated." Export Council of Europe, *Report by the Chairman on the First Two Years and the Future: Achievement and Challenge*, London, 1961.
[88] *Times* (London), May 5, 1961, p. 12.
[89] The *Director*, Vol. 13, No. 10 (April 1961), 51.
[90] *Guardian* (Manchester and London), June 23, 1961, p. 15.

Market?" only two ABCC associates, representing 642 firms, voiced the answer "no," while 75 percent of the Association's membership expressed support for EEC entry. Nevertheless, the ABCC opposed entry on just "any terms," and emphasized the importance of securing advantages for Commonwealth and EFTA members, as well as British agriculture, before placing a British signature on the Rome Treaty. However, the delegates did not consider these obstacles to be insurmountable. In a memorandum of July 13, 1961, the ABCC forwarded these views to the Prime Minister. This document summarized the Association's replies from its questionnaire to members, together with the recommendations made at its annual conference the previous month.[91]

In a pamphlet the FBI published in July 1961 after the Grand Council had debated the question of EEC membership, a bid by Britain to join the Common Market received provisional approval. The statement acknowledged that the Federation's goal was a "European-wide multilateral trading system." [92] According to the statement, however, many FBI members believed that "it is right not to become committed to formal negotiations with the Six until existing differences over major problems have been so far narrowed as to offer the prospect of a satisfactory outcome."

The problems which concerned the FBI were those of temperate zone foodstuffs from the Commonwealth, British trade with EFTA, and the institutions, as well as the "political implications," of the Rome Treaty. Not unlike a broad segment of British opinion, the Federation was opposed to any "solution which in effect meant that the Commonwealth was to pay a substantial part of the price for British association with the Common Market." Secondly, the Federation declared, "it is imperative that Britain's obligations to EFTA, to which this country is not only contractually but morally committed, must be honored in full." According to the FBI, Britain's "abiding interest in Commonwealth development makes it important to us that any association should lead to expanding markets for Commonwealth producers, particularly those in the developing countries." Nevertheless, subject to the aforementioned caveats, the FBI supported the British application for Common Market membership.

In sum, by August 1961, there existed among British industrial

---

[91] *Times* (London), July 3, 1961, p. 19.
[92] Federation of British Industries, *British Industry and Europe* (London, 1961), p. 5.

leaders considerable sentiment in support of a Common Market application. The prospect of increasing sales in a free trade area had whetted the appetites of business leaders, while the interest generated by the government's proposals several years earlier for a free trade area had focused attention upon the markets of the Six. Although it provided freer access to the markets of several European countries, EFTA had never furnished a home market of dimensions comparable to that of a broader free trade area or the Common Market. Moreover, perhaps in part because Britain's businessmen had "discovered" Europe, British exports to the Continent grew rapidly in the period preceding the government's Common Market application. At the same time, Britain's trade with Commonwealth countries failed to register impressive gains. Fears of the loss of Commonwealth preferences diminished as former colonial countries reduced or eliminated the preferential treatment accorded imports from Britain and even, in some cases, raised tariffs or imposed quantitative restrictions against British exports. Therefore, the loss of Commonwealth markets appeared less a danger to British businessmen in 1961 than in previous years, although industrial support for Common Market membership was tempered by apprehensions about the reduction of exports to Commonwealth countries.

Like most other British proponents of European free trade, the TUC General Council saw EFTA not as an end in itself, but as a device for reconciling the non-members with the Common Market. When the General Council considered the provisions of the Stockholm Convention, its members concluded, as they had in the proposals for a broader free trade area, that the provisions for full employment were less satisfactory than those requested. Moreover, the General Council expressed regret because of the failure of the Convention to stress that "the closing of the breach with the European Economic Community was an urgent objective of signatory Governments." The General Council was dissatisfied that the Stockholm Convention placed "overwhelming emphasis" upon trade matters, rather than social issues such as full employment which were of great importance to the TUC. In talks with British officials the General Council, so it declared, had emphasized the point that a Convention "confined" to trade issues to the neglect of social issues would not be satisfactory to the trade union Movement." [93]

In the spring and summer of 1961, the General Council found itself

---

[93] TUC, *Report 1960*, pp. 262–263.

cautiously in favor of Common Market membership. After consultations with the labor leaders from other European and Commonwealth countries, the General Council expressed agreement "in principle with the government's decision to open negotiations with the European Community with a view to joining the Community, but insist that satisfactory arrangements must be made to meet the special needs of the United Kingdom, of the Commonwealth, and of the EFTA." [94] The General Council was not prepared to give full endorsement to the British bid until "negotiations with the members of the EEC have disclosed more clearly the conditions on which Britain could join and the extent to which her special needs could be met." Moreover, the General Council called for the protection of living standards for agricultural workers and "terms which are satisfactory to British agriculture." However, the TUC was prepared to take a "pragmatic, rather than a theoretical, view of supranationalism," since the "full gains of closer economic association cannot be obtained unless the countries concerned are prepared to adopt a more co-ordinated approach to the problems that confront them." Its guide in this matter would be the way in which the "interests of working people" would be affected by agreements reached during negotiations between Britain and the Six.

The policies toward European integration which the General Council adopted were not representative of the views of rank and file trade union members. If the attention that delegates to TUC annual meetings devoted to this question indicated the degree of interest among trade unionists, the General Council's level of interest remained throughout the period under consideration far above that of the membership of affiliated unions. In 1957, only two resolutions out of a total of eighty-eight listed in the TUC, *Report 1957*, for presentation at the annual meeting of that year, were concerned with European free trade. Both stressed the need for continued protection of the jute industry, together with "adequate safeguards for all workers in the industry," should Britain join a free trade area. However, the agenda of the TUC's annual meetings in 1958, 1959, and 1960, contained no resolutions on the question of free trade in Europe, despite the failure of the free trade area talks in 1958 and the negotiations during the following year which led to the formation of EFTA.

In its annual meetings of 1957, 1958, and 1961, the TUC discussed

---

[94] TUC, *Report 1961*, p. 468.

the question of Britain's relations with the European Community. In 1957 and 1958, supporters of the free trade area stressed the potential contribution of British membership to the maintenance of full employment and increased productivity and living standards in Britain. At the 1961 conference, proponents of Common Market membership referred to the benefits of a market of two hundred million people, as well as the possibilities which the EEC offered for increasing Britain's international influence.[95]

Within the trade union movement, opponents first of the free trade area and later of the Common Market viewed with alarm the prospect that Britain might lose control over economic planning. In addition to the often repeated apprehensions about full employment, they opposed the Common Market because of what they perceived to be reactionary governments in France and West Germany—an argument often put forward especially by opponents of EEC entry on the Labour left. Trade union opponents of EEC entry expressed fear of the possibility of lower living standards and the influx of large numbers of workers from southern Europe.[96] The specter of the reduction in trade with the Commonwealth and hence the loss of British jobs haunted others in the labor movement who opposed Common Market membership.

Even on the eve of the government's EEC announcement, however, support in the British trade union movement for such a step was confined by and large to the General Council and, in particular, to its economic and international committees. In these committees the implications for British trade unionists of the free trade area and the EEC had been considered in great detail. Nevertheless, a majority of delegates to the TUC annual meeting in September 1961 were prepared to endorse the General Council's position. The conference voted down a resolution which called Common Market membership "injurious to our

---

[95] *Ibid.*, pp. 325–338.

[96] Mr. Frank Cousins, General Secretary of the Transport and General Workers' Union, expressed many of these views at his union's annual conference in Brighton on July 12, 1961. Although he emphasized that the TGWU should not "get out of step with the rest of the labour movement" on the Common Market question, nevertheless, he warned that "the Labour movement would hesitate to give *carte blanche* to any politician on this issue for several reasons. There were insufficient safeguards for full employment, social services, wages and working conditions. There was a lack of clarity on political and military issues, and too little information about supranational institutions. If we put ourselves at the mercy of people whose expressed intentions were to beat us in the economic world, we could expect to suffer the consequences." *Times* (London), July 13, 1961, p. 8.

national interest." [97] The show of hands against the motion was said to be "about five-to-one or possibly four-to-one." [98]

Between 1950 and 1961 the TUC General Council had evolved a policy first in favor of British participation in a European free trade area, and later, Common Market membership. Among the factors which contributed to the development of attitudes favorable to the EEC among members of the General Council, were their contacts with labor leaders on the Continent. As a result of such meetings, British labor leaders gained a new awareness of the diminishing disparity between British and Continental living standards. Contrary to the earlier fears of British trade unionists, the British living standard might not be reduced if Britain joined the Common Market. Increasingly, TUC leaders saw gains to Britain's economy and to her industries from Common Market membership, which in turn might bring benefits to trade union members." [99] Therefore, the EEC gained considerable support among trade union leaders, if not among the rank and file of the labor movement.

In the private sector, however, it was the Europe-oriented groups such as Federal Union which pushed most actively for Common Market entry. By the summer of 1960 the Federal Union proponents of EEC entry had decided to organize the Common Market Campaign, an organization whose specific objective would be to press for British membership. As in the case of other "European" organizations sponsored and encouraged by Federal Union, the federalist founders of the Common Market Campaign wished to rally to their cause persons who might not necessarily share their commitment to European integration as a major step toward eventual world government, but who nevertheless, for other reasons, favored EEC membership. In January 1961, a Preparatory Committee of the Common Market Campaign was organized. Its organizers prevailed upon Lord Gladwyn, himself an ardent

---

[97] TUC, *Report 1961*, p. 338.

[98] *Financial Times* (London), September 6, 1961, p. 1.

[99] Trade union leaders came to share a view expressed by Robert Edwards, a Labour Member of Parliament and General Secretary of the Chemical Workers Union. "Revolutionary changes have indeed taken place on the social front of the Europe of the Six since the early debates on the Schuman Plan, when British workers enjoyed, in relative terms, so many advantages as compared with their European colleagues." Robert Edwards, "The Outlook for Labour," *European-Atlantic Review*, Vol. XI, No. 4 (September–October 1961), 34. Because he was a member of the Labour left, Edwards was exceptional in his support of British Common Market membership.

champion of British Common Market membership, to serve as chairman of the Campaign.[100] They chose Roy Jenkins as Deputy Chairman and Peter Kirk as Secretary, thus broadening the Campaign's base of support in order to appeal to members, respectively, of the parliamentary Labour and Conservative parties.

In the period before the government announced its Common Market decision, the Campaign's major effort consisted of a statement signed by 140 prominent persons from many walks of life, in support of a British EEC application. At a press conference held in London on May 25, 1961, the leaders of the Common Market Campaign issued their statement. This document, drawn up by Lord Gladwyn and a Preparatory Committee in which members of Federal Union were prominent, called upon Britain, after consultation with Commonwealth members and signatories of the EFTA Convention, to declare her "readiness in principle to join the European Economic Community and to accept the institutions of the Treaty of Rome." [101] Only by joining the Common Market could the "Commonwealth, of which the United Kingdom would remain the senior partner, be associated with a vast, new, outward-looking political organization, capable of accumulating and deploying the necessary capital for the development of less fortunate nations of the world. And only so can Britain ensure for herself the place which is her due in the Atlantic Community of the future." Unless Britain applied for Common Market membership she faced the danger of becoming a "backwater, both politically and economically" in the world.

The framers of the Common Market Campaign's statement claimed that they represented the views of persons from "many differing fields of activity." Such support should give the government "the assurance that if they decide to act as suggested they will enjoy widespread and influential support in the Nation." The signatories included fifteen Conservative, twenty-two Labour, and three present or former Liberal Members of Parliament. Among the signers were twenty-seven industrialists and bankers, eighteen academic figures, six trade unionists, twelve editors, publishers and journalists, and four churchmen and

---

[100] Lord Gladwyn, British Ambassador to France from 1954 to 1960 and previously, from 1950 to 1954, Britain's Permanent Representative to the United Nations, was in 1961 President of Britain in Europe. He was also a director of the banking firm of S. G. Warburg and Co. See Lord Gladwyn, *The European Idea.* Esp. 82–110; 129–141.
[101] Common Market Campaign, *Statement on Europe.* (London, 1961).

military leaders. Thus the statement had the backing of a small but impressive cross section of British opinion. Elaborating the views of the signatories in a covering letter sent with the Common Market Campaign statement to Edward Heath, Lord Gladwyn urged immediate negotiations for EEC membership. He also called upon the British government, in order to enhance the prospects for Common Market membership, to announce its acceptance of "the institutions and the political implications of the Treaty of Rome." [102]

CONCLUSION

The decision to apply for Common Market membership was preceded by the rise of support in Britain for such action. In considerable but not massive numbers, Englishmen perceived the need for their government to find for Britain a place in the European integration movement. The adequacy of the links of the past, especially those with other Commonwealth countries and the United States, to Britain's needs at the threshold of the 1960's, was questioned. Members of interest groups and press, as well as parliamentarians, developed expectations of gain from British membership in European integrative institutions. Support for EEC entry resulted from hopes of specific material rewards, such as greater markets, improved industrial efficiency, and increasing benefits for workers. In some cases, members of such interest groups were prepared to support a Common Market bid if they could perceive specific gains for themselves. In the period preceding the Common Market decision, certain members of political parties, and "European" organizations, as well as leading journals, provided strong and articulate advocates of EEC entry.

In the period between 1956 and 1961, the British government and major elites were engaged in a process of interaction from which emerged the Common Market decision of July 1961. The growth of European markets, together with the decision of the Six to press forward the development of European economic integration, had contributed to the British decision to propose a European free trade area. The free trade area negotiations of 1957–58 attracted considerable interest in Britain, and strengthened interest in European integration. The failure of these negotiations, together with the inability of EFTA to bridge the economic gap between the Six and Seven, gave rise to

---

[102] Common Market Campaign, Preparatory Committee. Letter to the Rt. Hon. Edward Heath, June 7, 1961.

increased support for Common Market membership. In this case the failure, rather than the success, of one integrative effort contributed to a growth in support for a still bolder initiative.

In opting for Common Market membership, the British government, to a far greater extent than in previous policies vis-à-vis western Europe, chose a policy which did not have a broad base of popular support. Although between 1956 and 1961, as this chapter has shown, sentiment in favor of Common Market membership had grown rapidly, important segments of the British electorate, together with elite opinion, remained opposed to, or accepted the idea of Common Market membership with reservation. Whereas British policy in support of a European free trade area had enjoyed strong bipartisan support, the Labour party withheld support, and each party contained vocal opponents of EEC entry. In the months ahead, the British government had the unenviable but challenging task of broadening the base of support for its Common Market policy, while at the same time reconciling the often conflicting interests of Commonwealth members and EEC countries. Although the British decision to apply for Common Market membership had been taken without a large-scale public debate, the government faced an electorate which became increasingly divided, and even hostile, as the terms of entry became known. Although the British political system made it possible for the Macmillan cabinet to decide to apply for Common Market membership without a thorough public discussion of the issues included, the British government now faced a major debate in negotiating the terms of entry.

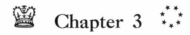 Chapter 3

THE FIRST COMMON MARKET DECISION

In the months preceding the announcement of the first British Common Market application, there was a particularly heavy flow of ideas and information between the British government and certain elites. The views of persons in the private sector were conveyed to the government. Governmental officials, in turn, helped to mold thought as membership in a European free trade area and, later, entry into the Common Market became the objective of the Macmillan cabinet. Such interaction enabled the government to gain needed information about the potential implications of EEC entry for key sectors of the economy.

In deciding to apply for Common Market membership, the British government formulated its policy after an examination of the views of labor organizations such as the TUC, industrial associations such as the FBI, pro-Common Market organizations, opinion within the parliamentary parties, and reference groups such as the press.[1] Although the growth of domestic support for Common Market membership contributed to the decision to seek EEC entry, a series of other factors as well played a role in the calculations of British policymakers.

According to Macmillan, the underlying issues facing Britain at the time of her Common Market application were "European unity, the future of the Commonwealth, and the strength of the free world."[2]

---

[1] Commenting upon the Common Market decision in his address to the 1961 Annual Conference of the Conservative party, Edward Heath declared: ". . . (T)he Government only took this decision after long, full and careful consideration. It has not been a hasty decision. . . . (I)n this last year we have had full consultations with Commonwealth Ministers, . . . numerous talks with the Ministers and officials of the Six countries and consultations with industry and others. So it is a decision which has been carefully weighed." National Union of Conservative and Unionist Associations, 80th Annual Conference, p. 52.

[2] Great Britain, *Parliamentary Debates* (Commons), Vol. 645 (August 2, 1961), col. 1480. In his statement of July 31, 1961, Macmillan declared:

This is a political as well as an economic issue. Although the Treaty of Rome is concerned with economic matters, it has an important political objective, namely, to promote unity and stability in Europe which is so

Shortly after announcing the Common Market decision, Macmillan expressed fear that the division of Europe between the Six and Seven, "although it superficially is of a commercial character, undoubtedly detracts from the political strength and unity of Western Europe." [3] British Common Market membership might heal the economic rift between EEC and EFTA. Moreover, Macmillan suggested, geopolitical considerations, as well as economic factors, had influenced the government in its decision. Britain could not find "in isolation a security which our geographical position no longer gives." [4] If Britain could no longer remain aloof from the European integration movement, her interests might best be served by a wholehearted commitment to the European Community.

THE FUTURE OF BRITISH TRADE

A major factor in the Common Market decision was the belief, widespread both in governmental and private circles, that EEC entry would give Britain access to the dynamic markets of western Europe.[5] If Britain's very survival depended upon the growth of exports, Common Market membership offered the most promising prospects for boosting trade. In fact, Macmillan pointed out that the "weight of opinion among British industrialists is that the balance of advantage for them lies in joining a unit which will be of a size comparable, let us say,

---

essential a factor in the struggle for freedom and progress throughout the world.

I believe that it is both our duty and interest to contribute towards that strength by securing the closest possible unity within Europe. At the same time, if a closer relationship between the United Kingdom and the countries of the European Economic Community were to disrupt the long-standing and historic ties between the United Kingdom and the other nations of the Commonwealth, the loss would be greater than the gain.
Great Britain, *Parliamentary Debates* (Commons), Vol. 645 (July 31, 1961), cols. 928–930.

[3] Great Britain, *Parliamentary Debates* (Commons), Vol. 645 (August 2, 1961), col. 1482.

[4] Great Britain, *Parliamentary Debates* (Commons), Vol. 645 (August 2, 1961), cols. 1480–94.

[5] According to Macmillan: "The development of the European Economic Community, the opportunity of the mass market which this has created for European industrialists, and the spur that this has given them to competitiveness and efficiency, present the British economy with a great challenge. . . . In the long-run, an island placed as ours is, where our need to export to other people . . . will always be greater than their need to export to us, cannot maintain the high standards that we want for our people in an isolated protective system." Great Britain, *Parliamentary Debates* (Commons), Vol. 645 (August 2, 1961) cols. 1485–1490.

to the United States or Soviet Russia." [6] By joining the EEC Britain would gain access to a vast new market, within which her industry could benefit from economies of scale.

Between 1956 and 1961 British expectations from the Common Market reflected trends in the pattern of British trade with western Europe and the Commonwealth. In this period British exports to EEC countries rose more than a third. (See Table 1) Although EFTA countries provided growing markets for British exports, the sharpest increases were recorded in two of the leading Common Market countries. By 1961, Britain's exports to Germany and Italy were almost double their 1956 rate.

TABLE 1

EXTERNAL TRADE

United Kingdom Exports to Europe
Monthly Averages of
Calendar Months
In Millions Pound Sterling

	EEC	EFTA	Sweden	Den-mark	W. Ger-many	Nether-lands	Belgium and Lux.	France	Italy
1954			7.8	6.9	5.9	8.3	4.6	5.3	
1955			7.9	6.2	6.4	8.8	5.3	6.0	
1956	35.7	27.5	8.8	6.9	7.7	9.9	5.8	7.4	5.0
1957	38.3	28.3	9.2	7.2	8.8	9.8	6.5	7.3	5.9
1958	34.9	29.2	8.7	6.4	10.3	8.2	5.0	6.0	5.5
1959	38.8	32.0	9.3	7.3	11.8	9.2	5.1	6.4	6.0
1960	43.3	35.9	10.9	7.5	13.6	9.7	5.4	7.3	7.3
1961	51.1	40.1	11.8	7.7	14.3	11.5	6.5	9.3	9.5
1962	60.0	43.1	12.9	8.6	16.6	12.6	7.7	11.5	11.6
1963	68.9	46.2	14.1	8.8	17.8	14.0	8.4	15.1	13.6

Source: Figures compiled from statistics in Great Britain, Central Statistical Office, *Monthly Digest of Statistics* (London: HMSO), 1954–1964.

During the same period British imports increased even more rapidly than British exports to the Common Market Six. (See Table 2). Although EFTA countries showed rapid advances, again the German Federal Republic and Italy experienced the greatest gains in exports to Britain. The contrast between British trade with western Europe and the Commonwealth is sharp. According to Table 3, between 1956 and 1961 British exports to the Commonwealth as a whole actually declined. Even if South Africa, which left the Commonwealth in 1961, is

[6] Great Britain, *Parliamentary Debates* (Commons) Vol. 645 (August 2, 1961) cols. 1489–90.

TABLE 2

EXTERNAL TRADE

Imports into the United Kingdom
Monthly Averages of
Calendar Months
In Millions Pound Sterling

	EEC	EFTA	Sweden	Den-mark	W. Ger-many	Nether-lands	Belgium and Lux.	France	Italy
1954			9.7	10.4	6.5	9.1	4.5	8.1	
1955			11.6	10.2	7.8	11.1	5.5	11.1	
1956	41.1	32.1	12.1	10.2	9.2	11.4	6.3	9.4	4.8
1957	40.9	33.1	13.1	9.6	10.4	11.0	5.1	9.2	5.2
1958	44.4	36.2	11.2	9.6	11.3	13.3	5.0	8.4	6.4
1959	46.6	39.0	10.7	11.1	12.0	13.3	4.8	8.6	7.7
1960	55.1	46.5	13.6	12.0	15.1	15.0	5.8	11.0	8.2
1961	56.4	46.2	13.4	11.8	16.2	14.4	5.5	11.9	8.5
1962	59.0	45.9	13.1	12.7	16.1	16.4	6.1	11.0	9.4
1963	64.1	50.3	13.6	13.7	17.4	17.4	7.4	12.8	9.2

Source: Figures compiled from statistics in Great Britain, Central Statistical Office, *Monthly Digest of Statistics* (London: HMSO), 1954–1964.

TABLE 3

EXTERNAL TRADE

United Kingdom Exports to Commonwealth Countries
Monthly Averages of
Calendar Months
In Millions Pound Sterling

	Common-wealth Total	Canada	South Africa	Rhodesia and Nyasa.	India	Ceylon	Aus-tralia	New Zealand
1954	121.5	11.0	13.0	4.0	9.6	1.6	23.1	10.5
1955	116.8	11.7	13.9	4.5	10.8	1.8	23.7	11.6
1956	121.5	14.8	12.9	4.9	14.0	2.2	20.0	10.6
1957	126.8	16.3	14.4	5.0	14.7	2.1	19.6	11.7
1958	120.4	15.7	15.5	4.3	13.4	2.3	19.6	10.7
1959	117.5	17.3	12.4	4.1	14.3	2.6	18.6	8.2
1960	125.0	17.9	12.8	3.9	12.5	2.4	21.7	10.1
1961	107.2 *	18.5	12.3	3.9	12.7	2.2	16.8	10.3
1962	99.2	15.7	12.2	3.4	9.7	2.1	19.0	8.9
1963	101.2	14.4	16.3	3.4	11.4	1.9	19.6	9.6

* Excluding Republic of South Africa
Source: Figures compiled from statistics in Great Britain, Central Statistical Office, *Monthly Digest of Statistics* (London: HMSO), 1954–1964.

included in that year's figures, the total Commonwealth market for British exports showed no growth. Australia and New Zealand, Britain's most loyal Commonwealth partners, i.e., the ones which voted with her in the United Nations at the time of the Suez crisis in 1956, also proved to be declining markets for British exports. Before she left the Commonwealth, South Africa failed to increase appreciably her share of imports from Britain. Although Canada, India and Ceylon increased their imports from Britain, they did not register advances as impressive as those of West European countries.

TABLE 4

EXTERNAL TRADE

United Kingdom Imports from Commonwealth Countries
Monthly Averages of
Calendar Months
In Millions Pound Sterling

	Common-wealth Total	Canada	South Africa	Rhodesia and Nyasa.	India	Ceylon	Aus-tralia	New Zealand
1954	134.4	22.7	7.0	7.2	12.4	3.4	19.7	14.7
1955	147.8	28.6	6.7	8.4	13.2	3.5	22.0	15.0
1956	145.1	29.0	7.6	9.0	11.8	3.3	19.7	16.4
1957	144.9	26.7	7.7	6.9	13.1	3.4	20.7	15.3
1958	128.7	25.7	7.5	5.7	11.6	3.9	16.6	13.4
1959	136.7	26.0	7.4	7.5	11.9	3.3	18.6	15.2
1960	146.1	31.2	8.0	8.6	12.4	3.4	16.4	15.3
1961	129.4 *	29.1	8.6	8.5	12.1	3.4	14.5	13.3
1962	116.4	29.1	8.6	8.0	11.3	3.5	15.4	14.1
1963	128.8	30.7	9.6	8.2	11.7	3.5	17.2	14.5

* Excluding Republic of South Africa
Source: Figures compiled from statistics in Great Britain, Central Statistical Office, *Monthly Digest of Statistics* (London: HMSO, 1954–1964).

In the period under consideration, Commonwealth exports to Britain, like British exports to the Commonwealth, declined. (See Table 4) Between 1956 and 1961, exports from Australia, India, and New Zealand to Britain fell, while exports to Britain from South Africa, the Federation of Rhodesia and Nyasaland, and Ceylon either rose only slightly or remained static. By 1961 Britain's exports to the German Federal Republic were greater than those to India and were exceeded, among the countries of the Commonwealth, only by sales to Canada and Australia. Moreover, British exports in 1961 to Sweden and the Netherlands each surpassed those to New Zealand. In short, compared to Europe, British trade with the Commonwealth showed little promise of gain in the years during which Britain moved toward a decision to apply for Common Market membership.

Table 5 reveals that the Commonwealth in 1960 furnished markets for 37.8 percent of Britain's exports, whereas the Common Market Six purchased 14.6 percent. In 1961, however, the Commonwealth's proportion of British exports dropped and that of the EEC rose. Similarly, the Commonwealth provided 36.3 percent of Britain's imports in 1960, and slightly less in 1961, while the EEC's share of exports to Britain rose from 14.6 to 15.4 percent in the same period. In 1960 and 1961, the

TABLE 5

United Kingdom Trade

	Percentage of Total U.K. Exports					Percentage of Total U.K. Imports				
	1952	*1956*	*1960*	*1961*	*1962*	*1952*	*1956*	*1960*	*1961*	*1962*
Commonwealth *	48.4	45.5	37.8	35.5	32.7	45.8	44.4	36.3	35.5	34.6
EEC	11.3	13.6	14.6	16.7	18.9	12.3	12.7	14.6	15.4	15.3
EFTA	10.2	11.9	10.7	11.7	13.6	9.2	11.6	10.1	10.4	12.0
Other (OEEC) Europe	4.4	2.3	5.1	6.0	3.2	3.6	2.3	4.7	5.5	2.3
Total W. Europe	25.9	27.9	30.4	34.3	35.8	25.1	26.6	29.5	31.5	30.6

* Excluding trade with South Africa, which left the Commonwealth in May 1961, and accounted for about 10 percent of Britain's exports to, and 6 percent of her imports from the Commonwealth.
Source: Great Britain, *Bulletin for Industry: A Monthly Review of the Economic Situation Prepared by the Information Division of the Treasury.* No. 150 (March 1962), p. 2. Figures for 1956 compiled by author from statistics in Great Britain Central Statistical Office, *Annual Abstract of Statistics.* No. 99 (London: HMSO, 1962), pp. 210–211. Figures for 1962 compiled from statistics in Great Britain Central Statistical Office, *Annual Abstract of Statistics.* No. 98 (London: HMSO, 1961), pp. 215–216. No. 100 (1963), pp. 210–211.

West European share of total British exports increased, while that of the Commonwealth in the same period declined. Thus, in 1961 the Commonwealth and western Europe each took similar proportions of British exports. Moreover, in that period the percentage of British imports from western Europe rose, while that of the Commonwealth fell.

Between 1952 and 1961 British exports to other OEEC members increased just less than 10 percent, while imports to Britain from these countries rose by about 5 percent. (See Table 5). The Common Market Six accounted for the greatest increases in British trade with western Europe, with exports rising from 11.3 percent in 1952 to 16.7

percent in 1961, and imports from 12.3 to 15.4 percent in the same period. As a percentage of total British imports and exports, EFTA trade did not gain substantially, although considerable increases were registered in commerce between Britain and European countries outside both the EEC and EFTA. The failure of British trade with the Outer Seven to grow, in contrast to that with the Six, undoubtedly accounts in part for British interest in Common Market membership. But the fact that trade with EFTA and other OEEC countries constituted, even in 1961, a percentage of commerce about equal to that with the EEC, gave substance to British interest in an "outward-looking" European Community consisting of many members and associated states. Finally, the fact that British trade with Commonwealth countries continued in 1961 to constitute just over one-third of total overseas commerce provided a powerful stimulus to British policymakers to retain wherever possible existing economic links with former colonies, while exploring the prospects for Common Market membership. Not only did policies designed to achieve this objective accord with British economic interest; they were in keeping with earlier British conceptions of the need to reconcile Britain's European and Commonwealth commitments.

Closely related to the future of export markets as an issue of great importance was the question of British economic growth. Greater access to the dynamic markets of western Europe would provide a stimulus to economic growth. In turn, the expansion of the British economy would contribute to the development of the modern industrial plant needed to make British industry more competitive in overseas markets.

The high growth rates of the EEC led to a reassessment of the importance to Britain of European integration. In growth of industrial production, Britain lagged behind each of the Six which, in the period between 1950 and 1961, registered greater increases than Britain in general indices of production. As Table 6 illustrates, the disparities were greatest between, on the one hand, the growth of industry in Britain, and on the other, industrial expansion in the three major EEC members—France, Italy, and Germany. Although EEC countries had enjoyed comparatively high growth rates even before the formation of the European Community, Common Market membership,[7] according

---

[7] See A. Lamfalussy, *The United Kingdom and the Six: An Essay on Economic Growth in Western Europe*, especially Chapter I.

to a widely held expectation, might contribute to a major increase in British growth rates.

If balance of payments deficits were the result of Britain's inability to increase the ratio of exports over imports and achieve sustained levels of economic growth, Common Market entry might provide the only satisfactory long-term solution to this chronic economic problem. Therefore, the mounting deficit in the balance of payments in 1961, then the latest of several such crises to plague Britain since World War II, may have provided an important motivation for the Macmillan cabinet to seek Common Market membership. On July 25, the Chan-

TABLE 6

GREAT BRITAIN AND THE EUROPEAN ECONOMIC COMMUNITY

General Indices of Industrial Production

	Bel-gium	Luxem-bourg	France	Ger-many	Italy	Nether-lands	The Six	United King-dom	U.S.A.
1950	93	89	89	72	78	88	80	94	82
1951	106	99	99	85	89	91	92	98	89
1952	100	109	98	91	91	91	95	95	92
1953	100	100	100	100	100	100	100	100	100
1954	106	103	109	112	109	111	110	108	94
1955	116	116	117	129	119	119	122	114	106
1956	123	124	128	139	128	124	132	114	109
1957	124	126	139	147	138	127	140	116	110
1958	116	121	145	152	143	127	144	114	102
1959	122	127	150	161	158	139	153	120	116
1960	129	138	167	178	182	157	171	129	119
1961	135	142	175	189	200	160	182	130	120
1962 *	139	134	193	194	216	167	191	128	126

* First quarter, seasonally adjusted.
Source: *OECD General Statistics*, July 1962, p. 2.

cellor of the Exchequer, Selwyn Lloyd, announced a series of measures designed to boost exports.[8] Several days later, on August 4, the International Monetary Fund (IMF) announced that Britain would draw an additional $500 million during the next twelve months.[9] In the five months preceding the IMF credit more than 1 billion in pounds sterling had been withdrawn from London, largely because, in anticipation of a

---

[8] They consisted of a pause in wage increases, reductions in public expenditures, including spending for British forces on the Continent and assistance to underdeveloped countries, and an increase in the interest rate of the Bank of England from 5 to 7 percent. *Times* (London), July 26, 1961, p. 12.
[9] *Times* (London), August 5, 1961, p. 6.

devaluation of the pound, foreigners holding British currency were converting their sterling balances. Undoubtedly, the Macmillan cabinet saw in Common Market membership a means of effecting long-range structural changes in the British economy and thus ending the recurring payments problem.

THE SUCCESS OF THE EEC

One of the reasons for Britain's initial reluctance to consider Common Market membership was the belief, shared by not a few Englishmen, that the EEC in all likelihood would fail to achieve the objectives set forth in the Rome Treaty. Perhaps because of the failure of EDC, the British found it difficult to envisage that the same six countries, which less than a generation earlier had fought each other and which retained differing economic structures, languages, and national traits, could form a customs union and achieve the other objectives to which they had committed themselves. Because its members might not be able to work together effectively within the framework provided by the Rome Treaty, the Common Market might be short-lived. Therefore, a British policy of aloofness might still commend itself, for historically European nation-states had shown little ability over the long term to evolve mutually satisfactory institutions and patterns of collaboration at the international level. Even in the postwar period the European integrative movement had a mixed history of success and failure.

By the summer of 1961, however, the British government had before it mounting evidence that the EEC, unlike the ill-fated EDC, was not doomed to failure. Since the beginning of the Fifth Republic, the French government had introduced reforms which strengthened France's economy and reinforced her commitment to the European Community. Since the founding of the Common Market, trade among its members had grown rapidly. Although the Six already enjoyed high growth rates, the formation of the Common Market contributed to even greater economic expansion in western Europe. Exports from the Six had registered impressive gains. Thus the economic dynamism the Common Market showed not only gave rise to British expectations of economic gains from Common Market membership; it cast doubt upon the initial British assumption that the Six could not achieve the objectives to which they had committed themselves.

The decision of the Six to speed up the transitional period to the completion of the Common Market, the Hallstein Plan [10] announced in March 1960, had an impact of considerable importance on British thought about the EEC. Not only had the Six shown an ability to meet on schedule the timetable set forth in the Rome Treaty; they were now prepared to move even more rapidly toward European economic integration.

If the EEC achieved the objectives set by its members, Britain might find it increasingly difficult, at some future date, to join the European Community. As the Common Market approached the completion of the timetable called for in the Rome Treaty, the terms for British entry would undoubtedly be stiffer, and the problems of adjustment greater, than if Britain applied for membership in 1961. By becoming a signatory of the Rome Treaty in the near, rather than the distant, future Britain might have a greater influence upon the shaping of EEC policy than if she remained an outsider.

Englishmen had viewed the Common Market not only as an organization which might be short-lived; they had seen the EEC as an institutional framework within which Britain might lose her freedom of action in economic affairs and eventually perhaps even in foreign policy. In addition to mounting evidence of the success of the EEC, the British found less cause for alarm that Britain, as a Common Market member, would cease to be independent.[10] Englishmen found that the French government, even though an EEC member, had retained great freedom of action. For all their pragmatism in the development of political institutions, the British had formed their conception of the European Community from an examination of the theories and goals of European federalism and supranationality, rather than from an assessment of the actual operation of EEC institutions. Whatever the framework set forth in the Rome Treaty and the objectives set by Continental proponents of European integration, the EEC was evolving as an organization in which member governments worked out differences and in some, but not all cases, upgraded national interests to form European economic policies. The locus of decision-making remained the nation-state, and national governments had little fear that their interests would be disregarded. President de Gaulle's conception of European political integration—a *Europe des patries*—found support in Britain. In fact, the British government committed itself to participation in a politically integrated Europe based upon an organizational framework similar to that favored by France.[11] As a Common Market

---

[10] Such fears were by no means absent. Opponents of EEC entry often based their case on such arguments. See Chapter 4.
[11] See the April 1962 statement by Edward Heath to Western European Union. Great Britain, *European Political Union*. Cmnd. 1720. The French proposals for European political integration included the following features: periodic meetings

member, Britain might contribute to the shaping of institutions of European political integration which would be compatible with British interests.

In one sector in particular, namely agriculture, early Common Market entry might make it possible for Britain to have a major influence upon the development of EEC policy. By 1961, British officials had reached the conclusion that Britain could reconcile her farming interests with Common Market membership. In fact, the Minister of Agriculture, Christopher Soames, had concluded that the cost of subsidizing Britain's farmers, under the deficiency payments system,[12] might rise to a figure as high as £400 million a year, as con-

---

of heads of government and ranking cabinet officials including ministers of finance, defense, and foreign affairs; meetings of a European assembly composed of delegates from national parliaments; co-ordination of foreign policies; development of common strategic doctrine; and collaboration in the development of advanced technologies. In such a framework each government would retain legal independence. See, for example, de Gaulle's press conference of September 5, 1960. *Major Addresses, Statements, and Press Conferences of General Charles de Gaulle*, pp. 92–93. In the Fouchet Plan, presented to France's EEC partners in July 1961 for consideration, the French government set forth its proposals for European integration. Another French proposal, the Fouchet-Cattani Plan, was presented to France's EEC partners in January 1962. For a detailed examination of these proposals, see W. W. Kulski, *De Gaulle and the World: The Foreign Policy of the Fifth French Republic*, 229–233.

[12] There are important differences between the agricultural policies of the EEC and Britain. According to the Treaty of Rome (Article 39), signatories agree to pursue a common agricultural policy having as its objectives: "(a) to increase agricultural productivity by developing technical progress and by ensuring the rational development of agricultural production and the optimum utilization of the factors of production, particularly labour; (b) to ensure thereby a fair standard of living for the agricultural population, particularly by increasing the individual earnings of persons engaged in agriculture; (c) to stabilise markets; (d) to guarantee regular supplies; and (e) to ensure reasonable prices in supplies to consumers." On January 14, 1962, after protracted deliberations, the Six reached agreement on means to place these objectives into operation in the EEC. They agreed that European agriculture would be treated fundamentally as the agriculture of a single community, inside which all quantitative restrictions, import duties and other barriers would be removed. However, EEC agriculture was to be protected from competition from other regions of the world. For example, in the case of important agricultural products such as cereals, at the end of the third stage of the transitional period provided in the Treaty of Rome, there would be a single target price within the EEC, together with a single levy for imports from outside the Community. This system differs from the British agricultural system in which there are relatively few tariffs or other restrictions against the importation of foodstuffs into the United Kingdom. The price to the British consumer is kept low, and the farmer in Britain is given a deficiency payment, fixed in annual price review, from general taxation. This payment or subsidy represents the difference between his guaranteed price and the cost of imports from the world market. For

trasted with the then prevailing annual cost of £270 million. Falling world commodity prices would widen the gap between Britain's costs of farm production and those of more efficient competitors overseas. Because taxpayers might be unwilling to bear the burden of increasing subsidies, the British government gave thought to the idea of adapting to Britain's needs the farm policy being developed by the EEC.[13] By EEC entry, the British government might contribute to the formulation of a European Community agricultural policy which reconciled the specific needs of British farmers with the general interests of British economy.

THE CHANGING BRITISH CONCEPTION OF THE COMMONWEALTH

Having maintained at the time of the free trade area negotiations that British entry into the Common Market was incompatible with Commonwealth commitments, British officials by 1961 asserted that there was no necessary incompatibility between the Commonwealth and European integration. Contrary to tenets once widely held in British official circles, Britain need not choose between the Commonwealth and the European Community.[14] In fact, Common Market membership, it was now argued, was essential to the preservation of the Commonwealth. According to Macmillan: "Britain in isolation would be of little value to our Commonwealth partners." [15] Far from destroying the Commonwealth, an enlarged Common Market which included Britain as a member might become an important trading partner and supplier of economic aid and technical assistance to Commonwealth countries. As a member of the EEC, Britain might strengthen her position as leader of the Commonwealth. Because Commonwealth countries were developing their own industries and lessening their dependence upon

---

the British to adopt the system of the Six would mean the reduction, if not the end, of certain Commonwealth agricultural imports, since Britain as a member of the Common Market would have adopted a farm policy under which levies would be imposed on all foodstuffs from outside the Community. Moreover, Britain could no longer have subsidized her own farmers with deficiency payments.

[13] In a statement to a group of MP's from farming constituencies, Mr. Soames expressed this viewpoint. *Times* (London), May 17, 1961, p. 14.

[14] For example, Duncan Sandys, then Commonwealth Secretary, declared: "I believe that my European friends will not misunderstand me if I say that if I were forced to make this cruel choice I would unquestionably choose the Commonwealth. Happily, we are not confronted with this dilemma." Great Britain, *Parliamentary Debates* (Commons), Vol. 645 (August 3, 1961), col. 1775.

[15] Great Britain, *Parliamentary Debates* (Commons) Vol. 645 (August 2, 1961), col. 1485.

imports from Britain, the system of Commonwealth trading preferences, which just a few years earlier the British government was unwilling to abandon, was of diminishing importance. In brief, by 1961 Commonwealth problems no longer presented an insuperable obstacle to British EEC membership.

Among proponents of Common Market membership, the idea gained currency that the Commonwealth had exercised a drag upon British thinking and upon the formulation of policy. Even though the Commonwealth, at the time of the Suez crisis of 1956, had not acted as a cohesive unit, the myth persisted that Britain, as the leader of the Commonwealth, was entitled to a voice in world affairs, if not the equal of, then only slightly less than that of the United States or the Soviet Union. During the Suez crisis most Commonwealth countries, while not hostile, were at best neutral with respect to British policy toward Egypt. Of Commonwealth members, only Australia and New Zealand voted with Britain in the United Nations. By 1961, however, a host of new states had achieved independence and Commonwealth status: Ghana and Malaya in 1957; Nigeria in 1960, and Cyprus in 1961. With the admission of new members, Britain and the old "white" dominions had become a minority. The new Afro-Asian states in the Commonwealth exceeded the older members both in numbers and population. South Africa's departure from the Commonwealth in May 1961, against the wishes of the British and Australian governments, illustrated the influence of the new Afro-Asian majority, for it was the representatives from "non-white" Commonwealth countries who forced the issue of South African membership because of her policy of *apartheid*.

Among Englishmen, especially within the Conservative party, there was a feeling that the "new" Commonwealth differed greatly from the "old" Commonwealth. Ties of family and sentiment linked Englishmen to Canadians, Australians, and New Zealanders. Such was not the case with the populations of India, Pakistan, Ceylon, Nigeria, or Ghana. Furthermore, the anti-British pronouncements of the leaders of such Commonwealth countries as Ghana met with displeasure in Britain. New Commonwealth countries, it was felt, sought the benefits of trade and aid which accompanied Commonwealth status, although they reserved the right to criticize British policy and to oppose British interests.[16]

---

[16] For British assessments of the changing importance of the Commonwealth, see Anthony Hartley, *A State of England*, 105–110; Michael Shanks and John

LIMITATIONS OF THE SPECIAL RELATIONSHIP

By 1961, the British assessment of the importance of the U.S. special relationship, the second pillar of postwar British foreign policy, had undergone a change of major proportions. The Suez crisis of 1956 had illustrated the limitations of the special relationship when the United States had failed to support British policy in the Middle East. Although Britain remained the principal ally of the United States, U.S. policy-makers no longer accorded London the deference the British had enjoyed during World War II. In fact, the retirement of President Eisenhower and the inauguration of President Kennedy in 1961 symbolized the transfer of power from an older generation of American leadership whose bonds of friendship had been forged and tested in wartime collaboration, to a new generation of U.S. political leaders who had no such ties with Britain. Not only was President Kennedy, in age, a whole generation removed from Prime Minister Macmillan; in marked contrast to his predecessor, during World War II President Kennedy had been an obscure commander of a PT boat. With the advent of a new U.S. administration, therefore, Britain might find her special relationship even further eroded.[17]

Shortly after its inauguration, the Kennedy Administration had begun to develop a framework for Atlantic Partnership.[18] The United

Lambert, *Britain and the New Europe: The Future of the Common Market,* 14–16; 23–24.

[17] See *Guardian* (Manchester and London), April 26, 1961, p. 10, May 23, 1961, p. 6, May 29, 1961, p. 10; *Daily Mail* (London), April 27, 1961, p. 1; The *Economist*, Vol. CXCIX, No. 6140 (April 29, 1961), 421. This view was held despite the Eisenhower Administration's opposition to British policy at the time of the Suez crisis, and the fact that as a young man Kennedy had spent several years in Britain when his father was U.S. Ambassador. Also see *Times* (London) April 21, 1961, June 7, 1961, p. 13; The *Spectator* No. 6929 (April 14, 1961), 499. In his eulogy at the funeral of Sir Winston Churchill in January 1965, President Eisenhower gave eloquent expression of the depth of the wartime links between the United States and Britain, and between Eisenhower and Churchill: "The loyalty that the fighting forces of many nations here serving gave to him (Churchill) during the war was no less strong, nor less freely given, than he had, in such full measure, from his own countrymen. An American, I was one of those Allies. During those dramatic months I was privileged to meet, to talk, to plan and to work with him for common goals. Out of that association an abiding—and to me precious—friendship was forged; it withstood the trials and frictions inescapable among men of strong convictions, living in the atmosphere of war." *New York Times*, January 31, 1965, p. 34.

[18] For a somewhat optimistic assessment and examination of the Kennedy Administration's proposal for an Atlantic Partnership, see Joseph Kraft, *The Grand Design: From Common Market to Atlantic Partnership.*

States was prepared to accord to an integrated western Europe a special relationship once reserved for Britain. Henceforth, the road to Washington might lie through Brussels, not London. Neither the United States nor the Common Market Six any longer had need for Britain to act as the interpreter of the United States to western Europe, and the interpreter of western Europe to the United States.[19] British entry into the Common Market was vital to the achievement of the Atlantic Partnership. To an even greater extent than its predecessor, the Kennedy Administration favored British EEC membership, and in the early months of 1961 urged upon Britain such a course of action.

ECONOMIC DIVISION IN EUROPE

As British expectations of gains from participation in the European integration movement grew in intensity, Britain found less acceptable the economic division of western Europe between EFTA and the EEC. Against their long-range wishes, the British, in leading in the formation of EFTA, had contributed to the perpetuation of West European economic division, even though British officials repeatedly had stressed the importance of EFTA as an interim device designed to bring the countries of western Europe eventually into one trading organization. By 1961 EFTA had not achieved this objective and western Europe, it was often pointed out, remained "at Sixes and Sevens." Moreover, EFTA had never provided a satisfactory alternative to the Common Market for British trade. To be sure, by joining EFTA Britain had extended her "home market," as she would have done as a member of the Common Market. But the total population of EFTA countries did not exceed eighty-eight million, of which more than fifty million were in the United Kingdom. Thus, as a member of EFTA, Britain had gained access to a market whose population, though not in all cases per capita income, was less than that of her domestic market. Therefore, Britain faced the need to abandon EFTA and instead join the Common Market if she was to achieve the objective for which EFTA had been created.

---

[19] According to one story which gained considerable circulation in Britain, when Macmillan expressed concern that Common Market membership might endanger the Anglo-American special relationship, Kennedy replied that he did not understand what special relationship Macmillan was referring to. See, for example, W. Horsfall Carter, *Speaking European*, 174.

DOMESTIC POLITICAL CONSIDERATIONS

In the months before the announcement of the first Common Market decision, the Macmillan cabinet had concluded that British membership in the European Community might revitalize not only Britain's economy, but also the Conservative party. By 1961, the government had become convinced that Britain must adopt new policies if the old notion of Britain's place at the center of three interlocked circles—the Commonwealth, the English-speaking world, and Europe—no longer accurately described London's position in the world. By joining the Common Market, the government would have adopted a fresh policy, which might have given to Englishmen their own "new frontier" for increasing British economic and political influence. If the Macmillan cabinet foresaw problems in adapting Britain's economy to compete more effectively with her industrial counterparts in Europe and elsewhere, Common Market membership might provide a means of accelerating necessary changes. Speaking at a political rally in Brighton on October 14, 1961, following the Conservative party annual conference, Prime Minister Macmillan had compared Britain's entry into the Common Market to a "bracing cold shower and not a relaxing Turkish bath." [20] Politically, it would be preferable to shift responsibility from London to Brussels for the inevitable, but hopefully temporary, discomforts which would accompany Common Market membership. Decisions resulting ultimately in the modernization and expansion of the British economy, which for political reasons could not be made in London, could be made in Brussels.

In the longer run, Macmillan believed, membership in the European Community would lead Britain to a new era of economic prosperity and political influence. Having presided over the transformation of Britain from an imperial power to the leader of an integrated Europe, the Conservative party would gain the image of a forward-looking, dynamic force. If Common Market membership had the effects Macmillan and other EEC proponents foresaw, the Conservative party might reap considerable electoral benefit from having pushed for, and achieved, British entry into the European Community. [21]

---

[20] *The New York Times*, October 15, 1961, Section 4, p. 2E.

[21] According to one Labour Member of Parliament: "So whereas foreign observers—particularly across the Atlantic—could regard the government's sudden conversion (to Common Market membership) as proof of Mr. Macmillan's statesman-

In sum, those in Britain, both within the government and in non-governmental elites, who favored first the idea of a free trade area and later, a British application to join the Common Market, held expectations of reward from such a policy. For the most part the expectations which Englishmen held were economic because of the nature of the Common Market, although British proponents of EEC membership anticipated political gains as well.

Economic expectations included: (1) larger markets for exports; (2) the strengthening, through greater competition, of British industry; (3) the modernization and expansion of industry; (4) increased industrial productivity; (5) rising living standards; (6) higher rates of economic growth; (7) greater reserves of capital for Commonwealth economic development; (8) new opportunities for Englishmen to make use of their skills; (9) the prospect of an end to the recurring balance of payments deficits of the postwar period.

Political expectations from Common Market membership included: (1) increased strength for Britain in world affairs as the leader of an integrated western Europe which might enjoy a special relationship with the United States; (2) a greater voice in the Commonwealth as a result of a new position of leadership in Europe; (3) an opportunity for Britain to strengthen the institutions of representative government on the Continent; (4) the possibility of exerting a moderating influence on East-West relations; (5) the prospect of strengthening the West in its struggle against communism. Although not all prospects were compatible, there was a consensus among EEC proponents that British membership in the European Community could provide for western Europe an influential role in world affairs and assure West European peoples sustained and even rising living standards.

In some cases the proponents of Common Market membership stated their expectations in negative terms: outside the Common Market, Britain could not survive as a major industrial power. Unless she joined the EEC, Britain would find herself excluded from Europe's burgeoning markets. Her economy would continue to register unimpressive

---

like vision, the opposition in Parliament was bound to view it in the first place as a party political gimmick—an attempt by a most adroit and ingenious politician to extricate himself from his domestic difficulties and maneuver himself into a situation where, having successfully negotiated terms of entry, he could appeal to the country posing as the greatest statesman since Disraeli." R. H. S. Crossman, "British Labor Looks at Europe," *Foreign Affairs*, Vol. 41, No. 4 (July 1963), 735. See also Kenneth N. Waltz, *Foreign Policy and Democratic Politics: The American and British Experience*, 257.

rates of growth. Increasingly, Commonwealth countries would rely upon other trading partners, and would look elsewhere for capital for economic development. Britain would lose irrevocably her special relationship with the United States. Thus, expectations of loss, as well as expectations of gain, gave substance to a British bid for Common Market membership.

By 1961, the British government had come to share many of the expectations held by EEC proponents in the private sector. Common Market membership might enable Britain to solve many of her most pressing economic and political problems. Yet the government did not have the unstinting support of all politically relevant strata on the question of Common Market membership. Only a small segment of the British electorate had expressed itself on behalf of EEC entry. Moreover, Britain faced opposition from other Commonwealth governments desirous of retaining their existing economic advantages. The Macmillan cabinet had before it the formidable task of convincing domestic opinion of the wisdom of its decision. In the absence of widespread popular support for Common Market membership, the British government found itself restricted in its ability, during the Brussels negotiations, to achieve agreement with the Six. Nevertheless, the existence of some support in Britain for EEC entry, as well as the conviction that Common Market membership provided a potential solution to many of Britain's most fundamental problems, led the Macmillan cabinet to enter negotiations in order to ascertain the terms for joining the European Community.

 Chapter 4

THE COMMON MARKET DEBATE

Seldom in Britain's long history has a governmental decision produced a debate of the magnitude of that touched off by Prime Minister Macmillan's announcement that Britain would apply for Common Market membership. In the eighteen months between Macmillan's House of Commons statement of July 31, 1961, and de Gaulle's veto of Britain's application in January 1963, Englishmen in many walks of life considered what to them was an issue of transcending importance. The question of Common Market membership produced in Britain divisions within each of the political parties and in the press, as well as among industrialists, economists, and trade unionists. The Macmillan cabinet was unable to develop a broadly-based national consensus in support of EEC entry. In fact, opposition to Common Market membership rose as the Brussels negotiations unfolded. The debate had several major focal points: the impact of Common Market membership upon British industry, agriculture, political institutions, the Commonwealth, and Britain's freedom of action in economic policy and foreign relations. Englishmen weighed Common Market membership against other policy options they thought remained open to Britain. In many cases, they concluded that it was not possible to reconcile Common Market membership, on terms set by the Six, with the preservation of British influence in the Commonwealth and the special relationship with the United States.

Before the announcement of the British EEC decision, discussion about Common Market membership was confined generally to the groups whose activities have been examined in Chapter 2.[1] Before July

---

[1] According to a report issued by Social Surveys (Gallup Poll) Limited in November 1961:

> In spite of all the attention given to the (Common Market) issue, in the press and elsewhere, there has been a substantial failure in communication. . . . Only one person in every three in Britain is aware that Britain is a member of the EFTA but not of ECM. One in five of the population are incorrectly informed about the present situation, either thinking that Britain is already a member of the ECM or a member neither of the ECM nor of the EFTA.

1961, by and large, knowledge about, and interest in, the Common Market did not extend beyond industrial and trade union leaders, the writers of press editorials, Europe-oriented organizations, Members of Parliament, and, of course, governmental officials. Only in the summer of 1961, immediately preceding the announcement of the decision, did British newspapers publish special articles, in contrast to pro-European editorials, designed to introduce a mass readership to the intricacies of the Rome Treaty. Nor did the British radio and television media concentrate upon the Common Market in their public affairs programs prior to the government's announcement.[2]

The opponents of Common Market membership did not marshall their forces until after July 1961.[3] This was understandable for at least two reasons: Not until 1960 had the British government given serious consideration to Common Market membership. Only as British policy-makers shifted course and opted for Common Market membership did the need arise for opponents to state their case clearly and effectively. Throughout much of the preceding period, British officials had set forth repeatedly the reasons why Britain could not sign the Rome Treaty. But there was, however, another reason for the seemingly belated articulation of opposition. The terms of entry which emerged from the Brussels negotiations contributed to the development of opposition to Common Market membership. These terms only became known after July 1961.

Unlike the preceding period, in the months after the government's announcement Englishmen in many walks of life debated the question of Common Market membership. Although the same groups which previously had considered EEC entry continued to do so, the Common Market debate engrossed other non-governmental elites and aroused, for the first time, considerable interest among the electorate at large. Interest in the Common Market was the result not only of the government's decision to apply for EEC entry, but also stemmed from public-

---

One-half of the population admit frankly that they just do not know what the present situation is.
Social Surveys (Gallup Poll) Limited, *Britain and the ECM*, London, November 1961, p. 6.

[2] The first major television program on the EEC was viewed by the British public on October 18, 1961. This broadcast, entitled "The Common Market and You," was produced by Associated-Rediffusion, Britain's commercial television network.

[3] One major exception was the Beaverbrook press which had intensified its editorial campaign against EEC entry in the months before Macmillan's July 31 announcement.

ity and support in the press, as well as the activities of trade associations and Europe-oriented groups. Such organizations held hundreds of meetings and established scores of study groups to acquaint Englishmen with the problems and prospects presented by the Common Market. In particular, industrialists, because of the economic potential of the Common Market, devoted considerable time to an examination of the implications of EEC entry.[4] Business leaders took comfort from the fact that most studies conducted by individual companies, industries or other organizations had concluded that British industry as a whole stood to gain from Britain's membership in the EEC. Moreover, businessmen were quick to observe that in the year preceding Britain's Common Market application British exports to the Six had risen rapidly. During 1962, they continued to rise as Englishmen discussed the question of EEC membership. During the Brussels negotiations, industrial organizations generally supported the government in its efforts to obtain satisfactory terms of entry. In fact, the Common Market announcement had come as a welcome relief to many industrialists, who now saw some of the uncertainties of recent months removed. As a result of the government's decision, businessmen could plan for the future with greater confidence that they would have continued access to the expanding markets of the European Community.[5]

Support for Common Market membership was greatest among larger industries and companies. Moreover, in highly competitive and dynamic industries which had advanced equipment and technologies, the idea of EEC entry found favor. Within the business community, the prospect of Common Market entry was highly attractive to bankers and financiers, and also insurance executives. Common Market mem-

---

[4] The proliferation of efforts to provide information on the EEC to businessmen led one commentator to write:

> If any British businessmen has not yet attended a Common Market conference, it can hardly have been because of a lack of an invitation. Scarcely a day passes without news of some fresh gathering to discuss the effects of "going into Europe," whether it is a mass jamboree by the seaside or a select house-party of two dozen industrialists in a provincial city.

Samuel Britton, "The Nation's Business," *Observer* (London), May 6, 1962. Meetings to acquaint groups such as businessmen with the potential implications of Common Market membership were held under the auspices of a variety of organizations including, for example, the United Kingdom Council of the European Movement, and the Federal Education and Research Trust. The latter organization had been founded by leaders of Federal Union. See Chapter II.

[5] See, for example, *FBI Review*, No. 136 (September 1961), p. 28.

bership would lead to greater collaboration among insurance companies in Britain and the Six.[6] In May 1962, British companies specializing in life insurance announced that they would establish a committee to study the prospects for increasing business in Common Market countries and examine legislation and regulations. It was anticipated that British life insurance companies might tap large new markets on the Continent.[7]

Both before and after the Macmillan cabinet made its decision to apply for Common Market membership, other business leaders had seen the need for such action in order to inject new vigor into the British economy.[8] In particular, spokesmen for two of Britain's largest industries—steel and chemicals—advocated entry into the European Community. The steel industry, it was anticipated, would experience indirect gains, since more steel would "flow into Europe in the form of steel-based exports—cars, machinery, domestic appliances, and the like —as British steel-using industries move to exploit the new sales opportunities opened to them by Britain's entry into the general Common Market." [9] The British Iron and Steel Federation also backed the British decision to join the European Coal and Steel Community, taken in conjunction with the application for Common Market membership.[10] According to the chairman of one of Britain's leading chemical companies, EEC entry was "likely to bring a healthy breath of fresh air" to British industry.[11] A second leader in the chemical industry declared that it was "essential for the well-being of Britain's economy that (Britain) join the Common Market." [12] Although such leaders saw specific gains to their firms and industries, they often spoke of the

---

[6] See, for example, the *Guardian* (Manchester and London), December 5, 1961, p. 12.

[7] *Times* (London), May 29, 1962, p. 18.

[8] According to the President of the British Iron and Steel Federation, "It is essential that ways be found of fostering the sources of dynamism in the British economy. Among the means to this end, closer relations with Europe must take a high place." Report of the President of the British Iron and Steel Federation, *Economist*, Vol. CXCVIII, No. 6135 (March 25, 1961), 1230.

[9] The British Iron and Steel Federation, *Into Europe?* Published statement (London, 1961), p. 5.

[10] Britain formally applied for ECSC membership on March 2, 1962. Negotiations began on July 17, 1962, when Edward Heath made his opening statement on behalf of Britain's application to the Ministers of ECSC countries.

[11] Statement by Mr. Paul Chambers, Chairman of Imperial Chemicals Industry, *Investors Chronicle*, January 5, 1962.

[12] Statement by Sir Miles Thomas, Chairman of Monsanto Chemicals, *Investors Chronical*, January 5, 1962.

potential benefits to the British economy in general from membership in the European Community.

A survey of industrial attitudes reveals support among the leaders of several other important industries. Provided it did not result in the loss of Commonwealth markets, the Society of Motor Manufacturers and Traders urged that Britain seek Common Market membership. Producers of vehicle parts, glass, machine tools, woolen textiles, high quality consumer goods, paper products, electronics equipment, rubber, and plastics tended to favor Common Market membership. Among the manufacturers of drugs, chemicals, automobiles, aluminum, components of electrical equipment, power cables, aircraft, furniture, and alcoholic beverages, including scotch and gin, there were numerous supporters of the British Common Market initiative. Members of the advertising industry, as well as shipbuilders, shipping companies, and producers of synthetic fibers, fertilizers, and agricultural equipment held expectations of new markets in the European Community.[13]

Some business and professional groups in Britain, however, harbored fears about Common Market membership. For example, some manufacturers of hosiery, shoes, textiles, and clothing saw the possibility of loss from EEC competition in Britain. In many cases such producers, it was thought, would face stiff competition partly because their products lacked adequate styling in the sophisticated markets of the Six.[14] Moreover, among members of the British Medical Association there were fears about the mutual recognition of qualifications by EEC countries and the removal of restrictions upon doctors practicing in other member countries. Doctors as well as dentists were concerned about provisions for labor mobility in the Rome Treaty. Such clauses might be unacceptable unless the health services of the Six offered benefits as extensive as those in Britain.[15]

Although greatest among larger, more dynamic, technologically advanced industries, support for Common Market membership could be found within smaller industries and firms. Not unexpectedly, however, the leaders of smaller industries and firms often had less knowledge

---

[13] For a survey of industrial attitudes toward EEC membership, see "Britain and Europe," *Financial Times Annual Review, 1962, of British Industry, Finanical Times* (London), July 9, 1962.

[14] See, for example, Colin Clark, *British Trade in the Common Market*, pp. 64–70; and Michael Shanks, "Britain and the Common Market: Who Will Lose?" *FBI Review*, No. 141 (February 1962), 31–33.

[15] See the *Sunday Times* (London), December 10, 1961, and *Times* (London), March 2, 1962, p. 6.

about the Common Market than their counterparts in large corporations and were less able to see precisely the potential gains or losses from EEC entry. For example, from a series of studies of the attitudes of merchants in its viewing area around London, completed in the autumn of 1961, the television network Associated Rediffusion published the following conclusions: In the case of all categories of merchants interviewed, a large percentage either had no opinions or saw no potential gain or loss to their particular business from Common Market membership.[16] It was to be expected that businessmen in smaller firms, as well as retailers, with less contact than their larger counterparts with the markets of continental Europe, would not have developed a keen interest in, or fixed opinions about, the European Community. Undoubtedly, their views did not differ greatly from those held by the majority of the British population, to whom the Common Market was an organization which only remotely affected them and therefore was not the object of great concern or interest.

In addition to the support industrial leaders gave the Common Market bid, the British government found within Europe-oriented organizations activists who, after the Common Market decision, stepped up their activities on behalf of membership in the European Community. In mid-July 1961, as part of its propaganda activities, the Common Market Campaign began publication of a monthly bulletin. Initially, the "Common Market Broadsheet" had the modest circulation of 2,000 copies per month, which had increased to 6,000 by October 1962. The Campaign provided copies to all Members of Parliament as well as to all known supporters, all major newspapers, and numerous individuals.[17] By October 1962, the Campaign had arranged some 200

---

[16] Among owners of gasoline stations, for example, three in ten had no opinion; another three in ten were neutral, believing that EEC entry would have no effect upon them. Of those who had any opinion, however, there was a preponderance of about three to one in favor of Common Market membership. Among dealers in automobile and cycle accessories, some three out of ten had no opinion and one in five expressed neutrality. The remaining dealers interviewed, believing that they would benefit from increasing sales, were favorably disposed toward Common Market membership. Retailers of liquor and cigarettes, as well as merchants selling meat, vegetables, men's wear, women's clothing, and confectionary, registered large percentages of persons having no opinion about the potential implications of Common Market membership for their business. Among these merchants, as in the case of other categories examined in this survey, those having opinions and knowledge of the Common Market tended to favor British entry into the European Community. For a more detailed analysis of the findings of this survey, see Associated-Rediffusion, *London Profiles* (Numbers 6-12), London, 1962.

[17] Common Market Campaign, *Report* (London, 1962), p. 2.

speaking engagements, had distributed thousands of copies of leaflets and booklets espousing Common Market membership, and had arranged meetings with Members of Parliament.[18] During the Brussels negotiations, the Campaign's activities ranged from contacts with MP's and Commonwealth Prime Ministers to efforts to form local action groups throughout Britain.

Literature distributed by the Common Market Campaign stressed several points: that a medium-sized nation such as Britain could not stand alone; that British exports to Europe were growing more rapidly than those to the Commonwealth; and that the Six, because of possibilities for economic specialization, would be able to cut their costs and make inroads into British markets even with Commonwealth countries.[19] The leaders of the Campaign attempted also to convince Englishmen that many Commonwealth governments no longer supported Britain, except on the rare occasion when British policies coincided with their own. But the Campaign's leaders envisaged the growth over the next decade of a federal structure in the Six. With their own foreign policy and nuclear capabilities, the Six would constitute a far greater power than Britain. If the time came when the Soviet Union and the United States were prepared to negotiate a settlement of outstanding Cold War issues, it would be the interests of the Six, with their greater strength and voice in Washington, rather than those of Britain, that the Americans would take into account. Using an argument adopted by many other British proponents of Common Market membership, the Campaign's leaders maintained that the United States would look to the Six rather than to Britain as the major American ally.

Before the government's announcement of July 31, each of Britain's political parties had strong supporters of Common Market membership. Officially, however, both major parties, with the consent of a majority of members inside and outside Parliament, accepted the assumption prevalent before 1961, that Commonwealth and other overseas interests and commitments were incompatible with British membership in the European Community. After the Common Market decision, cleavages developed within both the Conservative and Labour parties. Often for differing and even incompatible reasons, members of each party supported or opposed Common Market membership. Not in

[18] Common Market Campaign, *Report for the Period Ending 18th October 1962*, pp. 2-3.
[19] See, for example, Common Market Campaign, *Common Market Broadsheet, No.* 7 (August 1962).

keeping with textbook assumptions about British party unity and party discipline, the Common Market decision produced divisions of opinion in which members of one party found themselves in agreement with members of the other party and opposed to positions taken by colleagues in their own party.

Historically, the Conservative party had championed the special relationship with the United States and the preservation of Commonwealth links. As party leader, Churchill had stressed the Commonwealth and the special relationship as the principal British foreign policy interests. To many Conservatives, the Commonwealth remained an outstanding example of the British ability to achieve the orderly transformation of an empire into self-governing units which retained at least some of their British heritage and enhanced Britain's stature in world affairs. Between 1956 and 1961, however, a few Conservatives had begun to view with misgivings the development of the once predominantly white Commonwealth in which Britain was the undisputed leader, into an unwieldy organization of heterogeneous membership in which the newer African and Asian members formed a majority. If Britain could no longer find in the Commonwealth either support for her policies or expanding markets for her exports, she might turn to western Europe for allies and trade. By 1961, this shift in sentiment about the Commonwealth produced a cleavage within the Conservative party on the issue of Common Market membership.

Often disdainful historically of British imperialism, Labour members took pride in having presided, in the early postwar years, over the dissolution of much of the empire, and in the part played by their party in the creation, in its place, of a multiracial Commonwealth. According to many Labour members, as well as the party leadership, the Commonwealth represented not only a force for world peace, but a bridge between the West and less developed peoples. If the cost of Common Market membership was the weakening or destruction of the Commonwealth, the potential gains did not outweigh the likely losses.

Members of Parliament from all parties led in the creation of groups with the specific objective of advancing or opposing Britain's bid for EEC entry. The Common Market Campaign counted among its officers Peter Kirk and Roy Jenkins, leaders in the parliamentary Conservative and Labour parties of factions actively in support of Common Market membership. Shortly after the formation of the Common Market Campaign, its Labour members assisted in the creation of their own pro-European organization, the Labour Common Market Committee.

In an effort to gain wider acceptance of the idea of EEC membership, both groups worked in close collaboration.

The Labour Common Market Committee came into existence after a meeting in September 1961 which brought together Labour party members and trade unionists. The founders of the committee undertook to cooperate with other socialists and union members in western Europe in order to help strengthen the progressive forces within the Common Market. The committee held training sessions for persons who might, in turn, speak on behalf of EEC entry to local branches of trade unions and to party gatherings in the constituencies. From shortly after its founding until the collapse of the Brussels negotiations the committee, like the Common Market Campaign, engaged in a variety of activities, including publication of a newsletter and the dispatch of speakers to various parts of Britain to develop support, especially among trade unionists, for Common Market membership.

Several themes were dominant in the statements of the Labour Common Market Committee. It was held that Continental social services, contrary to British popular belief, were at least as advanced as those of Britain and that in fact some other West European countries spent more per capita than Britain on social security. Common Market entry, it was contended, would not prevent a future Labour government in Britain from engaging in national planning and the nationalization of industry, since the Rome Treaty made provisions for such planning. Some EEC members, the Labour Common Market Committee pointed out, had important sectors of their economies under national ownership, including companies in the steel, engineering, automobile and aircraft industries, as well as public utilities such as railways.

The committee sought to refute another notion about the Common Market: that British membership would result in the large-scale emigration of Continental workers to Britain. According to the Labour Common Market Committee, conditions in most EEC countries were such that few workers would be tempted to seek employment in Britain. The Rome Treaty only permitted a foreign worker to accept a job in Britain when a specific offer had been made to him. Thus Britain was unlikely to face an influx of unemployed persons who might compete with British workers for jobs. Moreover, the committee addressed itself to the contention that trade unions in the Six were weaker than in Britain. Admitting that Continental unions differed from those in Britain and that "the nature of the Common Market certainly leaves much to be desired from a socialist point of view, it should not be forgotten that its controlling institutions make specific provision for trade union representation." The task of British socialists and trade unionists was to help in the strengthening, where necessary, of the labor movement on the Continent. This objective could be achieved most effectively by Common Market membership. Similarly, if representative government in the major EEC countries was less firmly established than in Britain, the goal of Englishmen should be to assist in the strengthening of West European political systems. By joining the European Community, Britain might advance both the cause of socialism and representative government.[20]

Within the Conservative party there was no organization comparable to the Labour Common Market Committee. During the Brussels negotiations, cabinet members, including the Prime Minister himself, met with parliamentary Conservative party members in efforts to arouse support among wavering backbenchers. Government ministers and "European" Conservative MP's toured the provinces of Britain to make speeches on behalf of Common Market membership, and the issue evoked several full-scale parliamentary debates, as well as many written and oral questions in the Commons. Nevertheless, an air of mystery surrounded many of the government's activities during the tedious and protracted Brussels negotiations. On occasion the press, not without justification, complained that information was being withheld even from Commonwealth governments.[21]

If the Macmillan cabinet chose deliberately a policy of obfuscation, such a course of action was not without foundation. Undoubtedly, the cabinet foresaw considerable difficulty in reconciling with Common Market membership its obligations to the Commonwealth and domestic British interests. Instead of grasping firmly the nettle of leadership and embarking upon a massive program designed to broaden the base of support for EEC membership, the government chose a policy designed to keep the domestic debate well modulated until the terms of entry became clear, and until Britain was about to sign the Rome Treaty. Such a strategy, it may have been reasoned, would enhance Britain's bargaining position in Brussels. Otherwise, the Six might stiffen the

---

[20] See, for example, *Newsbrief of the Labour Common Market Committee.* London, March 1962, No. 4; January–February 1963, No. 13.

[21] See, for example, the *Times* (London), November 25, 1961, p. 9; *Daily Herald* (London), November 14, 1961, p. 8; November 27, 1961, p. 6; *Yorkshire Post* (Leeds), October 4, 1961, p. 6; November 25, 1961, p. 10.

terms for entry if Britain appeared overly eager to join. In any event, the Conservatives waited until the autumn of 1962 to initiate their most massive effort to place their case for Common Market membership before the electorate.

Into the void left by the government's apparent decision not to stir the electorate prematurely, stepped the numerous anti-Common Market groups formed during the summer of 1961. By mid-1962 several such organizations, with such descriptive titles as the "Keep Britain Out Campaign," the "Forward Britain Movement," the "Anti-Common Market League," and the "True Tories," disseminated propaganda, in written as well as oral form, designed to muster opposition to EEC entry. The principal anti-Common Market organizations had as their founders and leaders EEC opponents in the Conservative, Labour and Liberal parties, although in membership they cut across party lines, as was the case with Europe-oriented groups, and on occasion combined their efforts in opposition to the British government.

The Forward Britain Movement, founded by Mr. R. W. Briginshaw, General Secretary of the National Society of Operative Printers and Assistants, drew its membership largely from the ranks of trade unionists and the Labour party. The Forward Britain Movement brought together people who opposed EEC entry for a variety of reasons, ranging from Conservatives who feared the loss of British sovereignty, to members of the Labour left who believed that an enlarged Common Market would heighten Cold War tensions. However, the principal themes which characterized the Forward Britain Movement's opposition to the Common Market were those held most strongly by the Labour left. It was alleged that Britain might be admitted to the Common Market only if she agreed to several unacceptable concessions, including a decision to create an Anglo-French nuclear force. This would heighten the arms race and lead eventually to the acquisition of nuclear weapons by the Germans, since presumably the Bonn government would be asked to participate in such a force at some future date. In a Europe armed with atomic capabilities, the danger of war by accident or miscalculation would be increased. As a member of the Common Market, Britain would be unable to expand her trade with communist countries, since the EEC, "through its supranational institutions, collectively decides what kind and how much trade the EEC countries may have with the Socialist states." [22] As an alternative to the

---

[22] Forward Britain Movement, *The Alternative to Entering the Common Market.* Preliminary paper issued to all conference participants July 16–19, 1962. Reprinted in *Britain Should Stay Out* (London), 1962, pp. 6–13.

Common Market, Britain should attempt to increase trade with the communist world. Outside the EEC, moreover, Britain could assume the position of intermediary and peacemaker between East and West.

The Common Market was held to be the wrong grouping for Britain because it discriminated against imports from the less developed countries. The EEC was characterized as a protectionist bloc dominated by Germany. Britain not only would become an offshore satellite in a European union led by Bonn, but would sacrifice important Commonwealth interests. The underdeveloped nations needed markets in the industrialized countries if they were to raise their living standards. The EEC would increase trade among Western nations at the expense of the less developed countries. The rich would grow richer, while the poor states of Africa and Asia would be increasingly impoverished. British Common Market membership would weaken the Commonwealth as a bridge between races. Although some Commonwealth countries would seek associate membership in the Common Market, others would opt to remain outside. In any event, the Commonwealth would become a less effective force in world affairs.

Members of the Forward Britain Movement held that Britain, as a member of the Common Market, would be forced to accept decisions made in Brussels rather than in Westminster and Whitehall. No longer would the British government be able to engage in national planning. The Rome Treaty was unacceptable because it was held to be a device for the perpetuation of capitalism in the Six. In effect, the Forward Britain Movement advocated a neutralist Britain. Instead of joining the Common Market, Britain should place herself at the head of the "third world," since her interests lay in closer ties with Accra, Cairo, and New Delhi, rather than with Washington, Paris, and Bonn. The Germans were to be feared perhaps as greatly as the Soviets. Portugal's political leadership was to be condemned more forcefully than Tito's Yugoslavia.[23]

As an alternative to Common Market membership, the Forward Britain Movement proposed several economic measures. Bulk purchase agreements might be concluded between Britain and less developed countries to enable such states to expand their exports of industrial goods as well as primary products and earn some of the foreign exchange needed for programs of economic development. A Commonwealth payments union and development bank, which EFTA countries would be invited to join, might be established. A recommendation was

---

[23] *Ibid.*, p. 147.

offered to create a "Full Employment Club" among nations whose governments wished to co-ordinate their efforts to prevent recession or unemployment. Clearly, the leaders of the Forward Britain Movement saw the major problems of world politics as lying in the less developed countries rather than in a threat to the West from the communist world.

Shortly after Macmillan's announcement that Britain would apply for Common Market membership, Conservatives who found themselves at odds with such a course of action had formed the Anti-Common Market League, under the leadership of Mr. John A. Paul, an oil company director and former chairman of the South Kensington Conservative Association. Absent from the League's literature were the expressions of apprehension about the heightening of Cold War tensions found in the publications of the Forward Britain Movement. Nevertheless, some aspects of the Anti-Common Market League's case against British entry bore a marked resemblance to that of the Forward Britain Movement. It was alleged that Britain, as a member of the Common Market, would be dominated by a European Community government. Britain would be unable to retain existing links with the Commonwealth and the United States. London faced the loss of its "special influence" in the world. Moreover, membership in the EEC would constitute an infringement upon British sovereignty and upon the rights of Britain as a nation to make its own decisions and manage its own affairs.[24]

Of considerable concern to members of the Anti-Common Market League was the effect of EEC membership upon the older Commonwealth countries. It was held that Common Market membership would be tantamount to a betrayal of the older Commonwealth members—to those countries which had fought at Britain's side in two world wars. Britain could not forsake loyalties tested in conflict with countries populated by her own kinsmen. Of all Commonwealth countries, Britain owed special consideration to Australia, New Zealand, and Canada, to whose populations millions in Britain had family links. In contrast to the Forward Britain Movement, whose members feared the destruction of the multiracial Commonwealth, Anti-Common Market League pronouncements reflected a Conservative interest in the older Com-

---

[24] R. Hugh Corbet, (ed.), *Britain, Not Europe: Commonwealth Before Common Market*, (London: Anti-Common Market League, 1962), pp. 12–13. This symposium included articles by Sir Roy Harrod, Robin Turton, Peter Walker, and Sir Derek Walker-Smith.

monwealth populated by people of European origin, rather than the newer multiracial Commonwealth.

In British Common Market membership, members of the Forward Britain Movement saw a sinister American effort to create a United States-dominated bloc for the heightening of Cold War tensions. Anti-Common Market League members saw in the U.S. eagerness for Britain to sign the Rome Treaty a thinly veiled attempt to increase American influence in the Commonwealth. As Britain turned her attention to European affairs after joining the Common Market, the United States would gain political and economic predominance in Commonwealth countries. Those states which were once within the British sphere of influence would be obliged to turn to Washington.

According to the Anti-Common Market League, the EEC was unduly restrictionist in its trade policies. In addition to being forced as a Common Market member to buy much of her foodstuffs from western Europe rather than from lower cost sellers in the Commonwealth, Britain would face even more severe competition than previously for her exports. Rising food prices in Britain would stimulate wage demands and increasing costs of production that would adversely affect the competitive position of British exports. With the ending of preferential arrangements in the Commonwealth, Britain would face new competition from other industrial countries. At the same time, British industrialists would be confronted with an influx of manufacturers from the Six as Britain's own tariff levels were lowered. Economic distress and unemployment would follow British EEC entry. The result would be to speed the emigration of skilled workers from Britain.

The Anti-Common Market League urged the British government to take several measures to boost Commonwealth trade. The League called for increased market research and analysis, commodity stabilization agreements and greater research on the reserves of raw materials available in Commonwealth countries. Such steps might make it possible for Britain to reverse the decline in Commonwealth trade. With greater emphasis on the expansion of Commonwealth economic relationships, Britain could gain many of the benefits of dynamic markets which proponents of Common Market membership foresaw from entry into the European Community.

Although the Liberal party had been the first of Britain's political parties to advocate EEC membership, a small Liberal minority had seen such a course of action as a betrayal of traditional liberal principles of free trade. In 1961, Liberals who disagreed with their party's official stand on the Common Market had founded the Keep Britain Out Campaign. Its leader, Mr. Oliver Smedley, had long been active in efforts to promote in economic matters a liberalism akin to that of the nineteenth century Manchester School. According to Smedley and his followers, Britain's greatest period of achievement had come when she embraced the economic doctrine of free trade. As the world's largest single importer of foodstuffs and raw materials, Britain could not afford to purchase at any but the cheapest prices. Because of its policies, the EEC did not represent a step toward the freeing of international trade, but instead hampered the ability of Britain to maximize her comparative advantage in world commerce.

Those who supported the campaign opposed British EEC membership on several grounds. Like other opposition groups, they rejected the notion that the actions of Parliament might be superseded by decisions made in Brussels. Only Britain should have final authority to devalue sterling or to determine British tariffs and other trading policies. Unlike other EEC opponents, however, the Keep Britain Out Campaign stressed in its literature a faith in the ability of the British, through their "inherent qualities, if put to the test, to regain the vigour and enterprise which enabled them to maintain their political independence and defend the freedom of the world against tyranny for 500 years." [25] According to the Keep Britain Our Campaign, it was folly to attribute economic growth in the Six to the EEC. Such expansion had been the product of U.S. aid and a manifestation of belated recovery from the effects of World War II. Countries outside the Common Market, such as Austria and Japan, had experienced equally spectacular rates of economic growth. In place of Common Market membership, the Keep Britain Out Campaign offered a balanced budget, a freeing of the pound sterling from governmental controls, the elimination of all subsidies, the ending of tariff protection, and efforts to instill in Englishmen "the need for integrity in everything and for giving value for money received." [26]

Participation in anti-Common Market organizations included Liberals as well as prominent members of the Conservative and Labour parties. One such Conservative, Sir Derek Walker-Smith, a former Minister of Health, spoke out against the government at the first public

---

[25] Leaflet published by the Keep Britain Out Campaign (London, 1962).
[26] See "Common Market: Economists' Blunder." *City Press* (London), December 1, 1961.

meeting of the newly formed Anti-Common Market League on October 4, 1961,[27] and in the Commons. In the parliamentary debate of August 2–3, 1961, and at the Conservative Annual Conference in October 1961, Walker-Smith expressed fears about the future of Britain's relations with other Commonwealth countries, the "surrender" of sovereignty, the protection of British agricultural interests, and the reduction of Britain's role in world affairs if she joined the Common Market. Several months later, Walker-Smith, together with two other Conservative backbenchers, tabled an amendment to a House of Commons motion. The amendment, which some forty other Conservative Members of Parliament signed, called upon the government to seek an expansion of Commonwealth trade and not to enter the Common Market without "special arrangements to protect vital interests in the countries of our Commonwealth partnership." [28]

During the spring and summer of 1962, this "Commonwealth Group" within the parliamentary Conservative party took additional steps to publicize its views. One Conservative MP, Mr. Peter Walker, embarked upon a tour of Commonwealth countries. His objective was to alert business and political leaders to the dangers he foresaw in British Common Market membership. He sought to arouse opposition to the European Community by calling attention to the losses in trade which Commonwealth countries might suffer if Britain acceded to the Rome Treaty. By playing up opposition in the Conservative party as well as elsewhere in Britain, Walker believed he could rally Commonwealth leaders to an anti-Common Market stance and weaken the position of the Macmillan cabinet in the conference of Commonwealth Ministers scheduled to convene in London on September 10, 1962. Another such measure consisted of an open letter to the press, signed by fourteen members of the "Commonwealth Group" of Conservative MP's expressing displeasure with the terms agreed upon in Brussels late in the spring of 1962 for exports of Commonwealth manufactures to Britain.[29]

In a pamphlet published under their signatures in June 1962, Walker-Smith and Peter Walker outlined their proposals for a Commonwealth

---

[27] *Times* (London), October 5, 1961, p. 6.

[28] *Daily Telegraph* (London), March 26, 1962, p. 1.

[29] The signatories of this letter expressed fears that agreements such as this represented a "continual whittling away of the Commonwealth position (which) may in due course break Commonwealth trade on which 40 out of every 100 people in this country depend for their employment." *Guardian* (Manchester and London), June 6, 1962, p. 1.

alternative to the Common Market. They called for the creation of such institutional devices as a Commonwealth Economic Conference, an Economic Consultative Council, a Marketing Board, and a Commonwealth Court of Appeal to supplement the work of the Judicial Committee of the Privy Council.[30] In this fashion, it was suggested, the Commonwealth might be strengthened to the mutual advantage of its members. On July 30, 1962, moreover, a group of dissident Conservative MP's introduced in the House of Commons a motion urging the government to "insist on definite assurances for Commonwealth trade and on the continuance of the power of sovereign decisions by the British Parliament for our agricultural and horticultural policies." [31]

The anti-Common Market forces counted among their numbers persons who gave their cause a sophistication and intellectual appeal which most other opponents could not have supplied. Some of Britain's leading economists questioned a premise which had guided the thinking of many proponents of Common Market membership: that Britain would gain economically from the exposure of her industries to competition from the Six. One such critic, Sir Donald MacDougall, deputy director and chief economist of the National Economic Development Council, an official advisory group, declared that Britain might lose more exports than she would gain from Common Market membership. Additional trade with the EEC would not compensate for greater losses in Commonwealth markets. Membership in the European Community might harm rather than improve the British balance of payments. Furthermore, contrary to the expectations of Common Market advocates, Britain would not benefit from new economies of scale in the EEC.[32]

Other opponents of British entry criticized the Common Market because of its alleged political implications. Widely differing British and Continental political practices and assumptions about political systems might make it impossible to achieve the consensus necessary for Britain and the Six to work in harmony. For example, William Pickles, Senior Lecturer in Political Science at the London School of Economics and a student of European affairs, as well as an articulate and active

---

[30] Sir Derek Walker-Smith and Peter Walker, *A Call to the Commonwealth*. (London: 1962).

[31] *Guardian* (Manchester and London), July 31, 1962, p. 1.

[32] According to MacDougall: "The British market of over 50 million people, living at our high standard, together with our large export markets throughout the world, already made possible most of the economies of scale in most industries." *Reynolds News* (London), April 22, 1962.

opponent of British membership in the Common Market, warned, in a pamphlet published in April 1962, that in the Common Market Britain would be compelled to adapt herself to Continental practices. The adjustment would be long and difficult. Until Englishmen learned the ways of their European Community partners, Britain would not be able to influence the evolution of European integration. Even when Britain had become acquainted with Continental political and legal conduct" . . . in, say, a couple of generations—we shall *perhaps* be able to exert our due share of influence, but certainly no more. To believe anything else is to be guilty of stupid and insular arrogance." [33]

In his statement to the House of Commons on August 2, 1961, Prime Minister Macmillan had set as one of the conditions for British EEC entry the achievement of "satisfactory arrangements . . . with the (European Economic) Community which would assure the continued well-being of British agriculture. Our objective," he declared, "is to have a prosperous, stable and efficient agricultural industry, organized to provide a good life for those who live and work in the country-side." [34] By the autumn of 1961, it had become apparent that the British government was prepared, if satisfactory arrangements for the transitional period could be worked out, to adopt in substance the agricultural policy of the Six.

As the Brussels negotiations unfolded, the British government faced opposition from Britain's major agricultural organization, the National Farmers Union (NFU). At its annual meeting held on January 23, 1962, the NFU adopted with unanimous support a resolution opposing EEC membership unless the following conditions of entry were met: continuation of annual price reviews, maintenance of guaranteed prices for farm products, effective support for horticulture, and governmental support for producer-controlled marketing. This resolution did not receive approval until after the representatives in attendance had heard numerous statements urging that Britain refuse to abandon her existing

---

[33] According to Pickles:

Multi-party systems produce political habits of mind vastly different from those engendered by our two-party setup. So do conceptions of democracy based on interpretations of Rousseau instead of, as in Britain, the ideas of Locke. Written constitutions create rigidities and ways of getting around them unknown to pragmatic Britons.

William Pickles, *Not with Europe: The Political Case for Staying Out* (London: Fabian International Bureau, 1962), p. 8.

[34] Great Britain, *Parliamentary Debates* (Commons), Vol. 645 (August 2, 1961) cols. 1486–1488.

agricultural policy in favor of the EEC farm system.[35] Nevertheless, in January 1962, the NFU did not express outright opposition to British membership in the Common Market.

During 1962 the NFU became increasingly dissatisfied with the deliberations in Brussels on agricultural policy. On July 19, the NFU presented a resolution to the Minister of Agriculture, in which the Union repeated its earlier contention that satisfactory arrangements had still to be made for agriculture in an enlarged Community.[36] Apparently the resolution was intended as a reminder to the Macmillan cabinet that the NFU saw the need for changes in the EEC agricultural policy. The NFU focused its criticism on several specific features of Common Market farm policy. According to the NFU, the EEC agricultural accords were unsatisfactory because they had been worked out essentially on a commodity basis, with insufficient consideration having been given to the general economy and financial conditions in agricultural areas. Instead, the Union reminded the British government: "A comprehensive agricultural-economic review to establish the facts about the agricultural position in each country and in the Community as a whole, has always been regarded by the NFU as the first step in determining an effective and consistent agricultural policy." [37]

In another criticism, the NFU expressed the view that EEC commodity regulations would not provide adequate assurance of reasonable and stable returns to farmers. The European Community's existing arrangements, the NFU maintained, did not furnish, in the language of the British Agriculture Act of 1947, "proper renumeration and living conditions for farmers and farm workers in agriculture and an adequate return on capital invested in the industry." Moreover, EEC regulations for fruit and vegetables were matters of particular concern to the Union, since British producers of horticultural crops, however technically efficient they might be, could not be expected to compete with produce grown in areas more favourably suited. Finally, the NFU remained uncertain of the role which producer marketing organizations in Britain might play in commodity arrangements for an enlarged Community.[38] Another agricultural group, the Country Landowners' Association, expressed agreement with the NFU position that the terms

[35] *Times* (London), January 23, 1962, p. 6; 18.
[36] *Times* (London), July 20, 1962, p. 6.
[37] The National Farmers Union of England and Wales, *British Agriculture and the Common Market* (Part 1), London, NFU Information Service, 1962, p. 80.
[38] *Ibid.*

for agriculture worked out in Brussels were not satisfactory.[39] However, the association, whose 27,000 members claimed to hold about 70 percent of the farming land in England and Wales, continued in the summer and autumn of 1962 to withhold final judgment on EEC entry until the full terms were known.[40]

On August 23, the NFU issued a statement expressing opposition to British membership in the Common Market on terms then under consideration. Having concluded that the Six were unwilling to adapt their farming policy to suit Britain's needs, the NFU declared that the Common Market did not provide a satisfactory basis for British agricultural prosperity.[41] The NFU set forth an alternative agricultural proposal for the enlargement of the Organization for Economic Cooperation and Development (OECD) to include Australia, New Zealand, and Argentina. The NFU proposed worldwide commodity agreements which could have among their signatories the Six, the United States, Argentina, and such Commonwealth countries as Britain, Australia, Canada, and New Zealand. The world's major agricultural producers would agree to place quantitative restrictions upon exports of foodstuffs to Britain, and would contract for the use of surplus foodstuffs to assist less developed countries to meet shortages.[42] In return, the NFU was prepared to agree to quotas for British agricultural production.[43]

During the course of the Brussels negotiations, other agricultural interest groups worked to oppose EEC membership. In particular, the Farmers and Smallholders Association and the Cheap Food League, whose leaders sought a return to free trade even in agriculture, ranked among the opponents of EEC entry. In their efforts to oppose British EEC membership, the Liberal leaders of these groups had founded the Keep Britain Out Campaign. This organization used the same London offices as its "parent" interest groups, the Farmers and Smallholders Association and the Cheap Food League, which opposed the policy of governmental aid and controls contained in the Agricultural Acts of 1947 and 1957. The organizations sought to assist farmers in financial difficulty, organized petitions to the government, sent letters to cabinet members, had questions asked in Parliament, and issued

---

[39] *Times* (London), August 27, 1962, p. 5.
[40] *Times* (London), October 18, 1962, p. 23.
[41] *New York Times*, August 24, 1962, p. 7. See also *Financial Times* (London), August 24, 1962, p. 11.
[42] Asher Winegarten, "Agriculture—In or Out?", *Statist*, December 14, 1962, 744.
[43] The *Economist*, Vol. CCIV, No. 6209, August 25, 1962, 678.

propaganda critical of official British policy.[44] According to the leaders of these organizations, only by a return to free trade could British industry and agriculture attain once again the efficiency and prosperity of the period between 1840 and 1880 when the restraints upon competition were few.

During the final months of the Brussels negotiations, the NFU leadership remained convinced that the agricultural policy of the Six was unsuitable for Britain.[45] Even if the Six agreed to Britain's request for a lengthened transitional period for agriculture, it was contended, the longer term consequences for Britain would be harmful. Upon joining the Common Market, Britain's food bill would rise. Under the provisions of EEC agricultural policy, Britain would be forced to pay a levy on imported foodstuffs to support Continental rather than specifically British farmers. The EEC agricultural policy had been framed to meet the needs of the Six, less dependent than Britain upon imports of foodstuffs. This policy was unsuited, therefore, to the requirements of Britain, dependent as she was upon imports of cheap foodstuffs for her largely urban population.[46]

By no means were all who analyzed Britain's agricultural problems opposed to British Common Market entry. For the most part, those who believed Britain should enter the EEC maintained that British farmers had little to fear from Continental competition. It was suggested that, technologically, British farming was more advanced than that of EEC countries. Agriculture in Britain was more highly mechanized than on the Continent. On the average, Britain's farms were larger in acreage and therefore more efficient.[47] Hence, the British were unlikely to receive major concessions on agriculture in the Brussels negotiations. In some commodities, Britain even stood to gain as a result of Common Market membership. For example, Britain had surpluses in the production of barley which might find markets in an enlarged Community; there might also be new opportunities for sales of British lamb and beef on the Continent.[48]

Like members of the political parties, newspapers usually in opposi-

---

[44] Peter Self and H. Storing, *The State and the Farmer*, pp. 117–118.

[45] See *Christian Science Monitor*, January 10, 1963; *NFU News*, November 29, 1962; December 19, 1962; January 22, 1963.

[46] *NFU News*, January 29, 1963.

[47] Political and Economic Planning, "Agricultural Integration in Western Europe," *Planning*, Vol. XXIX, No. 470 (April 8, 1963).

[48] See, for example, Stanley Baker, "A Common Policy for Agriculture?" *Guardian* (Manchester and London), May 30, 1961, p. 8.

tion to one another on other major issues often found themselves in agreement during the Brussels negotiations. Some British newspapers, including such strange bedfellows as the Beaverbrook Press and the *New Statesman and Nation,* inveighed against the Common Market. Newspapers of the Labour left and Conservative right, in many cases, shared a disdain for the economic as well as political implications of Common Market membership. Both feared that Britain, as a member of EEC, would face a diminution of parliamentary authority. No longer could Britain maintain an independent foreign policy. Instead, the foreign policy of the European Community would be subordinated to the allegedly anti-communist interests of Germany, since an integrated western Europe, it was suggested, would be ruled from Bonn. Editorial writers in journals of the far left and far right shared the view that British Common Market entry was incompatible with Britain's obligations to the Commonwealth, and that domestic British agricultural interests would be jeopardized. Both saw the need for Britain to seek new markets in the Commonwealth and in the communist world. Both feared the loss of British political and economic independence in the European Community. Not unexpectedly, newspapers of the far left saw a danger to British socialism in a Common Market dominated allegedly by conservative, capitalistic, Catholic regimes.

One of Lord Beaverbrook's papers, the *Daily Express,* echoed the sentiment of many other opponents of Common Market membership, namely, that Britain was negotiating with the Six as a result of U.S. pressure.[49] The appeals of Beaverbrook's newspapers included repeated references to such terms as the British Empire, rather than the Commonwealth, and "Empire free trade," a cause which has few supporters in the present-day Commonwealth. Undoubtedly, such references to the past helped to preserve in the minds of patriotic Englishmen the vision of an era which is history, but they hardly contributed to the resolution of the pressing problems facing Britain in the world today. The *New Statesman and Nation,* although fearful that Britain was about to abandon the Commonwealth, used one argument fashionable among the British left, namely, that the Common Market was an iniquitous device for perpetuating capitalism and large-scale economic units. According to this viewpoint, moreover, "the Tories can permit

---

[49] *Daily Express* (London), January 6, 1962. Another of the appeals which this newspaper made to British chauvinism came in the form of a rhetorical question: "Do you want to be British? Or are you willing that you and your children should belong to some British-French-German-Italian hotch-potch?" *Ibid.*

Britain to collapse into Europe because they accept the economic assumption on which the Community is based: they believe that the function of government is to create the conditions in which big business can flourish." [50]

Throughout the period between July 1961 and January 1963, however, the bulk of the British press remained committed, as it had in the months preceding the government's decision, to Britain's membership in the EEC. Newspapers whose sympathies lay with one or another of the political parties lent their support to the British application. Their editorial columns voiced expectations of economic gain, greater industrial efficiency, a new role for London in European affairs, and as a result of the foregoing a new stature for Britain in the world. The declining importance both of the Commonwealth and the special relationship with the United States as sources of British power received considerable emphasis. Editorial writers reminded readers that the British rate of economic growth was lower than that of her counterparts in the Common Market, and suggested that industrial modernization, rising living standards, and new export markets, would accrue to Britain from EEC entry.

If not prepared to advocate membership in a "federal" Europe, most newspapers nevertheless continued, as they had in the months before July 1961, to urge the government to consider political links of a confederal nature, such as those proposed by President de Gaulle, once Britain became a member of the Common Market. According to widely held expectations of gain, Britain had before her the opportunity to bolster the Western world against communism, to achieve a new position of leadership in an integrated Europe, to strengthen the Commonwealth as a result of Britain's own revitalization, and to assist Continental countries in the development of more stable and representative political systems. By 1962 there was greater editorial support than previously for the sharing of British nuclear technology with prospective Common Market partners. By such action, it was suggested, Britain might demonstrate her interest in European integration, while keeping nuclear weapons under the control of as few nations as possible, since the British and French nuclear forces would be merged to form the nucleus of European deterrent.[51]

---

[50] New Statesman and Nation, May 4, 1962, p. 621.
[51] The Economist, Vol. CCIII, No. 6192 (April 28, 1962), p. 319; Vol. CCIII, No. 6194 (May 12, 1962), pp. 535–537. Daily Telegraph (London), April 24, 1962, p. 10; July 18, 1962, p. 10. See also Sunday Times (London), July 15, 1962, p. 10.

Even among those journals which supported the principle of British EEC membership, there were limits beyond which Britain could not make concessions to the Six. As the Brussels negotiations proceeded, misgivings appeared in British newspapers about Common Market membership under the terms then under consideration. In the press there was a consensus concerning the need for specific arrangements to assure markets for Commonwealth temperate agricultural producers after the ending of the transitional period for British membership.[52] Although prepared to accept the ending of preferential treatment for Commonwealth manufactured goods, British journals for the most part opposed the granting of concessions in Brussels which would jeopardize exports of foodstuffs, especially from Australia, Canada, and New Zealand. In general, the press urged the British government not to concede to the Six the point that the British system of deficiency payments to farmers must end no later than October 1964, the latest date for calling a general election to elect a new Parliament.[53] The agreements on Commonwealth trade which emerged from Brussels led to a perceptible cooling in editorial support for Common Market membership. In the case of the *Guardian*, one of the first newspapers to call for EEC entry, there was a switch from support to opposition. In the autumn of 1962, the editors of the *Guardian* found unacceptable the provisions negotiated for EFTA, British agriculture, and the Commonwealth.[54]

In the months following the Common Market decision, it was the official policy of the Labour party not to commit itself either to support or to oppose British EEC entry until the terms for membership were known. Such a policy had several advantages. Should the negotiations fail, or produce terms disadvantageous to certain groups in Britain, the Labour party might stand to make political gains. Furthermore, a policy of wait-and-see commended itself to those members of the

---

[52] See, for example, *Daily Telegraph* (London), June 6, 1962, p. 12; *Scotsman* (Edinburgh), June 7, 1962, p. 8; The *Economist*, Vol. CCIII, No. 6198 (June 9, 1962), 97, Vol. CCIV, No. 6206 (August 4, 1962), 419–421; *Times* (London), June 5, 1962, p. 13. The *Spectator*, Vol. 208 (June 8, 1962), 239; *Guardian* (Manchester and London), July 27, 1962, p. 10. See also *Scotsman* (Edinburgh), August 9, 1962, p. 6; *Daily Mail* (London), July 31, 1962, p. 1; *Daily Herald* (London), July 30, 1962, p. 6; *Yorkshire Post* (Leeds), August 6, 1962, p. 4; *Daily Telegraph* (London), August 8, 1962, p. 8.
[53] Before the election of 1959, the Conservatives had pledged that, if returned to office, they would maintain the existing system of deficiency payments for the life of the next Parliament.
[54] *Guardian* (Manchester and London), October 4, 1962, p. 6.

Labour party who had genuine doubts about the Common Market. Finally, not the least of the reasons for such a policy lay in the division of opinion within the party on Common market entry among those who had already decided either to support or to oppose this issue. In the weeks after the government's announcement of July 31, the cleavage within the Labour party on the Common Market question revealed itself in debates held in the Commons and at the party's 1961 Annual Conference. When pro-European Labour Members of Parliament sponsored a motion which would have expressed party support for the Common Market, they met with opposition. Although this Labour Common Market motion attracted some thirty signatories, its opponents claimed, not without justification, that at least as many Labour Members of Parliament were prepared to sign a countermotion against Britain's adherence to the Rome Treaty.[55] The latter group included in its number Douglas Jay, the parliamentary Labour party's leading specialist on international trade and economics. In the latter months of 1961, however, Labour party members opposed to the Common Market confined their parliamentary action to the formation of a committee to watch and review critically the Brussels negotiations.

During the early months of 1962, Labour opponents of Common Market membership stepped up their campaign. A second Labour anti-EEC faction, the left-wing Victory for Socialism group, whose members had failed in their efforts to commit the party to an anti-Common Market stance at its annual conference the previous autumn, issued a statement on January 18, 1962.[56] The group expressed a view British socialists had voiced in opposing British membership in other European organizations: that such a course of action would restrict the authority of a Labour government to nationalize industry and engage in economic planning. The same statement condemned the EEC as an instrument of U.S. policy in Europe. It expressed the framers' fears that Common Market membership would result in a sharp rise in Britain's cost of living.

According to parliamentary members of the Labour left, the alternative to Common Market membership was the revision of Britain's links with the Commonwealth. In a communiqué following a meeting with colleagues from Norway and Denmark in February 1962, left-wing

---

[55] *Daily Telegraph* (London), December 11, 1961.
[56] *Times* (London), January 19, 1962, p. 6.

British socialists set forth such a view.[57] In another statement, Douglas Jay, speaking for the non-leftist Labour faction opposing Common Market membership, proposed that Britain seek to preserve EFTA and Commonwealth trading arrangements, while also benefiting from tariff reductions on a most favored-nation basis between the Six and the United States under the Trade Expansion Act, then under consideration in the U.S. Congress. Thus by January 1962, three principal Common Market factions had been formed within the Labour party. Members on Labour's right and left wings established groups in opposition to British entry, while a faction of Labour Members of Parliament actively supported Britain's membership in the Common Market.

Hugh Gaitskell had as his immediate task, therefore, to avert a split such as had shaken the party in 1960, when opposing groups clashed on the issue of unilateral nuclear disarmament. During the early months of 1962, Gaitskell and his deputy, George Brown, held several meetings with dissident factions on the Common Market question in an effort to prevent a new breach within the party. Their aim was the difficult one of devising a position acceptable to most members. Moreover, Gaitskell himself wished to keep the party officially uncommitted on the Common Market issue until the terms of British entry were known.

On March 7, 1962 the Labour party's leadership produced a compromise statement which fulfilled the aforementioned conditions.[58] The party set forth five requirements to be met before it would support British Common Market membership: guarantees for domestic agriculture; safeguards for Commonwealth trade; agreements for EFTA trade; retention by Britain of her present freedom in the conduct of foreign relations and in the formulation of social policies and economic planning; and assurances that the products of underdeveloped countries would be given free entry into the Common Market.[59] Labour's stipulations probably reflected the sentiment of the majority in the parlia-

---

[57] The communiqué stated: "We believe that a better alternative (to Common Market membership) would be to combine the Commonwealth and EFTA systems of mutual tariff preferences into a comprehensive, up-to-date agreement." *Guardian* (Manchester and London), February 15, 1962, p. 5.

[58] As a result, the pro-Common Market Labour group agreed on March 7 to withdraw its own motion, originally signed by Mr. Roy Jenkins and thirty other Labour MPs. This motion, however, was tabled again on March 8 as a Liberal motion in support of Common Market membership. *Guardian* (Manchester and London), March 9, 1962, p. 10.

[59] *Times* (London), March 8, 1962, p. 8.

mentary Labour party, as well as the constituency organizations, who wished to remain uncommitted until the terms of entry were more clearly discernible. Comparatively few Labour MPs advocated Common Market membership regardless of the conditions, and few rejected outright the idea of joining the EEC. Hence, these five conditions enabled Gaitskell and his colleagues to resolve the dilemma in which they found themselves. But they also undoubtedly weakened the hand of Britain's negotiators at Brussels. With conditions such as those posed by Labour in mind, de Gaulle and other leaders on the Continent could conclude, not without justification, that large numbers of Englishmen were not prepared to accept Common Market membership even if the British government reached agreement with the Six.

If anyone could have committed the Labour party to Common Market membership, it was Gaitskell. But apparently he did not make up his mind on this issue until the early autumn of 1962. Aside from the tactical considerations which influence the behavior of a political leader, especially in a party with so diverse a membership as that of the Labour party, Gaitskell himself had genuine misgivings about the EEC. In his speech replying to the Prime Minister's statement to the House of Commons on August 2, 1961, Gaitskell had attached great importance to the retention by Britain of her economic links with Australia, New Zealand and Canada, as well as with the newer members of the multiracial Commonwealth.[60]

It was Gaitskell's belief that Common Market membership would not be an unmitigated blessing. In his estimation, much of the EEC's vaunted economic growth, as compared with Britain's economic sluggishness, was illusory. Since the formation of the Common Market, France had experienced high growth rates, largely because her wage levels were lower than those of Britain. As the labor costs of Common Market members approached those prevalent in Britain, whatever competitive disadvantage British goods currently suffered would diminish. Moreover, the Labour leader viewed with considerable alarm the prospect of damage to British farming and the substitution of agricultural imports from the Six for those from Commonwealth countries.

Gaitskell's fear for the future of the Commonwealth shaped his attitude toward European political integration. His belief that a federal Europe meant the end of the Commonwealth led Gaitskell into a clash

---

[60] Great Britain, *Parliamentary Debates* (Commons), Vol. 645 (August 2, 1961), cols. 1504–1507.

with socialist leaders from the Six at a meeting in Brussels in July 1962. In the estimation of such European socialists as Paul-Henri Spaak, Gaitskell had placed far greater emphasis upon safeguards for the Commonwealth than upon the contribution Britain might make to the European Community. At that time Belgium's foreign minister as well as a leading proponent of British Common Market membership and a "federalist," Spaak could not accept Gaitskell's views. In particular, Gaitskell's declaration that Britain could not consider joining a European federation for at least a generation deeply disturbed not only Spaak but other members of socialist parties in the Six.[61]

As the summer of 1962 drew to a close, Gaitskell moved toward his final position on the Common Market question—a position which was to place the Labour party in opposition to the terms being worked out in Brussels. Like many other Englishmen whose loyalties lay with the Commonwealth, Gaitskell found unacceptable the terms which emerged from the Brussels negotiations. On the eve of the Commonwealth Prime Ministers' Conference, which convened in London on September 10, Gaitskell met at Transport House, Labour party headquarters, with Labour leaders from other Commonwealth countries. The conferees had before them the White Paper which the government had issued in August summarizing the state of the Common Market negotiations just prior to their recess on August 5.[62] After the Labour conference, the delegates declared that they could not "regard the provisional outline of agreements so far reached in Brussels as safeguarding the relation of Britain with the Commonwealth and as adequately fulfilling the Prime Minister's pledge. . . ."

> The essence of our objection is that while there appears to be a firm commitment to end Commonwealth preferences not later than 1970, and to give European exports a preference in Britain against the Commonwealth, no precise agreements which offer compensating advantages to Commonwealth countries have been reached.[63]

The Commonwealth Labour delegates did not see in the "vague promises of comprehensive trade agreements" offered in Brussels be-

---

[61] *Financial Times* (London), July 17, 1962.
[62] This document was entitled: *The United Kingdom and the European Economic Community: Report by the Lord Privy Seal on the Meeting with Ministers of Member States of the European Economic Community* from August 1–5, 1962. (London: HMSO, 1962), Cmnd. 1805.
[63] *Times* (London), September 10, 1962, p. 5.

tween the Common Market and Commonwealth countries a satisfactory alternative to existing arrangements with Britain. Moreover,
the delegates objected to the proposed application of the Common
Market's agricultural policy to British farm imports. Finally, the
conferees derived little satisfaction from the offer of associate membership to African and Caribbean Commonwealth members. Instead, the
Labour delegates proposed, Commonwealth members should be accorded free entry into the Common Market for most, if not all, of their
tropical products. It was this meeting, together with the government's
White Paper of August, which brought Gaitskell firmly on the side of
those who opposed the Macmillan cabinet's EEC policy. However, it
was the terms of entry, not the principle of Common Market membership, which were decisive in determining his position and thus in
influencing the course the Labour party chose at its 1962 Annual
Conference.[64]

In response to the anti-European statements generated by the meeting between Gaitskell and Commonwealth Labour leaders, the Labour
Common Market Committee issued a declaration expressing its collective conviction of "the importance for this country, Europe, and the
Commonwealth of Britain's entry" into the EEC. The group urged the
British government to find special arrangements for New Zealand and
to conclude commodity agreements in the interest of other Common-

---

[64] The Labour Party Conference approved the statement on the Common Market
prepared by its National Executive Committee. This statement reiterated the
conditions set forth in the compromise agreement of the previous March of the
parliamentary Labour party for Britain's membership in the Common Market.
According to the National Executive Committee's statement,

> The Labour party regards the European Community as a great and imagina-
> tive conception. It believes that the coming together of the six nations which
> have in the past so often been torn by war and economic rivalry is, in the
> context of western Europe, a step of great significance. It is aware that the
> influence of this new Community on the world will grow and that it will be
> able to play—for good or for ill—a far larger part in the shaping of events in
> the 1960's and the 1970's than its individual member states could hope to play
> alone. It is these considerations, together with the influence that Britain as a
> member could exercise upon the Community—and not the uncertain balance
> of economic advantage—that constitute the real case for Britain's entry.

While Gaitskell's speech to the Labour Party Annual Conference stressed the
dangers of membership in the EEC to the Commonwealth and other British
interests, the National Executive Committee's statement emphasized also the
political and economic gains which might accrue to Britain from Common Market
membership. To this extent at least, Labour Common Marketeers appear to have
reduced the harshness of the party's position against the EEC. *Report of the
Sixty-first Annual Conference of the Labour Party*, Brighton, 1962 (London:
Labour Party, 1962), pp. 245–251.

wealth countries. As a member of the EEC, it was held, Britain could exercise decisive influence, both on her own behalf and on that of the Commonwealth. Outside the Common Market, however, Britain would face the "loss of influence and of prosperity for this country and the Commonwealth, coupled with the real possibility of Europe developing in the way we least want to see." The declaration contained sixty signatories, of whom thirty-six were Members of Parliament.[65]

Like the political parties, the British trade union movement did not speak with one voice on the Common Market question. In the months following the announcement of the Common Market decision, the TUC General Council retained its position of guarded support for EEC entry, and weighed the implications for British labor of agreements concluded in Brussels.[66] In addition to meeting regularly during the Brussels negotiations with British officials, including Mr. Heath, the TUC submitted a memorandum to the Lord Privy Seal in June 1962. This statement brought together in one document the conclusions the General Council had reached with regard to the safeguarding of its members' interests in the Common Market. It represented an elaboration of the statement on European economic unity to which the 1961 Congress had given approval. As that statement had done, this memorandum focused upon those sections of the Rome Treaty which dealt with economic union in Europe. The General Council stressed its belief in the necessity for planned economic growth in an enlarged Community. The foundation for economic expansion lay in the creation of "circumstances where European countries as members of a mainly industrial community were encouraged to make the fullest and the best use of resources, notably the skill of their working people." [67] For this reason, according to the TUC, member governments of EEC countries must be given the authority to "take measures of physical, financial and fiscal control, both on the domestic and external fronts, which are necessary to encourage or restrain selected sectors of activity."

[65] *Newsbrief of the Labour Common Market Committee.* No. 11 (London, October 1962).

[66] According to the Report to the TUC Annual Conference in 1961: "The General Council . . . agree in principle with the government's decision to open negotiations with the EEC with a view to joining the Community, but insist that satisfactory arrangements must be made to meet the special needs of the United Kingdom, of the Commonwealth and of EFTA." TUC *Report 1961*, London, 1961, p. 468.

[67] Memorandum to the Lord Privy Seal. Reprinted in TUC *Report 1962* (London, 1962), p. 261.

As it had in earlier statements, the General Council expressed fears about the ability of Britain, as an EEC member, to take steps to avoid a balance of payments crisis. The Rome Treaty, so it appeared to the TUC, limited or even removed a member country's right to impose controls unilaterally upon imports not only from other members of the EEC, but from third countries as well. A Common Market member, it was feared, was restricted in its power to suspend convertibility and to control capital movements to other EEC members or to third countries. The General Council was apprehensive of future balance of payments crises and their possible impact upon trade union members. Therefore, the TUC suggested that the British government might propose the creation of a European Reserves Union, in which member states would deposit a certain percentage of their currency reserves. In much the same fashion as the International Monetary Fund, the Union would grant assistance to member countries in short-term payments disequilibrium. In the absence of a European Reserves Union, the General Council believed that Britain, as a member of the Common Market, should retain its existing powers of control over capital movements.

As it had at the time of the free trade area discussions, the question of full employment in the EEC again commanded the attention of the General Council. Admitting that levels of employment had risen steadily in the Six, the TUC nevertheless continued to press for the inclusion in any British agreement for Common Market membership, of a protocol or declaration of intention that member states had an obligation to seek jobs for all who desired them. The assurance that, like Britain, all EEC countries sought in their national economic policies to maintain conditions of full employment did little to assuage TUC apprehensions.

Unlike the Labour party, however, the TUC did not condemn the agreements concluded in Brussels. Although not entirely satisfied that Britain had succeeded by August 1962 in protecting its interests, the General Council accepted assurances from Edward Heath that as a signatory Britain could work within the Community to achieve the TUC's objectives.[68] Thus in the autumn of 1962, the TUC remained in guarded support of the British Common Market bid, and at odds with the official position of the Labour party against EEC entry on the terms being worked out in Brussels.

---

[68] TUC, *Supplementary Report No. 3* (London, 1962), p. 9.

Although the General Council received the approval of a majority of the TUC membership for its EEC policy, there remained a sizable minority which was skeptical about, or opposed to, Common Market entry.[69] Some feared that Britain would come under the control of conservative groups and regimes in Europe. Others opposed the Common Market because of its agricultural policy and the disastrous effects which allegedly EEC entry would have upon trade with the Commonwealth, and the resulting loss of jobs in Britain. Still other trade unionists, giving evidence of their insularity, feared that EEC membership meant the sacrifice of hard-won social and economic benefits. Despite the assurances of Labor Common Marketeers to the contrary, some trade unionists had visions of an influx of unemployed Europeans in search of jobs, bringing with them lower wages and undesired changes in the British way of life.[70]

The guarded position of the TUC General Council on the question of Common Market membership was not conducive to the widespread development among trade unionists of expectations of gain from the European Community. The British labor movement did not have hopes of reward from EEC membership to an extent comparable to much of Britain's press and industry. The expectations of trade unionists, even where they existed, were neither highly developed nor clearly articulated. The caution with which the General Council advocated British membership in a free trade area and later the Common Market, suggested that TUC thinking moved along a course roughly parallel with, rather than ahead of, thinking in governmental circles in Britain.

With their party having registered officially its opposition to the terms at Brussels in the autumn of 1962, Labour party opponents of the Common Market stepped up their campaign against the government's policy. Speaking to a Labour party gathering on October 20, 1962, Douglas Jay declared that an agreement between the British government and the EEC would have no "moral basis unless it is first submit-

---

[69] At its 1962 annual Congress, no less than ten motions were offered in opposition to Britain's entry into the EEC on terms then under consideration by the British government. Although all were withdrawn or defeated, they had the support of the following unions: the Amalgamated Engineering Union, the Association of Cinematograph, Televisionist Allied Technicians, the Draughtsmen's and Allied Technicians' Association, the National Union of Tailors and Garment Workers, the Society of Technical Civil Servants, the Associated Blacksmith's Forge and Smithy Workers' Society, the National Union of Furniture Trade Operatives, and the Amalgamated Union of Operative Artists, Designers, Engravers, and Process Workers.
[70] TUC *Report 1962* (London, 1962), pp. 403–421.

ted to the electorate to decide." [71] If the government should try to sign the Rome Treaty without first holding an election, Jay suggested, "certainly a future Labour government would not be morally bound by it." On September 21, Gaitskell added his name to those who believed that a general election should precede Britain's entry into the Common Market.

With this as well as other features of Labour's anti-European arguments, the Labour Common Market Committee took issue. In a widely circulated newsletter, the committee held that it was impossible to conduct a general election on a single specific question. The committee admonished its Labour colleagues who opposed the Common Market for using this issue to "stampede the Labour movement into an official stand against the Common Market, in the hope of snatching a quick electoral victory." [72] According to the committee, such tactics might lead to Labour's defeat rather than victory in the next election, since in many constituencies the Liberals and Conservatives, both committed to the Common Market, were receiving together more votes in by-elections than was Labour.

Only in the early autumn of 1962 did the Macmillan cabinet undertake its greatest effort to build popular support for its Common Market policy. The government took the occasion of the Commonwealth Prime Ministers' meeting and the Conservative party's 1962 Annual Conference to mount a campaign designed to counter the efforts of EEC opponents and achieve a broadly based consensus in favor of Common Market membership. The government's campaign included a stepped-up schedule of speeches by cabinet ministers and the massive distribution of pro-Common Market tracts by the Conservative party.

In a television broadcast following the Commonwealth Prime Ministers' Conference, for example, Prime Minister Macmillan attempted to answer charges about the potential impact of British Common Market membership upon the Commonwealth. To those critics who held that the Commonwealth "would never be quite the same again" if Britain signed the Treaty of Rome, he replied that regardless of British policy

---

[71] *New York Times*, October 21, 1962, p. 14.

[72] According to the Labour Common Market Committee: "The fact is that our electoral system provides for people voting for Parties or individuals, but not for particular issues. Only a referendum could decide an issue such as Common Market entry, and this is something which has never yet found its way into British political or constitutional practice." *Newsbrief of the Labour Common Market Committee*, No. 8 (London, July 1962), 1.

the Commonwealth was bound to experience profound change.[73] In a pamphlet published on October 7, 1962, Macmillan declared that as a Common Market member "Britain would be the chief spokesman of the Commonwealth in Europe, and the interpreter of Europe to the Commonwealth, reconciling the interests of these very different systems and acting as a bridge between them." [74] In joining the Common Market, Britain need not choose between the Commonwealth and European integration. These points the Prime Minister pressed at the Conservative party's 1962 Annual Conference. Submerging earlier differences of opinion by turning down demands for stringent guarantees for the Commonwealth and British agriculture, the Conference voted almost unanimously to join the Common Market on terms the government deemed suitable.[75]

In the autumn of 1962, moreover, the government's case for joining the European Community stressed the contribution Britain could make to the reduction of international tensions. Macmillan declared that this was a function which Britain could perform most effectively as a Common Market member. Moreover, the Conservatives called attention to the impressive growth of British trade with the Six. In the first half of 1962, British exports to the Common Market were 18 percent higher than in 1961, and 35 percent above the 1960 figure.[76]

In the latter months of 1962, the government faced increasingly formidable domestic opposition to its Common Market policy. Even leading Conservatives voiced doubts about the Macmillan cabinet's approach to Europe. In the House of Lords, Lord Salisbury, who in 1957 had been influential in securing Mr. Macmillan's selection as Prime Minister, was fearful of the political as well as economic implications of British EEC entry. As had Labour party spokesmen, he suggested that the government should "consult the people" in an election before committing Britain to membership in the Common Market. Lord Avon (formerly Sir Anthony Eden) also expressed misgivings about the possibility that "once in the EEC, Britain might become a

---

[73] Conservative and Unionist Central Office, *Commonwealth and Common Market.* Reprint of Prime Minister Macmillan's television broadcast following the Commonwealth Prime Ministers Conference, September 10–19, 1962.
[74] Harold Macmillan, *Britain, the Commonwealth and Europe* (London: Conservative and Unionist Central Office, 1962), p. 5.
[75] National Union of Conservative and Unionist Associations *81st Annual Conference*, Llandudno, 10th–13th October 1962, 46–67.
[76] Harold Macmillan, *Britain, the Commonwealth and Europe*, p. 5.

member of a European Federation, in which three of the Six have not found it possible to practice the same continuing loyalty to parliamentary institutions as we have in this country." [77] Moreover, he was critical of the terms for British agriculture and Commonwealth trade which Britain might be compelled to accept as the price for Common Market membership.

During the Brussels negotiations Sir Winston Churchill, like many other Englishmen, had sought to weigh British Commonwealth commitments against European interests. While recovering in August 1962 from a broken thighbone he had suffered in a fall, Churchill authorized the release of a statement he had prepared just a year earlier setting forth his views.[78] Sir Winston claimed that in the year since he had written this letter his views on Common Market membership had not changed. Churchill's position appeared to differ from that of the British government. While Churchill remained cautious, weighing Commonwealth commitments against European interests, the Macmillan cabinet became increasingly optimistic, at least in public pronouncements, about the prospects for Britain's entry into the Common Market.

In the final months of 1962 the anti-Common Market faction in the parliamentary Conservative party pressed its opposition to the government. On December 13, 1962, a group of forty-seven Conservative backbenchers tabled a motion calling upon the government to "formulate as soon as possible an alternative policy based upon a major Commonwealth initiative" if progress could not be made in Brussels to achieve acceptable terms for British EEC entry.[79]

---

[77] Great Britain, *Parliamentary Debates* (Lords), Vol. 244 (November 8, 1962), cols. 412–425 and 436–445.

[78] At that time, in a letter to the chairman of his constituency organization, Churchill had declared that Britain might well play a great part in the Common Market:

> to the profit, not only of ourselves, but of our European friends also. But we have another role which we cannot abdicate, that of leader to the British Commonwealth. In my conception of a unified Europe I never contemplate the diminution of the Commonwealth. . . .
>
> I think that the Government are right to apply to join the European Economic Community, not because I am yet convinced that we shall be able to join, but because there appears to be no other way by which we can find out exactly whether the conditions of membership are acceptable.

Guardian (Manchester and London), August 15, 1962, p. 26.

[79] In addition to Conservatives who had previously expressed opposition to Common Market membership, among those supporting this motion was Sir Anthony Hurd, a leading Conservative party expert on agriculture. Previously, he had not generally been associated with the anti-Common Market faction. Now, however, he found himself unable to accept the provisions being considered in

At a time when the British government faced mounting domestic opposition to the terms being worked out in Brussels for EEC entry, the Conservative party received evidence in by-elections that its pres-- tige was waning. Four by-elections held in November 1961 revealed an average vote shift of 6.5 percent from the Conservatives to Labour, more than sufficient to return a Labour majority at the next general election. Early in 1962, the government suffered a greater setback when the Conservative party lost a theoretically "safe" seat in the Orpington constituency to the Liberal candidate. In other by-elections held in 1962, the Conservatives continued to lose ground.

In most of the by-elections held in the months between July 1961 and January 1963, the Common Market question was not a key issue. In Orpington, for example, a study undertaken for the Conservative Central Office indicated that the policy on a pay pause as well as sheer boredom with the government contributed to the debacle.[80] Such was not the case, however, in South Dorset, where on November 22, 1962 the Conservatives lost a parliamentary seat to the Labour party when the Conservative Constituency party became divided on the issue of British membership in the Common Market.

During the Brussels negotiations, the British government faced an increasingly divided electorate.[81] The debate in Britain on Common Market membership failed to produce a sizable increase in the percentage of those who favored British entry into the EEC.[82] Public opinion

---

Brussels for farming in an enlarged Community. *Times* (London), December 14, 1962, p. 12.

[80] See the *Economist*, Vol. CCIII, No. 6190 (April 14, 1962), 130.

[81] In a sample survey of British elite attitudes on EEC entry conducted in the spring of 1963, selected from *Who's Who*, the following conclusions emerged:

   ... (I)n every subdivision of the total elite, substantial numbers of opponents were to be found alongside substantial numbers of supporters: old Etonians, members of the Reform Club and the Athenaeum, civil servants and business- men divided in much the same proportions as the total sample. Supporters and opponents had very similar backgrounds, worked alongside each other, spent much of their leisure together, and turned to the same papers for their news and opinions about world affairs.

Mark Abrams, "British Elite Attitudes and the European Common Market." *Public Opinion Quarterly*, Vol. XXIX, No. 2 (Summer 1965), 244.

[82] Polls conducted in Britain by Social Surveys (Gallup Poll) Limited produced responses in which 40 percent of those questioned on July 31, 1961 favored a British application to join the Common Market. By mid-November 1962, affirmative responses to the same question numbered 42 percent of those queried. During the debate on the Common Market in Britain support had risen to a high point of 55 percent in December 1961. In another survey, conducted by National Polls Limited, of those questioned on October 6, 1961, a total of 45.9 percent

polls conducted on the eve of the breakdown of the Brussels negotiations did not register a sharp increase in support over that revealed in polls taken at the time of Macmillan's announcement of July 31, 1961. To be sure, between July 1961 and January 1963, the total number of those persons favoring Common Market membership increased. However, as more and more persons formed views on this issue, they appear to have placed themselves in greater numbers on the side of the opponents of British entry into the EEC, rather than joining the ranks of the Common Marketeers.

In the debate about Common Market membership both sides, in many cases, overstated their case. The proponents of EEC entry often expressed gains which in all likelihood would not have accrued—at least not immediately—to Britain if she joined the Common Market. Undoubtedly, in the European Community British industry would face stiff competition from the Six. In an integrated Europe, Britain might not assume a position of unchallenged leadership, for by 1961 the locus of West European political leadership had moved from London to the Continent.

The opponents of EEC entry, for the most part, gave expression to equally unrealistic expectations about the adverse effects of Common Market membership upon Britain. It is unlikely that Britain would have been subordinated to the European Community to the extent suggested by opponents of Common Market membership. The EEC had not produced such drastic changes in the political, social, and economic systems of its members that they lost their national identity. As in the case of persons who before 1961 had seen EEC entry as incompatible with other British interests and commitments, the opponents of European Community membership appear to have given less than adequate thought to the actual operation of Common Market institutions. Had the opponents of Common Market membership studied the impact of the Rome Treaty upon the political systems of the Six, they might have had fewer grounds for opposition.

The question of Common Market membership produced divisions of opinion in Britain which cut across party lines. Persons normally in

---

favored and 22.6 percent opposed Common Market membership. On this date 31.5 percent registered answers of "don't know." When this research organization took another poll on September 24, 1962, the percentage of respondents favoring Common Market membership had fallen to 40.8, with the percentage in opposition rising to 45.9, and those without opinions declining to 13.3. As in the aforementioned Gallup Poll, National Opinion Polls also registered a high mark (52.8 percent) in mid-December 1961 of British support for the Common Market.

disagreement about political, economic, and social issues found themselves in accord either in support of, or in opposition to, the European Community. By 1961 Englishmen in considerable numbers were prepared in principle to consider Common Market membership. In general, even the advocates of EEC entry attached important conditions to Common Market membership. Although the Commonwealth was of declining economic and political importance, few Englishmen were prepared to join the Common Market if such a policy might result in the disintegration of the Commonwealth. The inability of the government to achieve terms of entry at less than a cost that seemed prohibitive, contributed to the rise in opposition as the Brussels negotiations dragged on. By the autumn of 1962, the Macmillan cabinet found itself poised in a delicate and unenviable position between domestic forces arrayed against and with it, and conflicting external pressures from the Commonwealth and the Six. Neither the government's belated effort to arouse flagging domestic support, nor its attempt in the Brussels negotiations to reconcile Commonwealth and European interests was sufficient to build a broadly based consensus or to avert the failure of the Common Market bid.

♛ Chapter 5 ✦✦✦

THE FIRST PHASE OF THE BRUSSELS NEGOTIATIONS

Throughout the Brussels negotiations, the British government faced the problems of reconciling domestic and Commonwealth interests with the conditions for Common Market membership. In an interactive process, the problems of building a domestic consensus in support of Common Market membership affected the negotiating tactics and position of the British government in its talks with the EEC. In turn, the course of the Brussels negotiations had an effect upon opinion in Britain and other Commonwealth countries. As the terms of entry became known, opposition to the Macmillan cabinet's EEC policy increased, as evidenced in public opinion polls, the policy statements of interest groups and the Labour party, and the activities of anti-Common Market groups examined in Chapter 4.

After Macmillan's statement of July 31, 1961, in the Commons, the British government intensified its preparations for negotiations with the Six. On August 9, Britain made formal application for Common Market membership.[1] The EEC Council of Ministers responded on September 26 with an invitation to attend preliminary talks on Britain's application, to be held in Paris on October 10. At that time Britain was to give more detailed information as to what safeguards British officials deemed necessary for British agriculture, the Commonwealth, and EFTA.

In preparation for the Common Market negotiations, Britain held a series of talks with Commonwealth officials. For example, the meeting of Commonwealth finance ministers held in Accra in September provided one occasion for an exchange of views on Common Market membership. From the British standpoint, the purpose of such meetings

---

[1] Ireland had applied for EEC membership on July 31, and Denmark and Norway disclosed on August 10 that they would submit their applications. Austria, Sweden, and Switzerland affirmed on October 19, 1961, after a ministerial conference in Vienna, that they would seek some form of association with the Common Market.

was twofold: to assure Commonwealth members that Britain would not join the European Community without taking account of major Commonwealth interests, and to obtain from Commonwealth governments as detailed a statement as possible of their views about specific problems and interests to be safeguarded in British negotiations with the EEC.

In the weeks which followed the Prime Minister's announcement of July 31, the Six had shown fewer misgivings about British Common Market membership than had many Commonwealth officials. Even President de Gaulle had responded affirmatively to a question asking if he approved of Britain's decision, although he may have had doubts that the negotiations for Common Market membership would prove successful. At his press conference of September 5, 1961, de Gaulle had stated:

> All along the members of the Common Market, the six of them, have wanted other countries, and in particular Great Britain, to join the Treaty of Rome, to assume the obligations involved in it and, I think, to obtain the advantages deriving therefrom.
> We know very well how complex the problem is, but it appears that everything now points to tackling it, and as far as I am concerned, I can only express my gratification. . . .[2]

De Gaulle's carefully worded statement, however, revealed that it was French policy to accept a minimum of changes in the Treaty of Rome. Britain, rather than the Six, would have to make the major concessions and adjustments in order to achieve Common Market membership.

As they had during the negotiations for a free trade area in 1957–58, the French quickly showed themselves to be particularly tough bargainers. They proposed that before beginning negotiations Britain should submit to the Six a "shopping list." The British were called upon to specify the problems they wished to discuss and at the same time to outline possible solutions. France argued that such a procedure would make it possible to know in advance if Britain would propose major changes in the Rome Treaty. From the British standpoint, such a procedure would have placed Britain in the position of announcing in considerable detail her bargaining position before the negotiations had

---

[2] *Ambassade de France, Service de Press et d'Information.* Full text of President de Gaulle's Press Conference held in Paris at the Élysée Palace on September 5, 1961, p. 7.

begun. Since it could not be kept secret, it was feared in London that a memorandum such as the one proposed by France might have played into the hands of opponents of EEC membership both in Britain and the Commonwealth.

In talks which British officials held with their counterparts in the Six, it was agreed that Britain was not expected to propose specific formulas for Common Market membership. Instead, the British were requested to put forward ideas about how their needs might be met. Specific solutions might then be worked out in subsequent negotiations, provided Britain accepted the objectives and substance of the Rome Treaty.

The British government and the Six were in accord that the key problems to be solved included British domestic and Commonwealth agriculture; the level of a common external tariff in an enlarged Community; the future of manufactured exports from Commonwealth countries to Britain; the association of certain Commonwealth countries with the EEC; and the implications for EEC institutions of a broadening of the Community to include new members.

In an apparent effort to forestall the rise of opinion, both in Britain and other Commonwealth countries, in opposition to its Common Market bid, the British government did not immediately release Heath's statement either to the press or to Commonwealth governments. The cabinet felt obliged to seek EEC entry without appearing to sacrifice important Commonwealth interests. The secrecy in which the Macmillan cabinet shrouded its opening statement, far from quieting the opponents of Common Market membership, aroused suspicion that Britain was prepared to sacrifice Commonwealth interests on the altar of European integration. It was not until November that the British government yielded to popular pressure at home and official requests from Commonwealth governments, and agreed to release the text of its statement on EEC entry. The decision initially not to release this document is indicative of the problems which the Macmillan cabinet faced in reconciling its policies toward the Commonwealth and European integration. In point of fact, however, the Heath statement pledged Britain to safeguard essential Commonwealth interests before joining the Common Market. Therefore, a policy of greater candor might have helped to quiet, rather than arouse, fears for the future of Commonwealth trade.

Although subsequent negotiations were held in Brussels, the EEC Council of Ministers met in Paris on October 10 to hear Edward

Heath's statement of British policy.[3] The purpose of the speech was to place before the Six Britain's positon on the key problems which would be considered in greater detail in the impending Brussels talks. Although Heath revealed little that was not already known to EEC member governments, he stated in affirmative terms the view that Britain's future lay with Europe, and set guidelines for British policy in the Brussels negotiations.

After restating the considerations which had led the Macmillan cabinet to apply for Common Market membership, Heath declared that Britain saw no need for amendments to the Rome Treaty "except, of course, in those Articles where adaptations are plainly required consequent upon the admission of a new member." For the most part, however, Britain's special problems might be met by protocols to the Rome Treaty. Britain was prepared to accept the structure of the EEC tariff provided adjustments could be made to meet certain British needs. Moreover, the British announced their willingness to make, "in a single operation, the same cuts in tariffs on trade between member states as the EEC itself might have made by the date of Britain's entry." [4]

The British admitted that the problem of Commonwealth trade differed in magnitude from that posed by former colonies of EEC countries. As a percentage of total British trade, commerce between Britain and other Commonwealth members was greater than was the case with the Six and their former colonies. Certain Commonwealth countries, for example, New Zealand, still depended heavily upon trade with Britain for a major source of their livelihood. Despite the importance of Commonwealth trade, Britain did not request associate membership of all Commonwealth countries; instead, the British proposed to divide Commonwealth problems into several categories and to work out solutions for each.

The first category included the less developed members of the

---

[3] Heath acknowledged that the British decision to apply for Common Market membership "was a decision arrived at, not on any narrow or short-term grounds, but as a result of a thorough assessment over a considerable period of the needs of our own country, of Europe and of the Free World as a whole. We recognize it as a great decision, a turning point in our history, and we take it in all seriousness. In saying that we wish to join the EEC, we mean that we desire to become full, wholehearted and active members of the European Community in its widest sense and to go forward with you in the building of a new Europe." *Great Britain, The United Kingdom and the European Economic Community.* Cmnd. 1565 HMSO, (November 1961).
[4] *Ibid.*

Commonwealth, as well as remaining British colonies.* As an EEC member, Britain would not wish to be compelled to give preferential treatment to existing associate members of the Common Market, i.e., the former colonies of such countries as Belgium and France, while discriminating against imports from her own former colonies. Nearly all the states in this first category produced tropical products and raw materials which competed with the exports of existing associate members of the Common Market.

Therefore, Heath announced that Britain would "like to see the less developed members of the Commonwealth and our Dependent Territories given the opportunity, if they so wish, to enter into association with the Community on the same terms as those which will in the future be available to the present Associated Overseas Countries and Territories." Hence, arrangements should be made for this list of Commonwealth states and dependent territories. Some might be associated with the Common Market; for others, where association was not possible, agreements might be concluded which would enable them to "maintain unimpaired their rights of access to the United Kingdom market, in the same way as was done for Morocco's trade with France, or for Surinam's trade with Benelux, under the relevant protocol to the Rome Treaty." Finally, for this category Britain proposed that in some cases discussion on a commodity-by-commodity basis might be undertaken.

At this point Heath listed four principal groups of commodities: tropical products, materials, manufactures and temperate foodstuffs. For trade in tropical products, problems were not likely to arise unless the Commonwealth country in question did not enter into association with the EEC. Although the exports of Commonwealth countries in tropical Africa and the Caribbean were similar to the products of other associate members of the European Community, they did not compete —in contrast with the agricultural exports of such Commonwealth countries as Australia, Canada and New Zealand—with farm products grown in Common Market countries. Therefore, the Six, the British had correctly assumed, would offer associate membership to Commonwealth countries in tropical Africa and the Caribbean. Finally, for commodities which Heath grouped under the category of "materials,"

---

* In this category were Tanganyika, Ghana, Nigeria, Sierra Leone, India, Pakistan, Ceylon, Malaya, Cyprus, Malta, Gibraltar and Falkland Islands.

Britain would urge the Six to adopt a zero tariff in an enlarged Community.[5]

For manufactures, a third main group of commodities, it was admitted that "indefinite and unlimited continuation of free entry over the whole of this field may not be regarded as compatible with the development of the Common Market and we are willing to discuss ways of reconciling these two conflicting considerations." The problem of manufactures was of concern chiefly to the more developed Commonwealth members—Australia, Canada, and New Zealand—as well as certain Asian countries, including India and Pakistan, and Hong Kong. Although Heath did not propose solutions to this problem, he believed that it was of "manageable proportions."

Turning to the group of commodities known as temperate foodstuffs, Heath declared that Australia, Canada, and New Zealand had "vital interests in this field for which special arrangements must be made." New Zealand, in particular, was heavily dependent upon markets in Britain for her mutton, lamb, butter, and cheese, and would face economic disaster if she could not be assured comparable outlets for her exports. Other Commonwealth countries producing temperate foodstuffs faced commodity problems of the same kind, if not of the same degree. At this time, however, Britain was not prepared to propose specific measures for reconciling British membership in the Common Market with problems raised by Commonwealth temperate foodstuffs. Yet a major British objective in the Brussels negotiations was to obtain from the Six support in finding alternative markets for Commonwealth countries which, after Britain's admission to the European Community, would no longer enjoy preferential access to the British market.

Even by October 1961, the Macmillan cabinet had accepted the idea that as a Common Market member Britain would have to adopt much of the agricultural policy of the Six. While emphasizing the benefits which the consumer derived from the British farm subsidy system in the form of lower food prices, Britain was prepared to accept Continental methods of farm subsidization. But the British were anxious to obtain a transitional period extending from twelve to fifteen years after the date of EEC entry in order to bring Britain's agricultural policies into harmony with those of the Six. This issue was to dampen the

---

[5] According to Heath: "Five of them—aluminum, wood pulp, newsprint, lead and zinc—are of great importance to certain Commonwealth countries: on these five materials we would wish to seek a zero tariff." *Ibid.*

prospects for early British entry into the Common Market, for the EEC was not prepared either to make major concessions to Britain on agricultural policy or even to give Britain a transitional period substantially in excess of that which remained to the Six themselves.

The British suggested that those countries which could not become full Common Market members should find an appropriate relationship with the Community. In his statement, Heath reiterated the British pledge made at the EFTA Council meeting in London in June 1961, that Britain could not join the Common Market "until satisfactory arrangements have been worked out . . . to meet the various legitimate interests of all members of EFTA, and thus enable them all to participate from the same date in an integrated European market." [6] If such arrangements could be made, Britain would be content to see EFTA disappear.

In the formation of policy first on a European free trade area and to a lesser degree on Common Market membership, the British addressed themselves for the most part to economic issues. Conceivably, they erred in not relating economic policies to a broader political framework for European integration. Had the British viewed participation in European economic integration as part of a basic reorientation of Britain's foreign policy from a global to European focus, the economic issues might have seemed less important and Britain's entry into the EEC speeded. The British government might have grasped firmly the nettle of leadership and called for a full commitment, politically as well as economically, to European integration. To have done so, however, the Macmillan cabinet would have had to experience a conversion to the European cause, which at that time had not yet occurred in the Conservative party. Even if such a conversion had enabled the government to provide bold leadership, it is by no means certain that having "given the country a lead," the country would have followed. Therefore, British policymakers proceeded cautiously with their Common Market application, and attempted to convince the electorate, and themselves, that membership in the European Community accorded with other British interests.

Yet the Macmillan cabinet did not ignore the political implications of Common Market membership. After Britain joined the Common Market, she was prepared to collaborate with other European countries in the achievement of political unification. To be sure, Britain, like

---

[6] EFTA *Bulletin*, July 1961, p. 8.

France, did not contemplate membership in a United States of Europe organized on federal principles. Instead, as Macmillan had declared in the Commons on August 2, 1961, the British envisaged "a confederation—a Commonwealth if you like—what General de Gaulle called *l'Europe de Patries* . . . of European countries and with our own." [7]

In all likelihood, Macmillan discussed the question of political unification when President de Gaulle met with him at the Prime Minister's estate in Sussex on November 24 and 25, 1961. But it was Heath who, during a meeting of the Western European Union Council in London on April 10, 1962, provided the most detailed statement of British policy towards European political integration.[8] Whatever hesitation Britain displayed about European integration was in part the result of the fact that London had not one, but two hurdles—one economic and the other political—to surmount. Heath contended that, unlike the Six, Britain was compelled to think at the same time of Common Market membership and accession to a potential political union. Britain "had always assumed that the existing European Community would be the foundation on which Europe would be built." Like France, Britain favored "more concentrated Ministerial machinery, especially of Ministers responsible for political questions. Periodic meetings of Heads of Government and of Foreign Ministers would promote and set their seal on the day-to-day consultation which already exists." Although the British government had no "fixed views" on the subjects to fall within its purview, a European political community might consider questions of defense. While holding that "any European point of view or policy on defense (should be) directly related to the Atlantic Alliance," Heath looked forward to the development of defense collaboration among West European countries.[9]

It is difficult to assess the extent to which this section of the Lord

---

[7] Great Britain, *Parliamentary Debates* (Commons), Vol. 645 (August 2, 1961), col. 1491.

[8] Great Britain, *European Political Union*, Cmnd. 1770, HMSO (April 10, 1962).

[9] Heath contended: "But, of course, as the European Community develops, the balance within the Atlantic Alliance is going to change. In the course of time there will be two groupings of the West: North America and Europe. The growth of this European point of view in the defense field will not, we believe, be long in making itself felt. Already we have seen the signs. We have the Western European Union itself, and we have the beginnings of cooperation in joint defence projects. There is no doubt in my mind that, with the closer integration of our industries which will follow British accession to the European Economic Community, we shall see great advances in European cooperation over defense production, research and development," *Ibid*.

Privy Seal's statement may have raised French expectations of British scientific assistance, particularly in the field of nuclear development. It is conceivable that Britain, whether intentionally or not, may have led France in the months before the Nassau Agreement to anticipate British participation in a European defense arrangement which included cooperation in the building of nuclear weapons.[10]

The British statement to the WEU Council stressed Britain's interest not only in the "central nucleus" of the Six, but also in the relationship of neutral EFTA countries with the core area of West European integration. Although the British did not propose ways of associating such countries with a politically integrated Europe, they suggested that "their association with the community could be arranged in such a way as not to weaken the political and economic cohesion of the central nucleus of full members or impede their progress."

The British contended that West European countries should avoid rigid formulas and blueprints for achieving political integration. To a considerable extent their criticism of such means of obtaining political integration resembled their earlier critique of the Rome Treaty. Even though the Six had displayed great flexibility and pragmatism in their behavior within the EEC, the British apparently saw an elaborate, complex framework for European political integration as overly rigid and likely to restrict Britain's freedom of action in foreign policy. Instead, the British suggested that the "substance of political integration will grow most effectively out of the habit of working more and closely together." However, in an integrated Europe, Britain wished to see a considerable role assigned to the European Parliament. Such a preference is understandable, given the importance attached to parliamentary institutions in the British debate on Common Market membership. Both to the European Community and the Continental nations, the British felt that they had a superior parliamentary experience to pass on to peoples less versed in the intricacies of representative government.

In the concluding remarks of his statement to the WEU Council, Heath suggested that inasmuch as Britain would be anxious to join a politically integrated Europe at the same time as she became a member of the EEC, London should have "the opportunity of consulting with (the Six) and commenting on the Draft (Political) Treaty before it is finally agreed." As an applicant for Common Market membership,

---

[10] See Chapter 6 for a discussion of the question of Anglo-French nuclear collaboration and the Brussels negotiations.

Britain should be invited to participate with the Six in discussions about the political future of western Europe then underway in the Fouchet Commission. However, the British were prepared to take part in the work of the Fouchet Commission only if the Six were unanimous in inviting them to do so.[11] The French, of course, were not prepared to admit Britain to these deliberations so long as her application for Common Market membership was still pending.

After the British government's opening statement in Paris, the negotiations for Common Market membership shifted to Brussels. To an even greater extent than at the time of the free trade area negotiations, Britain faced the Common Market Six, who formed one negotiating unit. The long and complex Brussels negotiations, which began on November 8, 1961, were held at essentially three levels. At the highest level was the EEC Council of Ministers and the leaders of the British negotiating team.[12] Ministerial meetings usually took place about once a month. Below this level were discussions between the deputies of the ministers which were held weekly between Tuesday and Thursday. Finally, there were expert working parties which dealt with technical problems and specific topics. Of course, bilateral contacts between Heath and his counterparts in the Six continued.

As the Brussels negotiations got under way, Britain and the Six set up technical committees, charged with the task of completing detailed studies of problems to which agreed solutions had eventually to be found before Britain could join the Common Market. For example, Britain and the Six set up a committee of experts whose task was to examine a list of products the British wished to exempt from the

---

[11] After a meeting of heads of government and foreign ministers in Paris on February 10 and 11, 1961, the Six set up a preparatory commission to develop specific proposals on political integration for consideration at a later meeting. This committee was under the chairmanship of Christian Fouchet, France's Ambassador to Denmark, and came to be known as the "Fouchet Committee." During the next several months, the Fouchet Committee attempted, without notable success, to reconcile federalist and confederal approaches to European political integration. For a detailed account of the work of the Fouchet Committee, see *Political and Economic Planning* (PEP), *The Negotiations on Political Union Planning* (London: PEP). October 1, 1962.

[12] The Council of Ministers included Couve de Murville, Foreign Minister of France; Paul-Henri Spaak, Foreign Minister of Belgium; M. Luns of the Netherlands; M. Beck of Luxembourg; Signor Colombo, Italian Minister of Trade; Dr. Erhard, Deputy Chancellor and Minister of Economics in the Federal Republic; and Dr. Rolflahr of the German Foreign Office. In addition to Mr. Heath, the British delegation included Mr. Duncan Sandys, Secretary of State for Commonwealth Relations and the Colonies, and Mr. Christopher Soames, Minister of Agriculture.

common external tariff.[13] Moreover, the committee was requested to undertake a detailed statistical analysis of Commonwealth economies and specific Commonwealth exports. The complicated task of preparing studies on these products and on Commonwealth trade in general slowed the progress of the Brussels negotiations. In this committee, in particular, Britain and the Six turned their attention to an examination of the difficult problem of reconciling Commonwealth trade with the EEC external tariff.

Shortly after the first round of ministerial discussions held in Brussels on November 9, de Gaulle and Macmillan met for the first time since Britain had applied for Common Market membership. On November 25 and 26, the French President visited Mr. Macmillan at his private estate in Sussex. Although the two leaders issued no official statement at the close of their deliberations, it was reported that the governments of Britain and France had each gained a greater appreciation of the problems confronting the other in the Brussels negotiations.[14] The talks are said to have included an examination of the relationship of an integrated Europe to NATO, as well as the future of West Berlin. Macmillan appears to have made an effort to convince the French President that Britain was determined to join the Common Market and that the British government shared France's views about the appropriate framework for European integration. As a result of this meeting, British suspicions that France wished to keep Britain out of the Common Market allegedly were allayed. At the same time, French fears that Britain might seek to hinder progress toward European political integration, based upon French proposals, were said to have been allayed.[15]

By the end of January, 1962, Britain and the Six had made progress in the development of a framework for negotiations on the substantive problems of Common Market membership. They had produced two categories of less developed Commonwealth countries: those which would suffer from the application of a common tariff in an enlarged Community, and those which would face direct competition from countries currently associated with the Common Market. The second

---

[13] This list included petroleum products, jute yarn, jute goods, a few chemicals (such as calcium carbide and silicone carbide), semi-processed leathers, certain ferro-alloys, cadmium, raw silk, some types of sulphur, aluminum, wood pulp, newsprint, lead, zinc, plywood, cobalt oxide, hand-knotted carpets, casein, vegetable tanning extracts, coir mats and matting.
[14] See the *Times* (London), November 27, 1961, p. 10.
[15] *Ibid.*

category of Commonwealth members could be granted associate membership in the EEC.[16]

Although the British and the Six had achieved a consensus on the question of associating certain Commonwealth countries with an enlarged Common Market, the working out of specific arrangements was postponed while the EEC explored the problems of renewing the agreement, scheduled to expire at the end of the year, for the association of their own former dependencies. The Six were not prepared to offer specific terms for associating Commonwealth countries until they had completed arrangements with their existing associate members. In turn, the British did not wish to offer a list of candidates for association until they knew what the terms were likely to be.

During the course of the Brussels negotiations, Britain and the Six faced delays as a result of the many technical problems before them. In addition, the progress of negotiations was slowed because the Six had not yet reached accord among themselves on such questions as a new agreement for associated states and the development of a Common Market agricultural policy, and therefore could not negotiate as a unit with the British. Of particular importance in the early months of the Brussels negotiations the Six were engaged in discussions aimed at reaching agreement on a common agricultural policy. France had added to the importance of these discussions by insisting that the Six reach accord on the framework of the EEC agricultural policy before the Common Market moved into its second transitional stage, scheduled to begin on January 1, 1962. Basic to the resolution of this problem was the ability of the Six to devise an agricultural accord which would help France find markets for farm surpluses without rendering undue harm to less efficient farmers in Germany. In turn, the Bonn government opposed an EEC agricultural policy which would flood the German market with cheaper imports from France.

Early on the morning of January 14, after an all-night session, the Six agreed on a set of agricultural regulations for the Common Market, thus allowing the EEC to pass into the second transitional stage.[17]

---

[16] They consisted primarily of producers of tropical agriculture in the West Indies, tropical Africa, and certain Pacific territories such as Fiji. The EEC had virtually excluded the possibility of association for such temperate producers as Australia, Canada, and New Zealand.

[17] The compromise solution provided a set of regulations for cereals, pork, wines, eggs, poultry, fruit, and vegetables. The Six established procedures for fixing minimum import prices in member countries for applying common rules of competition in agriculture, and for pricing farm products in the EEC. Moreover,

When the British returned to Brussels for the resumption of negotiations in January, the Six had resolved some of their major agricultural
problems. For the British, the EEC agricultural accord of January 1962
had at least two important consequences. On the one hand, having
reached agreement among themselves, the Six could negotiate with the
British with greater specificity about the adaptation of Britain's agricultural policy after joining the Common Market. On the other, the
Six had worked toward the completion of an agricultural policy suited
more to their needs than to Britain's. Excluded from negotiations on
the EEC farm policy because she was not a Common Market member,
Britain was unable to use her influence, as each of the Six had done, to
hammer out an agricultural policy which reconciled her farmers' interests with those of the European Community.

   Not until May did the Council of Ministers turn to the discussion of
the major substantive issues of British Common Market membership.[18]
Until then the negotiators had concerned themselves primarily with
such procedural questions as the allocation of studies of technical
problems to groups of experts and the development of categories of
products for examination in the negotiations.

   In the early months of the Brussels negotiations, the Commonwealth
problem had been divided into several principal parts for detailed
examination by the working parties. Since November 1961, a working
party had been studying the impact of British Common Market membership on manufactured imports from Australia, Canada, and New
Zealand. It was concluded that such goods, comprising but 1 percent of
Britain's imports from Commonwealth countries, could not be accorded special treatment in the European Community. The same working party considered the list of commodities, consisting of most British
imports of raw materials from the Commonwealth, for which Britain
sought the elimination of EEC tariffs. For most such imports the EEC
itself imposed no tariff, but for some products of particular interest to

---

the Six agreed to establish "target prices," which would be brought to a common
level in a period not to exceed seven and one-half years. Maximum and minimum
points were established, within which the common price must be found. It was
left to later negotiations to work out agricultural prices within the limits agreed
upon in January 1962.

[18] The Chairman of the Ministerial meetings of May 11 and 12 was Signor Emilio
Colombo of Italy. He opened the meetings with the statement: "The period of
investigation is over, the period of negotiation is beginning. We must attempt to
obtain a broad overall view of what the solutions for British EEC membership
could be by the end of July." *Christian Science Monitor*, May 12, 1962.

Commonwealth countries the Six levied duties and were unlikely, the working party advised, to remove them in an enlarged Community. Some of these tariffs reflected a delicate balance of compromises which had been achieved only after long negotiations among the Six.

In February 1962, a working party had examined another problem: the future of exports of manufactures from Asian Commonwealth countries if Britain became a Common Market member. Until February 1962, the British had clung to the hope that India and Pakistan might even be granted associate membership in the European Community. In April, the working party considering Asian Commonwealth exports reported that the Six could not give special treatment to manufactured products from these countries.[19] At the Ministerial meeting held on May 11 and 12, Britain conceded that the common tariff would take effect, with another 30 percent at the beginning of 1967 and the remainder by 1970. Britain also accepted certain features of "economic union" in the EEC, including provisions for labor and capital mobility, comparable standards for social benefits, antitrust legislation, and equal pay for men and women. Thus, although the major part of the negotiations on substantive matters lay ahead, by the spring of 1962 Britain and the Six had developed, at least in broad outline, many of the terms for British Common Market membership.

Early in June 1962, Macmillan and de Gaulle had another series of discussions. At this meeting, held near Paris, Macmillan is reported to have convinced French officials that Britain was willing to relinquish Commonwealth preferences and to attach reduced importance to her special relationship with the United States.[20] Macmillan attempted to assure de Gaulle of Britain's determination to join the Common Market and to persuade him that the British shared France's official position about the framework for European political integration. Moreover, British officials allegedly stated that they did not oppose the French policy for developing an independent national nuclear force. In their communiqué issued at the end of this meeting, the two heads of government agreed that the Brussels negotiations would be pursued in the spirit of "the community of interests between France and the U. K." [21]

By the end of June 1962, agreement had emerged from the Brussels

[19] See "Europe's Missing Link," *The Economist*, Vol. CCIII, No. 6191 April 21, 1962, p. 234.
[20] *Manchester Guardian Weekly*, Vol. 86, No. 23, (June 7, 1962), p. 7.
[21] *Ibid.*

negotiations that transitional arrangements ending in 1970 should be
made for Commonwealth exports of temperate agriculture products,
and that the enlarged EEC should attempt to negotiate worldwide
marketing arrangements to take the place of markets in western Europe. During the transitional period which would end in 1970, Commonwealth exports of temperate agricultural commodities to Britain
would gradually decline. The Common Market Six conceded that in
the absence of world agreements by 1970 an enlarged Community
should "enter into consultations with countries ready to conclude such
agreements—especially Commonwealth countries—to find solutions
for these countries." [22] Furthermore, the EEC was prepared to conclude before 1966 general trade agreements with Ceylon, India, and
Pakistan if Britain joined the Common Market. The EEC was willing
to reduce to 1 percent its 18 percent tariff on tea to offset losses to
Asian Commonwealth countries from the ending of preferential treatment in the British market. However, the Six insisted upon the application, as soon as Britain joined the EEC, of 30 percent of the common
external tariff on imports of cotton textiles from Asian Commonwealth
countries, to be increased to 60 percent of the common external tariff
eighteen months later. [23]

Proposed arrangements such as these aroused the opposition of Commonwealth governments, as well as Englishmen who feared that the
Macmillan cabinet, as the price for Common Market membership,
would be forced to sacrifice Commonwealth interests. In particular, the
tentative accord reached in May on manufactured exports from Australia, Canada, and New Zealand received criticism from Australia's
Prime Minister and New Zealand's trade minister. In a joint statement
the two leaders termed this accord a "disturbing development" which
must not under any circumstances be taken as a precedent for the type
of settlement which might be worked out for temperate foodstuffs. [24]
At the end of May, New Zealand's Deputy Prime Minister, Mr. J. R.
Marshall, visited the capitals of Common Market countries in order to
express his government's concern about the agreements which the
Brussels negotiations had produced. In a statement issued on May 29,
he insisted that Britain could not accept the agricultural policy of the

---

[22] *Financial Times* (London), July 2, 1962, p. 1.
[23] *Manchester Guardian Weekly*, Vol. 86, No. 26 (June 28, 1962), p. 7. This EEC
common external tariff was calculated on the basis of 18 percent of the value of
cotton textiles.
[24] *Financial Times* (London), June 2, 1962, p. 1.

Six without impairing Commonwealth trade. According to Marshall, "access to the Common Market for New Zealand's exports during a transitional period only—without the assurance of a market beyond that date—would be a threat to our livelihood and would be entirely unacceptable to us." [25]

Dissatisfaction with the terms thus far negotiated led Prime Minister Menzies to declare in London on June 12 that Australia would refuse to agree to abandon Commonwealth trading preferences by 1970 as part of the price of British Common Market membership. Yet despite the objections of Britain's Commonwealth partners, this was precisely the kind of agreement which now appeared likely for agricultural exports of vital importance to Commonwealth countries such as Australia, Canada, and New Zealand.

India raised objections to the proposed arrangements for industrial exports from India, Pakistan, and Ceylon. Indian officials claimed that the British proposal for the progressive application of the EEC external tariff to cotton textiles, India's major industrial export, would cut trade and reduce foreign exchange earnings needed to sustain programs of economic development. Instead Britain, it was suggested, should continue to grant India access to the British market and seek lower tariffs in the EEC for such products. Thus, the British government faced pressures not only from domestic groups opposed to Common Market membership, but also from Commonwealth governments fearful of the consequences for their countries of British entry into the European Community.

In an intensive round of negotiations in July 1962 the Six and Britain sought to complete the outline of terms before the August holiday recess. Such questions as the rules to be applied to regulate the price of eggs were discussed. Although agreement on this, as well as the issue of imports of temperate agriculture from Commonwealth countries, eluded Britain and the Six, the negotiators did reach accord that if Britain joined, the EEC would adopt the British procedure of annual reviews of farm prices and incomes.[26]

In the final days of the negotiations during the summer of 1962, little progress was made in reaching satisfactory arrangements for Common-

---

[25] *Manchester Guardian Weekly*, Vol. 86, No. 2 (May 31, 1962), p. 3.

[26] According to the British practice, the British government and the National Farmers' Union, Britain's principal farming organization, hold an annual meeting to discuss trends during the preceding year in farm prices and incomes. In the light of such discussions, the level of subsidization for farmers for the coming year is determined.

wealth temperate products. After initialing the accord for such Asian Commonwealth members as Ceylon, India, and Pakistan, the Council of Ministers turned again to a discussion of the problem of agricultural exports from Australia, Canada, and New Zealand. The talks dealt with amendments proposed by Britain to an EEC position paper on temperate foodstuffs. The Six had offered transitional arrangements under which preferences accorded Commonwealth exports of agricultural products in the British market would decline. Moreover, freedom of entry for commodities to which Britain did not accord preferential treatment to imports from the Commonwealth would be ended gradually if Britain joined the Common Market. In the event of a sudden disturbance in trade, the Six agreed to consult with Commonwealth countries in order to consider changes in arrangements for Common Market imports of farm products.

Britain had sought assurance that Commonwealth exporters would retain markets in an enlarged Community and that steps would be taken to minimize damage to them from the operation of the Common Market agricultural policy. The Macmillan cabinet strove to obtain for Commonwealth countries presently enjoying preferences in the British market access on the same basis as Community farmers until 1967, except in the case of wheat. Moreover, Britain proposed that the EEC enter into consultations with countries which were major exporters of farm produce, to consider measures to prevent sharp reductions in their sales. Finally, the British stressed the need for measures to assure markets for dairy products from New Zealand.

At this point in the negotiations the British met especially sharp opposition from France. Although the French did not have the full support of other members of the Council of Ministers, they did find agreement with their position in the EEC Commission. France based its case essentially on two points. First, it was suggested that Article 110 of the Rome Treaty obligated the EEC to strive for the development of international trade at satisfactory price levels. This should provide sufficient evidence to Britain and her other Commonwealth partners of the good intentions of the Six. Secondly, the French contended that the British amendments, if accepted, would deprive the EEC of its freedom in the formation of farm policy. Under British amendments, it was claimed that the Common Market would be obligated to freeze the existing pattern of trade with Commonwealth countries.[27]

---

[27] *Financial Times* (London), August 4, 1962, p. 1.

During the weekend of August 4–5, Britain and the Six held a session which ended at dawn on Sunday in a last effort to resolve the thorny problem of comparable outlets for exports of Commonwealth agricultural products which would no longer find markets in Britain. During this meeting the Six informed Britain that they regarded New Zealand as a special case. They were prepared, therefore, to make special arrangements for New Zealand, to be worked out in detail during later negotiations.

Whatever sense of optimism the British may have derived from the proposal of the Six on New Zealand must have been dulled by a draft statement which the French now introduced at Brussels. At 3:10 A.M. France presented the British delegation with a document concerning financial regulations for the common agricultural policy. When Mr. Heath read the statement, prepared at the request of France by Signor Colombo of Italy and Robert Marjolin of the Commission, he is said to have reacted with considerable indignation. He reminded the Six that his government had already agreed to accept the EEC agricultural policy but that he was "not prepared at 3 A.M., without legal advice, to sign interpretations of it which included references to other items, comments, and historical statements." [28] At 7:00 A.M. on August 5, after a session lasting sixteen hours, the Brussels negotiations recessed for the remainder of the summer.

In the final hours of the August Ministerial session France had tried to commit Britain to an agreement that after 1970, levies raised on foodstuffs imported into the enlarged Community would go to a common agricultural fund. The Six had already reached accord among themselves on such a provision in their discussions the previous December and January. As major importers of foodstuffs, the British wished to avoid such a commitment until agreement had been worked out for temperate agriculture.

The question of levies on agricultural imports after 1970 arose in part because of a legal difference in the interpretation of the Rome Treaty. In their talks of December 1961 and January 1962, the Six had agreed in principle to establish a levy to be paid to a common agricultural fund. At issue was the question as to whether an agreement in principle requires a second unanimous decision by the Council of Ministers before the necessary process of parliamentary ratification can begin. France and Italy held that a second agreement in the Council

---

[28] See, for example, Leonard Beaton, "Brussels Meeting Broken Off," *Manchester Guardian Weekly* Vol. 87, No. 6, August 9, 1962, p. 3.

was not needed, while Belgium, Germany, and Luxembourg contended that the ministers must make another unanimous decision.

France, anxious to seal the accord on import levies, probably saw the final hours of the summer session at Brussels as offering an opportunity to do so. Apparently, the French believed that the desire of Britain and some EEC countries to bring the negotiations to a favorable conclusion would cause them to yield to pressure from France. Or conceivably the French, knowing that Britain could not agree to a detailed financial plan on such short notice, saw an opportunity to demonstrate to her partners Britain's lack of fidelity to objectives of the Rome Treaty. In any event, the British returned to London with only a partial outline of terms to present to Parliament and the Commonwealth before the resumption of negotiations in the autumn.

Whatever private apprehensions British officials may have had, their public statements had a tone of cautious optimism about the ultimate results of the Brussels talks. In a speech delivered in London on July 31, Lord Home minimized differences between Britain and the Six. Commenting on the apparent deadlock over long-term arrangements for Commonwealth temperate agriculture, the Foreign Secretary maintained that the Macmillan cabinet had "always anticipated this present situation would arise." The negotiations presented "a problem which must be resolved and one to which we must all apply our minds." [29]

In a statement issued after the negotiations recessed, the British government summarized the results achieved thus far.[30] After setting forth the agreements which had been reached for association and describing the accord for manufactured imports from Ceylon, India, and Pakistan, the British government assessed the state of negotiations on temperate agricultural products:

> There was a prolonged discussion on arrangements for trade in temperate agricultural products from Canada, Australia, and New Zealand and much common ground was established. A good deal of work remains to be done, however, both as regards individual commodities and in order to give greater precision to some of the proposed arrangements.

---

[29] *New York Times*, August 1, 1962, p. 7.
[30] Great Britain, *The United Kingdom and the European Economic Community: Report by the Lord Privy Seal on the Meeting with Ministers of Member States of the European Economic Community from August 1-5, 1962.* (London): HMSO, 1962, Cmnd. 1805.

While admitting that important decisions were yet to be taken in British domestic agriculture and horticulture as well as imports of temperate agricultural products from the Commonwealth, the British statement expressed satisfaction at the progress "made on major questions affecting the Commonwealth association under Part IV of the Treaty of Rome, the particular interests of India, Pakistan, and Ceylon, and temperate agricultural products from Canada, Australia, and New Zealand."

In sum, as of August 5, provisional agreement had been reached on the following problems: manufactures from Australia, Canada, and New Zealand would be subjected to a common external tariff in three stages: 30 percent upon Britain's accession to membership, another 30 percent on January 1, 1967, and 40 percent on January 1, 1970. Britain and the Six had agreed to hold consultations with Ceylon, India, and Pakistan in 1966 and 1969 to work out agreements for the future development of trade. On imports of textiles from these Asian Commonwealth countries, Britain would apply the common external tariff of 18 percent in eighteen months' time, 30 percent a year later, and 30 percent when the common tariff took effect in the European Community. The EEC tariff on tea would be eliminated.

It had been decided that Commonwealth countries in Africa and the Caribbean would be offered associate membership.[31] The details of association were to be worked out after the Six had completed their own negotiations for a new agreement with states presently associated with the EEC. Less progress, however, had been recorded on the problems of temperate foodstuffs from Australia, Canada, and New Zealand. The Six and Britain were in accord that as members of the European Community they would work toward world commodity agreements, designed to balance the interests of European farmers and agricultural producers outside Europe. Under such arrangements, exporters from Commonwealth countries such as Australia, Canada, and New Zealand were to be accorded "reasonable opportunities" in the EEC for exports of foodstuffs. The Six, moreover, had expressed a willingness to make special arrangements for New Zealand because of that country's heavy dependence upon exports to Britain for her

---

[31] Gambia, Kenya, Mauritius, Zanzibar, Seychelles and British dependencies in the Caribbean except Jamaica and Trinidad, together with colonial territories in the South Atlantic and western Pacific were offered association. Further studies were to be made to determine suitable arrangements for Aden, Swaziland, Basutoland, Bechuanaland, Singapore, Sarawak, Malta, Hong Kong, Trinidad, Uganda, and Jamaica.

livelihood. Nevertheless, much work remained before detailed provisions satisfactory to all parties could be worked out.

There were other matters upon which Britain and the Six had not yet reached accord. A decision had not been made regarding Britain's request that no tariffs be applied to imports of several products. The negotiators had not yet decided upon a policy toward imports of processed foodstuffs from Australia, Canada, and New Zealand, in which Britain had requested the abolition of EEC tariffs.

Much work remained to be completed before an accord on British agriculture could be initialed. Although Britain and the Six were in agreement on the need for an annual EEC price review for farm products, transitional arrangements for agriculture had still to be worked out. Marketing regulations for several kinds of agricultural produce, including eggs and pig meat, had not yet been developed. Finally, many questions concerning other EFTA countries in an enlarged Community had to be resolved before Britain, given her pledge to assure satisfactory arrangements for essential EFTA interests, could accede to the Rome Treaty. Thus, in the summer of 1962, the British returned from the Brussels negotiations with only a partial outline of terms for Common Market membership to present to Parliament, the British electorate, and other Commonwealth governments.

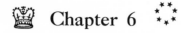

Chapter 6

THE BREAKDOWN OF THE BRUSSELS NEGOTIATIONS

In the autumn of 1962 the Macmillan cabinet faced the formidable task of convincing the British electorate as well as Commonwealth leaders that vital interests would be safeguarded. From September 10–19, the British government was host to the Commonwealth Prime Ministers Conference which convened in London. Although the Macmillan cabinet had hoped to present to the Commonwealth prime ministers the terms for British Common Market membership, the slow progress of the Brussels negotiations made it possible only to make available a partial outline of the conditions for EEC entry. As domestic opposition to the agreements already initialed in Brussels increased, Britain now faced the prospect of Commonwealth governments opposed to the British EEC bid attempting to use the conference to fan the flames of Common Market opposition in Britain. Moreover, manifestations of discord among Commonwealth governments, and domestic British opinion, might weaken Britain's negotiating position when the Brussels negotiations resumed, if it appeared that the British negotiators no longer enjoyed the support and confidence of Commonwealth governments and important segments of the public at home. Thus, in reconciling Commonwealth interests with its Common Market policy, the Macmillan cabinet had two immediate objectives: to restrain the Commonwealth Prime Ministers Conference from expressing opposition to the Common Market bid on terms already worked out in Brussels, and to avoid giving Commonwealth governments a veto over the final terms for EEC entry upon which Britain hoped, in the months ahead, to reach agreement with the Six.

In the attainment of both objectives, the British government enjoyed a measure of success. Instead of condemning outright the British Common Market application, the Commonwealth leaders issued a communiqué which acknowledged that "after full and continuing consultation with the other countries of the Commonwealth, and in the light of the furthur negotiations to be held with the members of the Community, the responsibility for the final decisions would rest with the British government." [1] Macmillan scored yet another success in avoiding a veto by Commonwealth governments of terms already worked out in Brussels. He did not allow his government to be maneuvered into a position in which Britain would be compelled as a result of Commonwealth pressure to seek changes in agreements already initialed. Nor did Britain commit herself to convene another Commonwealth Prime Ministers Conference to pass judgment on the final terms for British Common Market membership. Thus the British adroitly averted pledges to other Commonwealth countries which would hamper them when the Brussels negotiations resumed.

When the negotiators reassembled on October 8, 1962, the British sought to bring the talks to a speedy conclusion. The longer the negotiations dragged on, the more British industrialists, as well as businessmen in the Commonwealth and other countries, would face uncertainty in planning for the future. The greater the uncertainty about the outcome, the more doubtful British and Commonwealth opinion might become about the chances for entry on satisfactory terms. Nevertheless, with the resumption of the negotiations, Heath attempted, before moving to remaining topics for discussion, to obtain slightly improved terms on an issue upon which agreement had already been reached. After calling for consultations with Ceylon, India, and Pakistan in order to conclude comprehensive trade agreements as soon as Britain entered the EEC, the Lord Privy Seal then asked that Britain be permitted to suspend tariffs against these Asian Commonwealth countries until such agreements could be negotiated. It will be recalled that Britain had already agreed to apply progressively the EEC tariff against manufactured imports from Asian Commonwealth countries as soon as she entered the Common Market. Moreover, Heath reminded the Six that the governments of countries such as Australia, Canada, and New Zealand were dissatisfied with agreements reached so far for their manufactured exports to the Common Market. They were also apprehensive that the EEC might become self-sufficient in temperate agriculture and that the levy system, which formed a key element of the Common Market's farm policy, might serve to lower world prices of foodstuffs to the detriment of Commonwealth farmers. The British effort to improve the terms for Commonwealth exports of manufac-

---

[1] *Times* (London), September 20, 1962, p. 8.

tures and temperate agriculture undoubtedly reflected the opposition voiced by Commonwealth governments and domestic opinion, which the British government wished to placate.

During the autumn of 1962, the British negotiators and the Six made little progress in resolving the major problems confronting them.[2] They were unable to reach agreement on the timetable to be applied to the change from the British system of deficiency payments for farmers to the Common Market agricultural policy. The Six remained opposed to a transitional period extending beyond December 31, 1969, while the British declared that for domestic political and economic reasons they needed a longer time to phase out their present farm policy. The Six refused to accede to a British request for duty-free entry for aluminum and newsprint; they were equally unwilling to accommodate the British on imports of textiles from India and Pakistan. However, it was decided in the ministerial meeting held in the last week of October, that the EEC, in response to Heath's request several weeks earlier, would begin talks on comprehensive trade agreements with Ceylon, India, and Pakistan within three months after Britain joined the Common Market. But the Six were unwilling to agree to the British request that the common external tariff against imports from Asian Commonwealth members should not be applied until long-term agreements with these countries had been negotiated. In its negotiations with the Six, Britain thus faced a dilemma: The Conservatives had pledged not to dismantle the existing Agriculture Act before the next general election. If they were to keep this promise to the British electorate, they would weaken their chances for admission to the

---

[2] On October 29, 1962, moreover, the EEC Commission published a plan for speeding up the transitional period for the creation of a customs union among the Six. This plan called for the elimination of remaining internal barriers to trade and the completion of a common external tariff by January 1968, three years ahead of schedule. All passport controls and administrative trade restrictions were to be abolished among the Six. A program of highway construction to link capitals and major cities of the EEC was to be undertaken. The Commission also recommended compulsory consultation by member countries before changes in monetary policies and exchange rates; a common policy on wages and incomes, and collective bargaining in major industries; a commitment by each of the Six to assist another EEC member to eliminate deficits in its balance of payments; a plan for Community-wide economic expansion; harmonization of governmental budgets and systems of taxation; and a joint policy on foreign assistance. The introduction of such changes before the completion of negotiations for British EEC entry could hardly have lessened the problems confronting Britain in her bid for membership in the Common Market. See the *Christian Science Monitor* (Boston), October 23, 1962; and the *New York Times*, October 29, 1962.

Common Market, the importance of which the government had stressed during the autumn of 1962.

Nor did the Six and Britain register progress on the important problem of assuring markets for New Zealand's exports after British entry into the Common Market. In fact, during the debate among the Six on November 17, the French had insisted, as they had during the final hours of the summer session of the Brussels negotiations in August, that Britain accept EEC financial regulations for a common farm policy. While agreeing that the financial burden of the Community should be borne equitably, the French government wished to make certain that levies imposed upon agricultural imports to the EEC from third countries would become the property of the Community.[3] As important importers of foodstuffs, the British would become major contributors to EEC funds derived from levies.

The Six brought to Britain's attention another problem, namely, the relationship between British pledges to EFTA and membership in the Common Market. The Council concluded that negotiations for the association of European neutrals which were EFTA members, namely, Austria, Sweden, and Switzerland, would probably not be completed by January 1, 1964, the date on which Britain, it was assumed, might enter the EEC. Two other EFTA countries, Denmark and Norway, however, might be able to complete their negotiations for entry soon after Britain became a Common Market member. Thus, at that time Britain might be forced to begin to apply the common external tariff against her former partners in EFTA.[4] In fact, the Six informed Britain that she must apply tariffs against imports from other EFTA countries on the day of her entry into the Common Market. According to the EEC Council, such a step would be necessary because in all likelihood the negotiations on association for Austria, Sweden, and Switzerland would not be completed by the date of British entry. For Britain to discriminate in such a fashion against other members of the Outer Seven would violate the pledge she had made not to enter the Common Market until arrangements had been worked out for EFTA members. Such decisions from Brussels led the British to inform the Six that Britain would be compelled to review her defense commitments to the Continent if she was barred from the Common Market.[5]

---

[3] *Times* (London), November 19, 1962, p. 9.

[4] See the *Times* (London), December 6, 1962, p. 11.

[5] Nevertheless, the British declared that if they joined the Common Market they would not invoke Article 234 of the Rome Treaty, which provided for the

Although they remained at odds on many other questions, the EEC Ministers and Britain reached agreement in November 1962 on trade arrangements for those Commonwealth countries which were willing to accept associate membership in the Common Market. In addition, the Six offered to permit countries such as Ghana, Nigeria, and Tanganyika, which had refused association, to negotiate long-term trade agreements. On the question of association, agreement was comparatively easy to reach; the outlines of an accord had emerged in talks held earlier in the year. Although the Six and Britain made no headway on the British request that an enlarged Community levy no tariffs upon newsprint and aluminum, the EEC offered concessions on some 70 percent of the processed foods Britain imported from other Commonwealth countries.

In short, during the autumn of 1962 it became increasingly clear in Brussels—and in Britain itself—that the British were unprepared, and perhaps politically unable, to join the Common Market on just any terms. However eager to enter the European Community, Britain could not accept terms in effect dictated by the Six. In fact, British negotiators informed their counterparts that it was impossible to abandon the deficiency payments scheme for agriculture as soon as the United Kingdom joined the Common Market. The British tempered the enthusiasm shown by the Conservatives at their 1962 Annual Conference and in the official statements prepared by the government in the autumn of 1962 for domestic consumption, with the warning that Britain could not sacrifice other principal interests for the sake of EEC membership. Such statements were undoubtedly designed to reduce domestic fears—expressed in the Labour party, the press, and interest groups including the National Farmers' Union—that Britain would agree to Common Market entry on disadvantageous terms. Moreover, the British government, it appears, sought to strengthen its bargaining position in Brussels by informing the Six that Britain could not make further major concessions in order to obtain agreement on EEC membership. In London it was feared that by appearing eager to join the Common Market, the Macmillan cabinet had led the Six to stiffen the terms for entry.[6]

---

continuation of obligations incurred by member states under previous treaties, in order to retain economic ties with other EFTA countries. By this announcement, the British government sought to dispel rumors then current in Brussels that Britain would make use of this provision after joining the Common Market.

[6] See the *New York Times*, November 16, 1962, p. 8.

By mid-November, optimism in Whitehall about the prospects for Common Market membership had diminished as British economic interests clashed with those of the EEC, and of France in particular. The Macmillan cabinet had also to take account of pressure from Parliament and public opinion in Britain not to make concessions to the Six, especially on domestic agriculture. At the same time the returns from by-elections showed a considerable decline in popular support for the Conservative government.[7]

Perhaps to prepare public opinion for the possibility of failure or to bolster Britain's bargaining position, cabinet members in December 1962 played down the consequences to Britain of a breakdown in the Brussels negotiations. On December 8, the President of the Board of Trade, Frederick Erroll, declared that "we should not overnight be reduced to starvation and rags" if Britain was not admitted to the Common Market. Moreover, during a speech to the Foreign Press Association in London, Chancellor of the Exchequer Maudling remarked: "We want to join the Six and hope very much to do so. But on the other hand we have all said from time to time that it is not a question of disaster if we don't."[8] If she were excluded from the Common Market, Britain had "the whole of the rest of this world" in which to make a living.

At a meeting on December 10, the Ministers of the Six and Britain again considered, without notable success, the question of transitional arrangements for British agriculture. During these discussions the EEC made a concession by recognizing the British government's obligation, for the duration of the existing Parliament, to maintain its system of deficiency payments. Although this shift in EEC policy would have enabled the Macmillan cabinet to fulfill the letter of its pledge to Britain's farmers, it would not have given the time deemed necessary to adjust the British agricultural system to that of the Six. Since the existing Parliament was to end no later than October 1964, and Britain would have entered the Common Market early in 1964, the British would have had less than a year before the end of the deficiency payments farm policy. In order to examine in greater detail the agricultural proposals offered by Britain and the Common Market Six, the conferees agreed to establish a special committee consisting of their ministers of agriculture. Under the chairmanship of Dr. Sicco Man-

---

[7] See Chapter 4 for an examination of parliamentary bi-elections held during this period.
[8] *Financial Times* (London), December 11, 1962, p. 1.

sholt, Vice President of the EEC Commission, the so-called Mansholt Committee was charged with the task of presenting to the principal negotiators a detailed assessment of the effect of both British and EEC proposals upon farmers in Britain during the projected transitional period after Britain joined the Common Market. Two principal tasks confronted the Mansholt Committee: to assess the effect of an increase in market prices upon British farmers, and to examine ways in which producer prices in the United Kingdom could be brought into harmony with those of the Common Market. The Mansholt Committee was to report to the Council within the next month.

As in the case of the free trade area negotiations several years earlier, the British devoted their attention primarily to the economic problems associated with Common Market membership. Given the nature of the EEC, such a preoccupation was understandable. Nevertheless, problems which were essentially political in nature had a profound effect on the outcome of the Brussels negotiations and, in a broader context, on the European integration movement and the American "grand design" for Atlantic partnership.

Early in December 1962, attention turned to the meeting between de Gaulle and Macmillan to be held at Rambouillet, the French President's country estate, during the weekend of December 15–16. There is considerable evidence that French officials saw this meeting as offering an opportunity to make progress toward British Common Market membership.[9] In the week preceding the Rambouillet talks, the French State radio had given a prominent place to an interview with M. Robert Marjolin, a Frenchman and a Vice President of the EEC Commission, who had declared: "Tomorrow Britain will be in the Common Market. We are working on the assumption that Britain will

---

[9] For example, on December 13, Premier Pompidou declared: "In a few hours the British Prime Minister will be the guest of the President of the Republic. We shall receive him in the most friendly and most constructive spirit, ready to rejoice in all the efforts Great Britain is making in order to get closer to Europe, to which she is bound by so many interests and recollections. We are ready to make her transition easier, while, of course, upholding the view that Great Britain's entry should not destroy the structure, slow down the achievements, or compromise the results which we have gained, in particular, regarding the defense, vital in our eyes, of our agricultural interests." *L'Année Politique, Economique, Sociale et Diplomatique en France*, 1962. Paris: Presses Universitaires de France. Quoted in W. W. Kulski, *De Gaulle and the World: The Foreign Policy of the Fifth French Republic*, p. 242. For similar statements by President de Gaulle and M. Peyrefitte, Minister of Information, see the *Financial Times* (London), December 13, 1962, p. 5.

become a member." [10] Thus, despite their tough stance during the
Brussels negotiations, the French spoke, publicly at least, as if they still
saw the possibility of reaching an accord on British Common Market
membership.

When the two leaders met, Macmillan appears to have told de Gaulle
that the decision as to whether Britain could join was for the Six to
make. De Gaulle, however, maintained that Britain would be welcomed
to the Common Market if she was prepared to accept the Rome
Treaty, by which he meant the interpretation of the Treaty rendered
in the Brussels negotiations by the Six. De Gaulle sought from the
British Prime Minister assurance that Britain was prepared to place
Europe, rather than the Commonwealth or the special relationship with
the United States, at the top of her list of priorities. If the British were
willing to subordinate other interests to those of her relations with the
Six, she would have little difficulty in accepting the terms set forth by
the EEC.

The communiqué issued at the end of the meeting had the tone of
optimism. According to this statement, "General de Gaulle and Mr.
Macmillan . . . considered the stage reached in the current negotiations
on the subject of the Common Market. These negotiations have been
conducted and will be carried forward, in spite of the difficulties which
have been encountered, in the spirit to which definition was given at
the time of the Prime Minister's visit to Champs last June." [11] During
the Champs meeting, M. Couve de Murville is said to have stated that
France did not expect Britain to betray American nuclear secrets.
Nevertheless, at that time he is said to have alluded to the possibility of
European cooperation in nuclear defense and a changed role for Europe vis-à-vis the United States within the Atlantic Alliance. The
French felt the British must end their special relationship with the
United States in defense and foreign policy if western Europe, with
Britain as a Common Market member, was to achieve a more influential
role within the Atlantic Alliance. [12]

Without access to official records of the Rambouillet meeting, it is
difficult to determine to what extent de Gaulle and Macmillan dis-

---

[10] Quoted in *Financial Times* (London), December 17, 1962, p. 1.
[11] *Financial Times* (London), December 17, 1962, p. 1. At the Champs meeting of
June 2–3, the Prime Minister and the President had agreed that the Brussels talks
would be pursued in the spirit of "the community of interests between France and
the United Kingdom."
[12] *Financial Times* (London), June 4, 1962, p. 1.

cussed the question of Anglo-French nuclear sharing. It is equally difficult to ascertain the kind of accord the two leaders might conceivably have reached in their discussions. However, at the very least, they appear to have considered nuclear strategy in general terms, for their communiqué stated: "They found themselves in close agreement about the conclusions to be drawn as regards Western policy and Western defense."

If de Gaulle sought evidence of Britain's commitment to Europe, he might have found it if the British had offered to join with France in the development of an Anglo-French nuclear capability, which would reduce western Europe's military dependence upon the United States. Because of the importance de Gaulle attached to atomic weapons, France had pressed forward the development of the nuclear *force de dissuasion*. With British help, France might have cut considerably her expenditures for research and development and hastened the completion of her nuclear program.

Although not prepared to make a specific commitment to participate in a European defense scheme after Britain joined the Common Market, British officials had hinted that one day the European Community might concern itself with military problems. On April 10, 1962, in what was then the most detailed statement of British policy towards European political integration, Heath discussed the question of European defense collaboration. While affirming the necessity for "any European point of view or policy on defense (to be) directly related to the Atlantic Alliance," Heath envisaged the development of closer collaboration within Europe on military matters.[13]

It is difficult to assess the extent to which Heath's statement may have raised French expectations of British scientific collaboration, particularly in the field of nuclear development. Intentionally or not, in the months before the Nassau Agreement, Britain may have led France to anticipate a European defense arrangement which included Anglo-French collaboration in the building of nuclear weapons.

On July 3, 1962, the British government had made formal application for membership in Euratom. At that time, despite Heath's April 1962 statement on the possibility of European defense collaboration, Britain

---

[13] He declared: "There is no doubt in my mind that, with the closer integration of our industries which will follow British accession to the European Economic Community, we shall see great advances in European cooperation over defense production, research and development." Great Britain, *European Political Union* Cmnd. 1720 HMSO (April 10, 1962).

had specified that her nuclear defense program would remain outside any accords she might reach with the Six on atomic energy.[14] Nevertheless, the British press had given hints that Britain should consider linking her nuclear program to a broader European effort.[15]

On July 13 and 16, 1962, changes in the Macmillan cabinet were announced. Peter Thorneycroft, with a reputation as a "European," replaced Harold Watkinson as Minister of Defense.[16] In a speech to the Western European Union Assembly in Paris on December 4, Thorneycroft had spoken of the "barrier" to communism provided by a "happy and prosperous Europe, whereas a weak and divided Europe would pose a difficult defense problem." He sought to refute the notion Secretary of Defense McNamara had put forward in June 1962 in a speech in Ann Arbor, Michigan, that European national nuclear deterrents, and the British force in particular, had little value in a world of superpowers.

> I must touch on this point that the British deterrent can be regarded as dangerous and expensive, prone to obsolescence, and lacking in credibility. Indeed, it is prone to obsolescence certainly —so is everybody and everything. It is certainly expensive, for the price of deterring war is not cheap.
>
> The forces of Europe will demand—whether they are deployed on the central German plains or in the Persian Gulf—more and more sophisticated equipment. . . . What is needed for larger projects—and we are talking here of very large projects indeed—is capital resources and large markets, and it is these attributes which facilitated solutions which have been reached in Soviet Russia and the United States of America. Europe could find the same solutions. The combined capital and technical resources of Europe are equal to anything that can be found outside. The problem is how best to use them.[17]

---

[14] *Christian Science Monitor*, July 3, 1962.

[15] See Chapter 4 for a discussion of such proposals in the British press. It should be recalled, however, that on July 5 Mr. Heath had announced, somewhat ambiguously, in a speech in his constituency, that British membership in the Common Market did not necessarily mean a "giveaway of atomic secrets," reports to the contrary notwithstanding. *Times* (London), July 6, 1962, p. 12.

[16] See *Manchester Guardian Weekly*, Vol. 87, No. 3 (July 19, 1962), p. 1.

[17] Assembly of Western European Union, *Proceedings Eighth Ordinary Session*, Second Part (December 1962), IV, pp. 87–91.

After hearing Thorneycroft's address, the Assembly met in closed session for a question period. At this meeting the British Defense Minister is reported to have suggested that there were two ways in which a European nuclear capability might be established: by purchasing weapons from the United States or by Anglo-French joint production of such a force.[18] This comment, together with Thorneycroft's address itself, provided evidence that Britain was indeed prepared to explore the possibility of nuclear collaboration with other European powers.

A few days before Macmillan's Rambouillet meeting with de Gaulle, the United States had announced that the program for the development of the Skybolt missile would be discontinued. Early in December, there were reports from Washington that the United States had not included funds for the Skybolt in the Defense Department's budget for 1963–1964.[19] On December 11, Defense Secretary McNamara conferred with Thorneycroft, with Skybolt their principal topic of discussion. Several days later, on December 17, Thorneycroft informed the Commons that the future of Skybolt was uncertain. At the beginning of November, he declared, McNamara had advised him that the future of Skybolt was under examination. Thorneycroft then remarked: "From the point of view of the United States, the weapon is proving more expensive than originally estimated; secondly, it looks as though it will be late and possibly not as efficient and reliable as had at first been hoped; and thirdly, alternative weapons systems available to the United States government have proved relatively more successful." [20] McNamara contended that in five test flights Skybolt had developed power failures. The United States had already invested nearly $500 million in the development of Skybolt. In order to perfect Skybolt an investment of $2.8 billion would be needed. After the Blue Streak project for the development of a British intermediate range missile was abandoned in 1960, Britain had decided to purchase Skybolt missiles from the United States. If British aircraft could be equipped with the air-to-ground Skybolt missile, the life of Britain's strategic bomber force could have been lengthened by several years. By abandoning the

---

[18] Clare Hollingworth, "Nuclear Prospects for Europe," *Manchester Guardian Weekly*, Vol. 87, No. 23 (December 8 and 10, 1962), p. 3.
[19] *Financial Times* (London), December 8 and 10, 1962.
[20] Great Britain, *Parliamentary Debates* (Commons), Vol. 669 (December 17, 1962), col. 894.

Blue Streak and relying instead on the Skybolt, Britain had placed the future of her nuclear force, and hence decisions about her national security, in the hands of the United States. By cancelling Skybolt, the United States had jeopardized the future of the British nuclear force.

Just after his meetings at Rambouillet, Macmillan traveled to Nassau for discussions with President Kennedy which lasted from December 19 to December 21. In their communiqué following the conference the two leaders announced that the Skybolt program would be scrapped. The United States offered to continue the program, provided Britain was willing to assume half the costs. Such an arrangement was unacceptable to the British, who agreed instead to purchase Polaris missiles, for which Britain would supply the nuclear warheads and build the submarines. In return for the U.S. offer to supply Polaris missiles the British government agreed that the purpose of the joint Anglo-American Polaris program "must be the development of a multilateral NATO nuclear force in the closest consultation with other NATO allies." According to the Nassau communiqué, the British Polaris-equipped force "will be used for the purpose of international defense of the Western alliance in all circumstances." However, the British government retained the authority to withdraw its nuclear force from NATO command in times when "supreme national interests are at stake." [21]

Upon his return to London on December 23, Prime Minister Macmillan announced that he had made "a good deal" with President Kennedy. Macmillan had before him the task of convincing domestic British opinion, including members of his own party, that the Polaris offer would serve a purpose similar to that of Skybolt. He had also to assuage British feelings which had been injured by a U.S. decision which appeared to take little account of Britain's special relationship with the United States.

Although the British found reason, as a result of the Skybolt affair, to question the value of their special relationship with the United States, Britain signed an agreement which, in de Gaulle's estimation, tied her even more tightly to U.S. decisions in defense. On December 21, President Kennedy, in a letter to President de Gaulle, offered to provide Polaris missiles to France on the same terms as to Britain. Rejecting this offer, de Gaulle maintained that the United States was

---

[21] Quoted in U. W. Kitzinger, *The Politics and Economics of European Integration*, pp. 223–224.

prepared to extend special assistance to Britain in building submarines for delivering Polaris missiles. Since the United States had not indicated that it was prepared to give similar help to France, the offer was of little value to the French government. Instead, France would concentrate upon the building of her own nuclear force.[22]

Whatever Macmillan had offered, or refused to offer, during the Rambouillet meeting with de Gaulle, he had worked out a far-ranging agreement with President Kennedy just a few days later at Nassau. The seemingly interminable delays in the Brussels negotiations, in which Britain haggled over the tariff for such imports as canned kangaroo meat, and carefully weighed Commonwealth commitments against European interests, contrasted sharply with the speed with which Britain worked out a far-reaching defense agreement with the United States. This contrast, together with the extent to which Britain was prepared to maintain her technological-military dependence upon the United States, could hardly have escaped de Gaulle.[23] Moreover, the extent to

---

[22] In his celebrated press conference of January 14, 1963, the French President remarked: "France has taken note of the Anglo-American Nassau Agreement. As it was conceived, undoubtedly no one will be surprised that we cannot subscribe to it. It truly would not be useful for us to buy Polaris missiles when we have neither the submarines to launch them nor the thermonuclear warheads to arm them. Doubtless the day will come when we will have these submarines and these warheads. But that day will be long in coming. For the World War, the invasion, and their consequences have slowed us down a great deal in our atomic development. When we will one day have these submarines and these warheads, what will the Polaris missiles then be worth? At that time we will probably have missiles of our own invention. In other words, for us, in terms of technology, this affair is not the question of the moment.

"But also, it does not satisfy the principle of maintaining our own right to dispose of our deterrent force. To turn over our weapons to a multilateral force, under a foreign command, would be to act contrary to that principle of our defense and our policy. It is true that we too can theoretically retain the ability to take back in our hands, in the supreme hypothesis, our atomic weapons incorporated in the multilateral force. But how could we do it in practice during the unheard of moments of the atomic apocalypse? And then, this multilateral force necessarily entails a web of liaisons, transmissions and interference within itself, and on the outside a ring of obligations such that, if an integral part were suddenly snatched from it, there would be a strong risk of paralyzing it just at the moment, perhaps, when it should act." Ambassade de France à Londres, Service de Press et d'Information. *Text of the News Conference Held by General de Gaulle on January 14, 1963*, p. 11.

[23] According to André Fontaine, "À Paris, la volunte de defendre la lettre et l'esprit du traites de Rome se trouve encore renforcée par des considerations strategiques-politiques. D'une étude approfonde de l'accord des Bahamas, nos dirigeants retiendraient que la Grande-Bretagne à accepté en fait d'integrer completement sa défense nationale dans le systemme américain. Le guidage des fusées Polaris serait en effet d'une telle complexité qu'il exigerait le recours

which Macmillan informed de Gaulle of the kind of deal he proposed to work out for Britain at Nassau is uncertain. The failure to advise the French President of his intentions during Macmillan's forthcoming talks with U.S. officials, as well as the substance of the Nassau Agreement itself, could have weighed heavily in de Gaulle's decision to exclude Britain from the Common Market.[24] But the chief significance of the Nassau Agreement lies in the fact that it demonstrated to de Gaulle the durability of Britain's special relationship with the United States, and the extent to which the British were willing to entrust to a non-European power the major decisions about British security. Because Britain was not yet prepared to cast off the American hegemony, she had not become sufficiently "European" in orientation to qualify for Common Market membership.

French statements issued after the failure of the Brussels negotiations suggest a close relationship between the Nassau Agreement and de Gaulle's veto of the British Common Market application. On February 5, 1963, Premier Pompidou declared that the Polaris arrangement reflected Britain's preference for the United States over the Six. On the same day, de Gaulle informed members of the National Assembly, at an Elysée reception, that Macmillan told him in their Rambouillet meeting: " 'You are right to make a nuclear strike force. We ourselves are trying to make our own. We should try to associate them within the European framework, independent of America'. Thereupon he leaves me to go to the Bahamas. That brought forward my press conference a little and changed its tone." [24] Later, Michel Habib-Deloncle, then France's Deputy Foreign Minister, suggested in an address to the Assembly of the Council of Europe on September 23, 1963 that Britain and France might eventually cooperate in the development of European nuclear capabilities, and that such collaboration and British participation in the European Community were related.[25]

---

constant au support logistique americain. Dans ces conditions la possibilité pour les Britanniques de disposer de leur force, au service des 'interets nation-aux supremes' qui pourraient être mis en peril, serait purement théorique." *Le Monde* (Paris) January 10, 1963, p. 1.

[24] *Times* (London), February 6, 1963, p. 10.

[25] Habib-Deloncle declared: "Already, the mere fact that France has made a start in this direction (developing nuclear weapons) means that we can look forward to the possibility of an alteration, to Europe's advantage, in the present allocation of costs and responsibilities between the members of the Atlantic Alliance. I would even add that if Great Britain decides her future lies with the Community of Europe, this is a field in which she has the opportunity of making a positive contribution to that community—provided, of course, that she makes the choices

Factors other than the nuclear question may have contributed to the French decision to veto the British Common Market application. As a result of events in France in the autumn of 1962, de Gaulle's position was strengthened. On November 11 the French government had leaked to the press a sector-by-sector survey of industry in France. British companies, it was suggested, were in many cases at least twice as large as their French counterparts. Britain's leading producers of chemicals, automobiles, and electrical products were larger than their counterparts in France. Prices for such manufactures as machine and hand tools, office and refrigeration equipment, and farm tractors were lower in Britain than in France. In Britain, the process of merger had gone farther than in France. According to this study, British industry had surplus capacity in many sectors which might be utilized to create intensive price competition in an enlarged Community. British firms were said to have benefitted from links with U.S. industry.[26] French steel producers expressed apprehension about the implications of British Common Market membership. Speaking in Paris on October 16, René Damien, chairman of the French steel industry's trade association, declared that the existing disparity between steel tariffs in Britain and the Six was "particularly shocking." He suggested that French steel tariffs were less than half as high as those of Britain. Moreover, according to French producers, British steel prices on the Continent were such that Britain might dump her surpluses in markets across the Channel. Although M. Damien did not oppose Britain's entry into the European Community, he called for as short a transitional period as possible for Britain after joining.[27]

De Gaulle was strengthened by other developments. In a referendum held on October 28, 1962, he had sought approval of his proposal for the election of the French President by popular vote. On November 18, the Gaullist Union de la Nouvelle Republique (UNR) received a majority in the National Assembly, a feat unparalleled in recent French history. More than 5.8 million votes were cast for the UNR, as opposed to only 3.6 million in the 1962 election, when the UNR gained 31.9 percent of the votes cast.[28] Although more than twelve million

---

implied in such a decision." Council of Europe, Consultative Assembly, *Official Report*, Session 15, Part 1–2, (May 6–September 24, 1963), p. 510.

[26] *Financial Times* (London), November 12, 1962, p. 1.

[27] *Financial Times* (London), October 18, 1962, p. 5.

[28] See *Manchester Guardian Weekly*, Vol. 87, No. 18 (November 1962), p. 2; Robert Kleiman, *Atlantic Crisis: American Diplomacy Confronts a Resurgent Europe*, pp. 72–74.

persons—as against just under eight million "no's" and six million abstentions—voted in favor of this proposal, de Gaulle's majority was sharply reduced below that which he had obtained for his policy of peace in Algeria in the referendum held the previous April. Nevertheless, these two electoral successes bolstered de Gaulle's position both in domestic affairs and foreign policy. He could oppose Britain's Common Market bid with less concern about adverse repercussions in France.

By the autumn of 1962 public opinion in Britain had become deeply divided on the issue of EEC entry. In contrast to de Gaulle's strengthened position, the Macmillan cabinet faced a divided electorate which was losing confidence in the Conservative government. Undoubtedly, de Gaulle took note of cleavages within Britain on the Common Market question. In fact, his contention during his Press Conference of January 14, that Britain was "insular, maritime, linked through its trade, markets, and food supply to very distant countries" and hence different in economic structure and political outlook from the Six, bore a marked resemblance to many of the statements of British anti-Common Market groups. By revealing major differences of opinion, the debate in Britain about Common Market membership reinforced de Gaulle's doubts about Britain's qualifications for the EEC entry.

French statements about the Brussels negotiations after the Nassau Agreement reveal a cooling in French interest in British Common Market membership. For example, in his New Year's message on January 1, 1963, de Gaulle discussed the question of British membership in the European Community. He spoke of the strengthening of France's ties with Germany and of the development of political unity among the Six. He declared that during the year to come France would strive for "the union of western Europe with respect to its economy, its policies, its defense, its culture, thus establishing a balance with the United States, reinforcing thereby the alliance of the free world, ready to receive, and definitely aiming at organizing with the countries of the East—should they one day come to a complete easing of the tension— the peace and the life of our whole continent.[29] Apparently de Gaulle did not believe that Britain would soon become a member of the EEC.

[29] Ambassade de France, Service de Press et d'Information, New York. New Year's Message delivered by General de Gaulle, President of the French Republic, over French Radio and Television on December 31, 1962, p. 2.

Instead, Britain would join the Common Market at some future date when she could meet the obligations imposed by the Rome Treaty.

Early in 1963, other expressions of pessimism about the future of the Brussels negotiations appeared in Europe. On January 9, the Netherlands Foreign Minister, Dr. Luns, informed the Dutch Second Chamber that negotiations for British Common Market membership had reached "a dangerous stage." [30] Unless important decisions were taken soon, he feared that the talks would result in total failure and that European countries would drift apart. At the same time French sources suggested a stiffening of British as well as French attitudes on Britain's entry. French officials are reported to have concluded that in the Nassau Agreement Britain had strengthened her special relationship with the United States. British Common Market membership would give the United States a "Trojan Horse" in Europe.[31] Such reports accorded with de Gaulle's own statement about the effect of the Nassau Agreement upon the French veto of the British application.

Despite such expressions of concern, the Six and Britain prepared for the resumption of the Brussels negotiations. In his preparations for the forthcoming Brussels round, Heath visited Paris for discussions with French officials on January 11. Although Foreign Minister Couve de Murville had just informed the Foreign Affairs Commission of the French National Assembly that Britain must make important concessions, including acceptance of the agricultural policy as defined by the Six, Heath apparently had little indication of the course de Gaulle would adopt in his Press Conference of January 14.

After discussing constitutional changes in the Fifth Republic and prospects for French economic expansion, de Gaulle responded to a question about France's position concerning the entry of Britain in the Common Market and the political evolution of Europe. He described the Rome Treaty as an agreement between "six continental states which, economically speaking, are, in short, of the same nature." In their industrial and agricultural production, in foreign trade, in liv-

---

[30] *Financial Times* (London), January 10, 1963, p. 5.
[31] *Le Monde* (Paris), January 10, 1963. "On conclurait en haute lieu que les 'liens spéciaux' entre Londres et Washington se trouvent encore renforcés et que, de ce fait, la venue de la Grande-Bretagne dans le marche commun risquerait de plus en plus d'ouvrir ses portes a un 'cheval de Troie' américain. La crainte de voir, sous l'influence de l'Angleterre et de la 'caravane' qu'elle entrainerait à la suite, la Communauté des Six dégénérer en une vaste zone de libre-échange est d'autre part toujours aussi vive à Paris."

ing and working conditions, the Six had many more similarities than differences between them. De Gaulle then termed the Six "extensions of each other through their communications," which belong together because of their many transactions with each other.[32]

In the Common Market it had been possible to link those countries which "from the standpoint of their economic development, their social progress and their technological capability . . . are, in short, in stride with each other and . . . are moving forward at more or less the same pace." No serious political problems divided the Six. Instead, de Gaulle maintained, the EEC countries possessed a "feeling of solidarity between them, first owing to the awareness they have of together possessing an important part of the origins of our civilization, and also with regard to their security, because they are continental countries and they are confronted by the same single threat from one end of their territorial grouping to the other."

In contrast, Britain retained important links with other Commonwealth countries and the United States. "Its (England's) activities are essentially industrial and commercial, and only slightly agricultural. It has, throughout its work, very marked and original customs and traditions. In short, the nature, structure and economic context of England differ profoundly from those of the other states of the Continent." If Britain joined, the Common Market would be transformed from a tightly-knit unit to a grouping in which some members had interests in conflict with those of the original members. According to de Gaulle: "It is foreseeable that the cohesion of all its members, who would be very numerous and very diverse, would not hold for long and that in the end there would appear a colossal Atlantic Community under American dependence and leadership which would soon completely swallow up the European Community."

Turning to a more detailed examination of the question of agriculture, de Gaulle contended that France "cannot conceive of a Common Market in which French agriculture would not find outlets commensurate with its production, and we agree, moreover, that, among the Six, we are the country for which this necessity is the most imperative." The EEC farm policy, de Gaulle pointed out, had been formulated only after long and detailed negotiations. He noted that the governments of the Six, not the Commission, had taken the necessary

---

[32] Ambassade de France à Londres, Service de Presse et d'Information. *Text of the News Conference Held by General de Gaulle on January 14, 1963.*

decisions. However, he paid the Commission the delicate compliment of having "worked in a highly objective and pertinent fashion."

According to de Gaulle, the economic structure of Britain and the Six, including the place of agriculture in their economies, differed profoundly. On the one hand, the Six, and France in particular, grew a large part of the food they consumed. The Common Market had worked out an agricultural policy which, as de Gaulle succinctly summarized it, "consists of making a pool of the agricultural products of the entire Community, of strictly determining their prices, of forbidding subsidizing, of organizing their consumption between all the members, and of making it obligatory for each of these members to pay to the Community any savings they might make by having foodstuffs brought in from outside instead of consuming those offered by the Common Market."

In contrast, de Gaulle described Britain's agricultural policy: "The means by which the people of Great Britain nourish themselves is in fact by importing foodstuffs purchased at low prices in the two Americas or in the former dominions, while still granting large subsidies to British farmers. This means is obviously incompatible with the system the Six have quite naturally set up for themselves." Far from being prepared to abandon their agricultural policy in favor of that of the Six, Britain had requested exceptions to the EEC farm policy in order to accommodate British interests: "The question is to know if Great Britain can at present place itself, with the Continent and like it, within a tariff that is truly common, give up all preferences with regard to the Commonwealth, cease to claim that its agriculture be privileged and, even more, consider as null and void the commitments it has made with the countries that are part of its free trade area." This, de Gaulle implied, Britain was not prepared to do.

Britain, he contended, had at last decided to apply for Common Market membership after having refused initially to assist in the formation of the European Community. Instead, the British government had created EFTA, and had even "put some pressure on the Six in order to prevent the application of the Common Market from almost getting started." After having pursued such policies, Britain "requested membership, but on its own conditions." Nevertheless, de Gaulle suggested that Britain might "one day come round to transforming itself enough to belong to the European Community without restriction and without reservation." When that day arrived, "France would place no obstacle in its path." For the moment, however, Britain "is not yet prepared to do this, and that indeed appears to be the outcome of the long, long Brussels talks."

De Gaulle had never looked with particular favor upon Britain's Common Market application.[33] Conceivably, de Gaulle saw in British Common Market membership a challenge to French leadership in western Europe. The Macmillan Cabinet, as well as other British advocates of Common Market membership, had looked upon the European Community as a means of restoring British power and prestige through leadership of an integrated western Europe. The United States, as well, saw Britain's Common Market bid as part of a "grand design" for an Atlantic partnership. This, in turn, de Gaulle viewed as a design for perpetuating Anglo-American supremacy in NATO. Differing conceptions of Atlantic and European unity clashed and for the immediate future the French view prevailed, since no member was willing to risk the destruction of the European Community in order to obtain British entry. De Gaulle saw confirmed his long-standing suspicions about Britain and the United States. Conceivably, at this time the French President might have been willing to make a place for Britain in his scheme for European unity had the British shown a willingness to cast aside old habits of cooperation with the United States and join with France in building a nuclear force and a Europe freed from the hegemony of the United States.

In the aftermath of President de Gaulle's press conference several delegations in Brussels issued statements in support of British membership in the Common Market. German Foreign Minister Schroeder declared that for both political and economic reasons, Britain must become a member of the European Community. According to Schroeder, Britain had made economic concessions beyond those anticipated

---

[33] In his memoirs he wrote of the design which he evolved during World War II for achieving French influence and security:

I intended to guarantee France primacy in western Europe by preventing the rise of a new Reich that might again threaten its safety; to cooperate with East and West and if need be contract the necessary alliances on one side or the other without ever accepting any kind of dependency; to transform the French Union into a free association in order to avoid the as yet unspecified dangers of upheaval; *to persuade the states along the Rhine, the Alps and the Pyrenees to form a political, economic and strategic bloc;* to establish this organization as one of the three world powers and, should it become necessary, as the arbiter between the Soviet and Anglo-American camps. Since 1940, nearly every word and act had been dedicated to establishing these possibilities; now that France was on her feet again, I tried to realize them. General de Gaulle, *War Memoirs: Salvation, 1944–1946,* 178–179. Italics added.

by de Gaulle. The British had expressed their willingness, at least in principle, to accept a common external tariff, to abolish Common-wealth preferences, to adopt the Community system on agriculture, and to give up special links with other EFTA countries upon joining the Common Market. Speaking for Belgium, Foreign Minister Spaak found it difficult to accept de Gaulle's contention that Britain was not an integral part of Europe. In fact, Europeans could discuss integration today "largely because of the attitude of Britain in 1940–41 when she was practically isolated." [34] This view Dutch Foreign Minister Luns supported.

Other expressions of hostility toward French policy were forthcoming. On January 24, the Belgian Senate voted unanimously in favor of continuing negotiations for British Common Market membership. Spaak termed the French action a *Diktat*. Speaking in the Italian Chamber of Deputies, Premier Amintore Fanfani characterized France's action as "a menace to the internal equilibrium of NATO." [35] On January 25, the German cabinet issued a statement that British membership in the EEC was necessary for political and economic reasons, and that the talks in Brussels "can and should be continued with the aim of reaching a positive conclusion." [36] The Germans sought to avoid a choice between France and the United States, which full support for French policy would have entailed. Official German statements in support of Britain's entry reflected divisions of opinion in the cabinet and elsewhere in the Federal Republic.

During the week of January 14 the Ministerial session continued in Brussels, almost as though de Gaulle had not held his press conference. By January 16 the British and the "Friendly Five," as France's EEC partners came to be called, had put forward proposals on several outstanding tariff questions, as Britain and the EEC countries, except France, attempted to avert the collapse of the Brussels negotiations. Heath informed the EEC that Britain was willing to modify her earlier request for zero tariffs on aluminum, certain kinds of canned fruit and heavy jute goods. Instead, the British were now prepared to accept a lowered Common Market tariff on these items. At the same time, the Commission recommended that Canadian newsprint be admitted to the EEC under the same terms as those to be accorded Sweden if she became an associate member. For aluminum, the Commission proposed

[34] *Manchester Guardian Weekly*, Vol. 88, No. 3 (January 17, 1963), p. 3.
[35] *The New York Times* (European Edition), January 27, 1963.
[36] *Observer* (London), January 27, 1963.

reductions in tariffs from 9 to 7 percent if the EEC received similar concessions in the forthcoming talks provided by the United States Trade Expansion Act of 1962. This recommendation the French opposed because they feared the effect of a tariff of 7 percent upon their aluminum industry.

In an effort to forestall French efforts to end the Brussels negotiations, the Friendly Five offered proposals for continuing the talks until major outstanding problems could be resolved. In one proposal the German government called upon the EEC Commission to prepare a progress report on the state of the negotiations and to propose solutions to remaining problems within about two weeks. According to the German plan, the Brussels talks would be resumed as soon as the Commission had submitted its report. This proposal had the support of the Benelux countries and Italy. Althought the French opposed the compromise, the Five reached agreement late on Tuesday afternoon, January 29, on the text of a draft mandate, which called upon the Commission to prepare a report on the state of the negotiations.[37]

After a meeting during the evening of January 14, in a session which did not adjourn until 3:20 the following morning, the Mansholt Committee finished its report on British agriculture. This report Dr. Mansholt presented to the Ministers of the Six and Britain on January 15. At this time the British, in a concession to the Six in agriculture, announced that they would accept in 1970 the full EEC agricultural policy for pigs and eggs.

After Mansholt's presentation, Spaak put two questions to Heath. First, he asked if the British were prepared to seek solutions on a commodity-by-commodity basis to the problems posed by British agriculture. This question Heath answered in the affirmative. Next, the Belgian Foreign Minister suggested that if Britain accepted 1970 as the final date for full adherence to the EEC farm policy, the Six might be able to make concessions regarding the adaptation of British agriculture to the EEC system during that period. Heath replied that Britain would agree to the 1970 deadline, provided the arrangements for individual commodities were acceptable. This statement the Five welcomed, while France's delegation offered no comment.

In effect, the British were accepting the EEC timetable, provided they could work out suitable terms for agriculture. In this exchange with Spaak, however, the British did not offer to accept the Common

---

[37] *Guardian* (Manchester and London), January 30, 1963, p. 1.

Market agricultural transitional period ending in 1970, and then to make arrangements for individual commodities. In a sense, Heath and Spaak each put different priorities first. In agriculture, as in other negotiations, the British were only willing to commit themselves to the EEC if they were satisfied with the terms. In short, in this instance, Heath appeared to have made a concession in principle in accepting the 1970 date without, however, having abandoned his position on individual commodities, for which a longer transitional period might be needed.

As their EEC partners strove to keep the negotiations going, the French sought to end them. On January 17, Couve de Murville asked for the indefinite suspension of the talks and reiterated de Gaulle's contention in his press conference that major economic questions, not to speak of political problems, remained to be resolved. During the discussions Couve de Murville suggested, as de Gaulle had done in his Press Conference of January 14, that Britain seek associate membership in the Common Market. In the Ministerial session held on January 18, the Five, nevertheless, lined up with Dr. Hallstein, representing the Commission, in opposition to de Gaulle.

At this time the objective of British policy was to avoid the onus of having caused the failure of the Brussels negotiations. London wished to place the burden for the breakdown of negotiations squarely on France. The British were prepared to continue to negotiate as long as the EEC remained willing to do so. Outwardly, at least, the Macmillan cabinet avoided expressions of pessimism about the prospects for Common Market membership. Commenting on the de Gaulle press conference, Macmillan acknowledged, during a Conservative party rally in Liverpool on January 21, that there had been "a setback—I trust and pray not a fatal setback. . . . Given the will, the remaining difficulties can be surmounted." He remarked that "We in Britain believe that we can be loyal Europeans, without disloyalty to our great Commonwealth tradition." In this speech, moreover, he sought to set the record straight about his conversations the previous month with de Gaulle.

> If there was an objection in principle (to British entry into the EEC) we should surely have been told so from the start. Indeed, at my meeting with him at Rambouillet, General de Gaulle himself reminded me that the length of the negotiations was inevitable in view of their complicated character. Similarly, it has been suggested that by making the Polaris arrangement with President

Kennedy a few days after I had seen General de Gaulle himself at Rambouillet, I did not treat him with absolute sincerity. On the contrary, we discussed this question and I explained that if the Americans decided to abandon Skybolt as unlikely to prove satisfactory I would do my utmost at Nassau to obtain an effective alternative. . . . I am sure he fully understood our position.[38]

Indeed, the French and British may not have understood each other's position, since official statements on both sides attached differing interpretations to the Rambouillet meeting and the Nassau Agreement.

From Brussels attention shifted back to Paris where, on January 21 and 22, Chancellor Adenauer conferred with de Gaulle. There was hope in Britain, as well as among France's EEC partners, that the Adenauer visit would provide an opportunity for the Bonn government to modify de Gaulle's views. However, Chancellor Adenauer had as his main priority to conclude a pact with France which would symbolize the burgeoning friendship between the two countries. Clearly de Gaulle's primary interest lay in unity between the two leading members of the Common Market, rather than enlarging the European Community to include Britain.

At the end of their talks on January 22, the two leaders signed the Franco-German Treaty, which embodied de Gaulle's conception of European integration. It provided for meetings between heads of government to be held at least twice a year; consultations at least once every three months between foreign ministers; periodic consultations between responsible authorities of the two countries in the fields of defense, education, and youth; and discussions at least every three months between the Ministers of the Armed Forces or of Defense.

The French and German governments agreed to "consult each other, prior to any decision, on all important questions of foreign policy, and in the first place on questions of common interest, with a view to arriving, insofar as possible, at a similar position." In particular, the consultations were to include problems relative to the European Communities and to European political cooperation, East-West relations, and other international organizations, including NATO. The Treaty provided for harmonization of strategic and tactical doctrine, joint programs of armaments, and exchanges of military personnel, including entire units. Both signatories undertook to increase the knowledge of

---

[38] *Financial Times* (London), January 22, 1963, p. 1.

each other's language, to cooperate in scientific research, and to exchange students.[39]

Following the signing of the Franco-German Treaty, the French reiterated their contention that, so far as they were concerned, the Brussels talks were adjourned. At the same time the French cabinet issued a communiqué warning the Five against reprisals because of opposition to French policy on British Common Market membership. It had been suggested that the EEC should refuse to approve a new protocol for French-Algerian trade, that the revised agreement for Associated States should be rejected, and that the agricultural accords among the Six themselves might be blocked. In this event, however, France was prepared to oppose other EEC countries on questions of importance to them. The French had concluded, correctly as it turned out, that their partners would not risk destruction of the Common Market over the question of British membership. Like France, the other members enjoyed benefits they were unwilling to jeopardize, despite disagreement with France for having rejected Britain's EEC application.

On January 29, the Brussels negotiations ended in failure. After hearing several statements which stressed France's responsibility for the failure of the talks, Couve de Murville replied that "in reality, the responsibility which we have taken is that of having made clear that the negotiations have been taking place in a vacuum since October, and of having said that it was preferable to face facts." [40] France's Foreign Minister repeated de Gaulle's contention that Britain was unprepared to accept the obligations imposed by the Rome Treaty. He then declared that "when Britain can accept all the requirements of the Treaty of Rome, nothing can stop her from entering the Common Market. But it is on her and not on us that the burden of proof lies." France's objective, he maintained, was to assure that "the Europe which we create is a Europe which is European."

The heads of delegations from other EEC countries spoke out against the French action. Each of the Five emphasized the gravity with which they viewed the breakdown of the Brussels negotiations. Spaak expressed dismay that the Six now gave evidence that the EEC was not, as they had contended, "outward looking." According to

---

[39] Ambassade de France, Service de Press et d'Information, *Texts of the Common French-German Declaration and of the Treaty between the French Republic and the Federal Republic of Germany of January 22, 1963.*
[40] *Guardian* (Manchester and London), January 30, 1963, p. 1.

Schroeder, German ratification of the Rome Treaty had been made contingent upon the eventual enlargement of the Community to include such countries as Britain. Luns saw the suspension of the Brussels negotiations as gravely weakening the Common Market.

In his reply, Heath reminded the Six that Britain was prepared to accept the proposal put forth earlier by Germany, calling for the resumption of negotiations after the Commission had prepared a progress report and suggested solutions for remaining problems. He emphasized that because Britain was "part of Europe by geography, history, culture, trade and civilization," the British would not turn their attention from the Continent. Expressing Britain's disappointment with the outcome in Brussels, Heath declared:

> We entered these negotiations sixteen months ago in good faith and have endeavoured strenuously to reach a successful conclusion. Five countries and the Commission have said publicly that all the remaining problems in the negotiations were capable of solution. I share that view. The five governments and ourselves all wished to continue the negotiations and bring them to a successful conclusion. The high hopes of so many have thus been thwarted for political reasons at the will of one man. The end of the negotiations is a blow to the cause of that wider European unity for which we have been striving.[41]

It now remained only for the chairman of the conference, M. Fayat, to announce his regret that the member states of the Community were unable to continue the negotiations, and to declare closed the seventeenth Ministerial Session devoted to Britain's EEC application. Thus the Brussels negotiations ended with Britain and the Five exchanging ideas about the feasibility of continuing contacts on either a multilateral or bilateral basis, possibly within the Western European Union.

The British government now faced the unenviable task of adjusting its policy and explaining to the electorate the reasons for the failure in Brussels. Having argued the merits of joining the Common Market, British leaders had now to acknowledge failure and to seek other means of achieving objectives which had inspired the EEC application. In a television broadcast on January 30, Macmillan attempted to explain to the British public what had happened in Brussels. He declared that Britain had entered the Brussels negotiations in order to unite and

---

[41] *Ibid.*

strengthen, not to divide, western Europe.[42] As Heath had done in his final statement in Brussels, Macmillan attempted to place the blame for failure squarely on France and specifically on de Gaulle. He maintained that the present government of France was "looking backward, not forward. They seem to think that one nation can dominate Europe." According to Macmillan, the negotiations had broken down "not because they were going to fail, but curiously enough because they were going to succeed." In short, France had chosen to veto the British application when it had become apparent that the remaining problems could be resolved. Such was not the conclusion, however, that the EEC Commission reached in its report on the state of the negotiations.[43]

The Commission acknowledged that many important points of difference remained. The question of the general level of a common tariff in an enlarged Community had still to be settled. Britain had reserved the right to determine at the end of the negotiations whether downward adjustments would still be needed. Moreover, the British, it will be recalled, had sought zero duties for twenty-six products. Agreement had been reached for ten of them, and tariff levels for sixteen items remained to be worked out. These included four products of major importance: newsprint, aluminum, lead, and zinc.

Turning to the Commonwealth, the Commission dealt first with Australia, Canada, and New Zealand. Although for the most part solutions for their industrial products had been found, problems remained in the case of agricultural exports from these countries. The Commission noted that the Brussels negotiators had decided to conclude "generous trade agreements" with Ceylon, India, and Pakistan to replace Commonwealth preferences accorded them. The EEC had offered associate membership to Commonwealth countries in Africa and the Caribbean, and had agreed that "those independent Commonwealth countries which did not wish to avail themselves of this offer were to be helped through the conclusion of formal trade agreements and transitional measures." However, the question as to how Britain was to participate in the Common Market Development Fund for associated overseas countries had remained unresolved.

---

[42] "We want to heal the division of Europe by a real unity and we want to see this freely united Europe use her strength and prosperity for the benefit of the whole world." *Challenge Accepted*, Text of Prime Minister Macmillan's Broadcast of January 30, 1963. (London: Conservative and Unionist Central Office, 1963.)

[43] European Economic Community Commission, *Report to the European Parliament on the State of the Negotiations with the United Kingdom*, COM (63) 70, Brussels, February 26, 1963.

For British agriculture, the Six and Britain had agreed to an annual review of farming problems. But accord had not been reached on many remaining measures to fit British agriculture into the Common Market agricultural policy. For several products, Britain had sought exceptions to the EEC farm policy. Special arrangements were requested for British wheat, barley, and oats. Most British proposals for changes in EEC farm policy were not acceptable to the Six. The British had asked for a time lag of five years before the first tariff reductions were applied to such horticultural products as fruits and vegetables. They sought a transitional period ending on January 1, 1973, together with assurance that Britain could provide financial assistance to its horticulturalists. The Commission noted: "The Six considered that in general there was no justification for the exceptional measures which the United Kingdom Delegation requested for horticulture." Nor had the British and the Common Market negotiators agreed on a plan for financing the agricultural policy of an enlarged Community.

In their detailed discussions of the problems of economic union with the Six, the British had agreed to accept Community law with three reservations. Britain wished further study of the rules of competition as they applied to agriculture. Moreover, the British wanted clarification of the position of Northern Ireland in regard to the free movement of labor. Finally, Britain sought a timetable for placing into operation the principles of equal pay for men and women workers in the United Kingdom.

In preliminary talks, institutional, legal, and financial questions had been considered. Here the negotiators had not anticipated special difficulties in British membership, although the admission of other states to the EEC would have required further study. Although the precise formula for voting in the institutions of an enlarged Community had yet to be worked out, there is no reason to believe that this problem would not have been resolved had the negotiations continued.

The future of other EFTA countries in the event that Britain joined the Common Market remained unsettled. The Commission recalled that Britain had made her own membership contingent upon the success of negotiations for her EFTA partners. Such a policy, the Commission suggested, had several effects upon Britain's application:

As regards the timing, Britain's accession was put off to a more uncertain date, which depended on the course of the other negotiations for accession or association. As regards the substance of the matter, Britain's accession itself became contingent upon the success of these other negotiations.[44]

The Commission concluded that in the case of Denmark, Ireland, and Norway, the prospects for EEC membership were promising. In the case of other EFTA countries, however, even greater problems remained to be worked out if Britain was to fulfill her pledge to them before joining the Common Market. For such countries "it was much more difficult to establish assumptions on either the timing or the nature of the solutions to be adopted."

Because their external economic relationships and political affinities were more complex than those of the Six, the British found themselves penalized for not having joined the Community as a founding member. Britain faced the difficult problem of reconciling her economic system and overseas commitments with the Rome Treaty. Of perhaps greater importance, the British had to adapt themselves to a Community which was changing even as they negotiated in Brussels. The British clearly faced a dilemma. In their belated bid for Common Market membership, the British were handicapped by the passage of time. Yet the state of public opinion in Britain, as well as the outlook of many leaders in government, precluded an application during the formative stages of the Treaty. Even in 1962 many Englishmen were not prepared to forsake relationships of consanguinity and loyalties tested on the battle-fields of Vimy Ridge and El Alamein for economic, and perhaps political, union with countries who, in some cases, had been historic and even recent enemies.

Nevertheless, in the period between 1961 and 1963 Britain had moved toward unity with the Continent to an extent unparalleled in her modern history. Her negotiators at Brussels had accepted tariff discrimination against industrial exports from Commonwealth countries, as well as the principle of weighted-majority voting in European institutions and, implicitly, the notion that decisions affecting the economic and political future of Britain would be taken in Brussels rather than London. To be sure, many outstanding issues remained. Had the British government yielded on these points, however, it might have eroded its already weakened domestic position. Given the division of opinion in Britain, at the next general election the electorate might have repudiated an agreement which appeared to be a "sell-out" to the Six. In sum, given the pressures against an agreement which might have

---

[44] *Ibid.*, p. 99.

jeopardized major British and Commonwealth interests, Britain was unprepared, in the Brussels negotiations, to make the economic concessions which might have been necessary to assure EEC entry. Politically, Britain was not prepared to make the choices implicit in a decision to build an Anglo-French nuclear force and to join France in reducing the U.S. hegemony in the Atlantic Alliance. Instead, many Englishmen recalled their country's intimate links with Commonwealth countries and the special relationship with the United States. Such memories conditioned British thought and contributed to the failure which the British experienced in the Brussels negotiations. But the failure was not Britain's alone. As part of its "grand design," the United States had pressed Britain to join the Common Market. Neither Britain nor the United States had anticipated the French veto of the British Common Market bid, or calculated accurately the effect of political-strategic decisions taken in Nassau upon economic negotiations in Brussels.

Chapter 7

TOWARD THE SECOND APPLICATION

The first reaction of Englishmen to the collapse of the Brussels negotiations was to recall other times of adversity in their long history.[1] Despite the Brussels debacle, British decision-makers and nongovernmental elites continued to reappraise Britain's international commitments and foreign policy orientation. With the breakdown of the negotiations, Britain enlarged her permanent mission to the European Community and arranged for consultations with the Six on issues related to European economic integration.[2] In July 1963, Britain and the Six agreed to meet in quarterly sessions under the auspices of Western European Union.[3] The British government looked to the reduction of tariffs in the then forthcoming Geneva trade negotiations, made possible by the U.S. Trade Expansion Act of 1962. Finally, British officials suggested that Britain should strengthen her own economy and adopt domestic policies designed to assure expanding markets for exports. This in turn might increase her political influence abroad.[4]

Although Britain was not prepared in the 1963–64 period to undertake a new initiative toward the Common Market, British officials

---

[1] Macmillan expressed this mood when on January 29, 1963, he answered a question in the Commons about the Brussels negotiations: "If and when they come to an end, a situation will have been created which we shall deal with. I am convinced that we shall deal with that situation as we have always dealt with difficulties facing us. We shall face it, I believe, as a united country." Great Britain, *Parliamentary Debates* (Commons), Vol. 670 (January 29, 1963), col. 758.

[2] See statement by Edward Heath. Great Britain, *Parliamentary Debates* (Commons), Vol. 671 (February 12, 1963), cols. 1159–1160.

[3] See the report submitted on behalf of the General Affairs Committee by the Hon. Maurice Edelman, Rapporteur, *Great Britain, EFTA and the EEC*. Assembly of Western European Union, Eleventh Ordinary Session (First Part) Document 341, 1965. In a speech on June 5, 1963, Edward Heath proposed that WEU should be the power in which to seek to develop closer European cooperation in defense and foreign policy. *Times* (London), June 6, 1963, p. 9.

[4] See, for example, Prime Minister Macmillan's statement to the House of Commons. Great Britain, *Parliamentary Debates* (Commons) Vol. 671 (February 11, 1963), col. 949.

stressed their continuing interest not only in the European Community, but also in European political integration. Successive governments
after 1963—Conservative and Labour—indicated that Britain wished to
participate from the beginning in any new discussions on European
political integration.[5] By taking part in such negotiations, Britain might
exert an influence on the future shape of a politically united Europe
which she had been denied by refusing to participate in the framing of
the Rome Treaty.

The years following the collapse of the Brussels negotiations were a
testing time for the European Community as well. In the period
1965–66, the Commission found itself the object of intense French
criticism. The dispute centered on conflicting views about the nature
of supranationality within the EEC, and in particular the position of
the Commission, the strengthening of the European Parliament, and
completion of regulations for the Common Market farm policy. During the latter months of 1965, the future of the EEC seemed uncertain,
since France had withdrawn from the deliberations of the Council of
Ministers. The French opposed the efforts of the Commission to link
the financing of the EEC agricultural policy to the strengthening of
the European Parliament. According to the Commission proposal, levies collected on agricultural imports into the Common Market would
have gone directly to the EEC to finance its agricultural policy. As a
result, the European Community would have gained a major new
source of revenue that would have lessened its financial dependence on
member governments. Although France pressed for completion of the
EEC farm policy, she was unwilling to link its financing, as the

---

[5] R. A. Butler, while foreign secretary in the Conservative government of Sir Alec
Douglas-Home, declared at a meeting of the WEU Council in London that British
participation at all stages in negotiations on European political integration would
be of benefit. *Guardian* (Manchester and London) January 25, 1965. Michael
Stewart chose the occasion of his first major address, on February 11, 1965, after
becoming foreign secretary in the Wilson cabinet, to emphasize Britain's interest
in European political integration: "It would not serve the cause of European and
Atlantic unity if important decisions affecting the political future of Europe were
taken by a restricted group. This is a matter on which the views of all European
powers who support the aims of a united Europe, including any members of the
European Free Trade Association who wish to participate, should be heard. We
for our part have always expressed our wish to join from the outset in any talks
aimed at political unity; and we regret that the latest proposals for such talks
envisage the participation of the Six European Economic Community countries
only." *The Labour Government and Europe*, mimeographed release by Labour
Party Overseas Department.

Commission wanted, to the strengthening of EEC institutions.[6] Nevertheless, the French government, like other member governments at the time of the Brussels negotiations, was not prepared to push its opposition to the point of destroying the Common Market. Before returning to the Council, France received agreement in January 1966 that the financial regulations would be completed without linking such action to the strengthening of Community institutions. Moreover, France's partners agreed that in preparing proposals for consideration by the Council, the Commission henceforth would "make the appropriate contacts with the governments of member states." The Council would seek to ensure that in cases where majority decisions could be taken, solutions would be sought "that could be adopted by all members of the Council in respect of their mutual interests and those of the Community."[7]

In May 1966, the Six reached agreement on financial regulations. Ninety percent of the revenues collected from levies on farm imports from third countries were to be paid to the EEC Fund for Agricultural Modernization and Guaranty. From this fund subsidies would be paid to Common Market countries for the modernization of their agriculture. Although France would be the chief beneficiary, the principle was established that the major part of levies on agricultural imports would be paid to the European Community, rather than to the member governments. This part of the agreement represented a victory for the proponents of a strengthened European Community.

During the Common Market crisis the idea of another British EEC bid gained currency. Reportedly, opponents of French policy in the Common Market, in particular Belgium and Germany, asked the Brit-

---

[6] Explaining France's withdrawal from the work of the EEC Council, de Gaulle, in his Press Conference of September 9, 1965, declared: "In Brussels, on 30 June, our delegation came up against a serious stumbling-block concerning the Five's definition of the financial regulation, as previously agreed upon. Shortly before, the Commission had suddenly abandoned its political discretion and formulated terms in connection with this financial regulation whereby it would have a budget of its own, possibly up to 20,000 million new francs [$4 billion], the states having made over into its hands the levies and customs receipts which would literally have made it a great independent financial power. And then those very states, having fed these enormous amounts to it at the expense of their taxpayers, would have no way of supervising it." Ambassade de France, *Speeches and Press Conferences*, No. 228.
[7] Ambassade de France, *Arrangements Made in Luxembourg between the Foreign Affairs Ministers of the Six on January 31, 1966*. (French Affairs—No. 188).

ish to commit themselves to the Rome Treaty.[8] Britain might not only
emerge as the leader of the EEC Five, but might offer proof of the
British commitment to an integrated Europe. At the very least, she
could strengthen the Five in their conflict with France. These views
were said to have the support of U.S. officials, who believed that
Britain might be letting a unique and historic moment slip by.[9] Even de
Gaulle, for reasons of his own, expressed interest in renewing at some
future date the question of Britain's relationship with the Six.[10]

Although the temptation was not absent from British discussions,
there was little inclination to exploit differences among the Six in order
to enhance Britain's position in Europe. Such a strategy might revive
latent Continental suspicion that Britain sought to exacerbate divisions
within the European Community. Moreover, the British conception of
a politically integrated Europe bore closer resemblance to that of de
Gaulle than to the ideas of the proponents of greater supranationality
against whom France was pitted. Finally, British policy at this time was
designed to build bridges between the EEC and EFTA, rather than to
drive wedges between France and other members of the European
Community.

Such a policy is understandable, since the Labour government
elected in October 1964 was not European in orientation.[11] Although at
the time of the Brussels negotiations Wilson was not opposed in

---

[8] *Financial Times* (London), December 29, 1965.

[9] *Ibid.*, November 16, 1965.

[10] Perhaps to blunt the campaign of his opponents for the French presidency and
to face down the proponents of supranationality in the European Community,
de Gaulle declared in a television broadcast: "We must take up again what France
proposed in 1961, and which did not succeed at first, that is to say, the organization
of a growing political cooperation between the states of western Europe. At that
moment, it is very probable that, a bit sooner or a bit later, England will join us,
and it will be quite natural. Of course, that Europe will not be supranational!"
Ian Davidson, "De Gaulle Treads the European Tightrope," *Financial Times*
(London), December 29, 1965.

[11] The cabinet included Patrick Gordon-Walker as Foreign Secretary; Denis
Healey as Minister of Defense; James Callaghan as Chancellor of the Exchequer;
Douglas Jay as President of the Board of Trade; and George Brown as Deputy
Prime Minister. Only Brown was strongly European, while Healey and Jay had op-
posed British entry into the Common Market. Several months before the election
Wilson had attacked the British government for having been prepared to join the
Common Market without proper regard for the interests of the Commonwealth.
He challenged the government to offer a pledge not to consider "entry into the
Common Market on any terms which would reduce Britain's existing freedom to
trade with the Commonwealth." Wilson declared: "On behalf of my party, I
give that pledge." Great Britain, *Parliamentary Debates* (Commons), Vol. 688
(February 6, 1964), cols. 1386–91.

principle to Common Market membership, he criticized the Macmillan cabinet for making its decision at a time when Britain was economically weak.[12] Wilson had stressed the importance of Labour's "five principles" as conditions which must be met before Britain could join the Common Market. By the autumn of 1962 Wilson, like Gaitskell, was convinced that they could not be met, and that the only option open to the Labour party was to oppose Common Market membership on the terms emerging from the Brussels negotiations.[13] Although prepared to discuss with the Six the idea of political integration, the Wilson cabinet, like the Conservative government before the first Common Market application, turned to EFTA as a device for reducing trade barriers between the Six and Seven. In other EFTA countries as well, the idea of using EFTA to achieve a single market in western Europe again gained currency.[14]

In a speech to the EFTA Ministerial Meeting in Vienna on May 24, 1965, Wilson called for the study of steps which might be taken to reduce differences between the Six and Seven. Although he had no detailed recommendations for the resolution of EFTA-EEC problems, he outlined several tentative proposals. A permanent standing consultative council, including representatives of EFTA and EEC, might be created. The Six and Seven might conduct special tariff negotiations for "European goods"—products traded more extensively in western Europe than elsewhere in the world. The idea that the Six, as one economic unit, might join a new trading unit in which EFTA countries would participate as separate governments should be examined. This proposal bore great resemblance to the British free trade area proposal of 1957. According to Wilson, the EEC and EFTA should attempt to remove non-tariff barriers to trade. Finally, the British

---

[12] Great Britain, *Parliamentary Debates* (Commons), Vol. 645, August 3, 1961, cols. 1651–67.

[13] Great Britain, *Parliamentary Debates* (Commons), Vol. 666 (November 8, 1962), cols. 1270–85; Vol. 669, December 13, 1962, cols. 658–675; Vol. 671, February 11, 1963, cols. 961–979. See also Harold Wilson, *Purpose in Politics: Britain's Role in the Post Colonial World*, Selected Speeches by Harold Wilson, 95–162.

[14] See, for example, the statement of Dr. Jose Goncalo Correa Oliveira, Chairman of the EFTA Council, on the eve of the meeting of EFTA Ministers held in Lisbon on May 9–10, 1963: "I am certain that our determination to provide EFTA with the possible economic potential—not only by abolishing customs tariffs but also by cooperating in a close and rational manner with the view to giving adequate consideration to the agricultural, industrial, technical, and financial problems on the solution of which the expansion of the member countries depends —will contribute both to the strengthening of EFTA and to the establishment of a single European market." *EFTA Reporter*, No. 72 (May 7, 1963).

Prime Minister urged that the problems of technological collaboration among EFTA countries should be explored.[15]

In the months following the return of the Labour government to office Britain faced immediate economic problems, including a balance of payments crisis, which outweighed the British interest in EFTA. At the time of Britain's last balance of payments crisis, the British government was preparing to announce its decision to apply for Common Market membership. This time, however, the government presented to Parliament a supplementary budget which included a temporary surcharge of 15 percent on imports of manufactured goods irrespective of their source. Because the British surcharge included imports from other EFTA countries, Britain was criticized for having set back the freeing of trade in western Europe. After a meeting on November 20, 1965, Britain's EFTA partners issued a statement expressing displeasure with the British trade restrictions as "inconsistent with the United Kingdom's obligation under the (EFTA) Convention and Association Agreement." [16]

The action of the Wilson cabinet was indicative of the weakness of the British economy as compared with the economies of the EEC and other EFTA countries, and gave evidence of Britain's inability to undertake the commitments and withstand the economic rigors that might be necessary if she were to join the Common Market. Moreover, British policy illustrated the apparent insensitivity of the new Labour government to the feelings of other Europeans on the issue of trade relationships in Europe. By imposing the surcharge without obtaining prior agreement, Britain, the largest and most important member of EFTA, had shattered the feeling of trust within EFTA and aroused latent suspicions in western Europe about the depth of the British commitment to European economic and political unity.

Whatever the effect of Britain's economic policies on the attitudes of her neighbors, the chronic economic problems facing Britain contributed to the strengthening of support within the parliamentary Labour party for Common Market membership. The economic crisis confirmed proponents of EEC entry in their conviction that Britain should apply again for membership and even increased their ranks. The Election of 1964, moreover, contributed to the change in attitude within the party. A large proportion of the Labour Members of Parliament

---

[15] *Ibid.*, May 31, 1965.
[16] *Sunday Times* (London), November 21, 1965.

who won seats in the elections of 1964 and 1966 were under the age of forty and were university educated and European in outlook. They represented a rising technocratic group in Britain, from which the Labour party had begun to draw substantial support. Like many others of their generation, background, and training, they did not view the Common Market with the suspicion and hostility often manifested by older Labour party members. Almost half of the sixty-six new Labour MP's elected in 1964 became members of the Labour Committee for Europe, whose objective was to promote support within the party for Common Market membership.[17]

At the same time the preconditions for EEC entry which Hugh Gaitskell, as leader of the party, had set forth in 1962 appeared to have less relevance in the light of changed circumstances. Especially after the return of Labour to office in 1964, there was a shift in Labour sentiment regarding the Commonwealth.[18] At the time of the Brussels negotiations, Labour spokesmen had stressed the importance of the Commonwealth as a link between developed and less developed nations. The multiracial Commonwealth, in whose creation postwar Labour governments had played a major part, was the object of great pride. In contrast, not a few Conservatives had become disenchanted with the Commonwealth, especially in the period preceding Macmillan's announcement of the British EEC application. With the admission of new members, for the most part from Africa and Asia, the Commonwealth, severely divided, no longer seemed to provide a major source of strength to Britain and no longer warranted being the primary object of British attention.

After 1964, Labour party attitudes toward the Commonwealth began to resemble those found in the Conservative party at the time of the first Common Market application. The Rhodesian question, including the unilateral declaration of independence by the government of Ian Smith in November 1965, and the India-Pakistan border conflict of

---

[17] "Edging towards Europe," *Socialist Commentary* (June 1966), p. 15. The Labour Committee for Europe was the successor to the Labour Common Market Committee, founded in 1961 by Labour "Europeans" to build support in their party for British EEC entry. The Labour Committee for Europe had as its president Sir Geoffrey de Freitas, who was also president of the Council of Europe. By 1967 it had among its membership ninety-seven Members of Parliament. See *Labour Left: Journal of the Labour Committee for Europe*, January 1967.

[18] See Sam Silkin, MP, "From Westminster to Europe," *Socialist Commentary*, September 1966, pp. 5–7; "Britain Faces Europe," *Socialist Commentary*, February 1967, pp. IV–X.

August–September 1965 were indicative of disintegrative tendencies in the Commonwealth. In both crises Britain was severely limited in her ability to furnish leadership and to effect a settlement. In protest against Britain's vacillation in meeting their demands for action against Rhodesia, some African Commonwealth governments severed diplomatic relations with London and even threatened to leave the Commonwealth. As a result, the idea of the Commonwealth as an alternative to Common Market membership seemed attractive to fewer Englishmen, even within the Labour party.

At the time of the Macmillan cabinet's application, proponents of EEC membership had pointed to the rapid increase in British trade with other West European countries, in contrast to the decline in trade with the Commonwealth as a percentage of total British commerce. As Table 1 illustrates, after the breakdown of the Brussels negotiations,

TABLE 1

UNITED KINGDOM EXPORTS AND IMPORTS
(Percentages)

	Exports			Imports		
	1961	1965	1966	1961	1965	1966
Commonwealth	35.5	28.4	25.9	35.5	29.8	27.6
EEC	16.7	19.1	19.0	15.4	17.8	18.5
EFTA	11.7	14.1	14.6	10.4	13.6	14.1
Other Europe (OEEC)	6.0	3.5	4.0	5.5	2.1	2.1
Total Western Europe	34.3	36.8	37.6	31.5	32.9	34.7

Source: Great Britain, Central Statistical Office, *Annual Abstract of Statistics* (London: Her Majesty's Stationary Office), Figures compiled from editions for 1961 and 1965. Monthly Digest of Statistics, No. 257, May 1967.

Britain's patterns of international trade continued to shift from the Commonwealth to western Europe. Although proponents of Common Market membership had argued that if Britain remained outside the EEC she might lose markets in the Six, trade trends after the collapse of the Brussels negotiations did not substantiate this claim. Even if trade with the Six did not rise as rapidly as would have been the case had Britain joined the Common Market, there was nevertheless a marked increase in commerce between Britain and the EEC. Still, the economic arguments which advocates of EEC entry had voiced at the time of the Brussels negotiations fell upon an increasingly receptive audience.

After 1963, many of the Commonwealth problems for which Britain had insisted on detailed solutions before entering the Common Market declined in importance. Not only did trade with Britain account for a diminishing percentage of their imports and exports, but Commonwealth countries began to make their own trading arrangements with the EEC.[19] Thus, the economic obstacles to Common Market membership posed by the Commonwealth became fewer in number.

At the time of the Brussels negotiations, Labour opposition was based to a considerable extent on dislike for the political implications of the European Community. Britain, it was feared, might join a European Community in which non-socialist governments held power in most member states. Gaitskell thought that a "federal" Europe would jeopardize the future of the Commonwealth.[20] After the breakdown of the Brussels negotiations, Labour opposition to the Common Market on these grounds declined. Between 1963 and 1967 the Six showed little political cohesiveness, and for the foreseeable future the prospects for the creation of a federal Europe appeared dim. In joining the Common Market, Britain would not become part of an integrative institution with clearly defined and generally accepted political objectives. Common Market membership would not place severe limitations on her independence of action in foreign policy.

Moreover, within the Labour party the idea, especially popular among the Labour left at the time of the Brussels negotiations, that the Common Market represented a right-wing, capitalist conspiracy designed to deprive Britain of her welfare state or to perpetuate East-West tensions, lost ground. More systematic study, as well as greater contact with Continental socialists, led party members to the realization that the economic and social welfare programs of Continental countries were not inferior to those of Britain. The efforts of France and other EEC countries to develop new links with eastern Europe lessened Labour fears that the EEC might serve to perpetuate East-West divisions. In the Labour party and elsewhere in Britain, there was a growing interest in the development of what was called a "wider Europe."[21] After the return of their party to office, several Labour M. P.'s formed the Wider Europe Group, which included people of

---

[19] In May 1966, Nigeria concluded an agreement for association with the Common Market. In 1967, the Six were engaged in negotiations for association with Kenya, Tanzania, and Uganda. See *Manchester Guardian Weekly*, May 12, 1966; *New York Times*, November 13, 1966, p. 16.

[20] For a discussion of Gaitskell's attitudes toward European political integration, see Chapter 4.

[21] See, for example, *One Europe, Is It Possible?* (London: BBC Publications, 1966).

various political orientations—right and left. Their objective was to study the implications of the Common Market for British domestic and foreign policy, the Commonwealth, and East-West issues.[22] The conclusion that Common Market membership was not necessarily incompatible with the building of a wider Europe contributed to the rise of support for EEC entry in the parliamentary Labour party.

At the time of the first British EEC application, Conservative party spokesmen had emphasized the potential economic gains, although some Conservatives, including Macmillan himself, had spoken of the benefits to be derived from British participation in European political integration. Subsequently, Sir Alec Douglas-Home, as Conservative party leader, had expressed support for Common Market entry because of potential political gains. In February 1965, Home had called upon Britain to join fully in the strengthening of European political, military, and economic integration, since the three must go together.[23] The selection of Edward Heath as party leader in July 1965 contributed to an increase in Conservative interest in Common Market membership and especially in European political integration. Heath's assumption of the party leadership, together with a widely-shared belief that few other options remained open, led the party once again to press for EEC entry. However, the Conservatives' statements no longer gave such great emphasis as the Macmillan government to the likely economic benefits. Instead, to a far greater degree than the Labour party, Conservatives stressed the potential political, technological, and military gains from Britsh participation in a larger European unit.

Younger members of the party, especially, began to advocate an integrated Europe, which would include Britain as a member, with a "European" foreign policy and even a European nuclear force. Only such a deterrent might enable Europe to regain control over its own defense and assure the future growth of European advanced technology. Britain's nuclear capability and technological achievements might provide powerful bargaining levers "to build for Europe a defense which will be viable whatever the future may bring." [24] Heath himself

---

[22] See Eric Heffer, "A Wider Europe," *Socialist Commentary*, (February 1967), pp. IX–XI.
[23] Conservative Research Department, *Conservative Election Manifesto and Statements by Leading Conservatives on the Common Market since January 1965*. (London: 1965).
[24] See, for example, the publication of the Monday Club entitled, *A Europe of Nations: A Practical Policy for Britain*. (London: Conservative Political Centre,

spoke of the need for "defense arrangements on a European scale, including Germany, with an Anglo-French arrangement in the nuclear field.[25]

Especially among the younger members after 1964, the Conservative party experienced a growth in "Gaullist" sentiment.[26] Whereas the older generation of Conservative leaders, including Churchill, Eden, and even Macmillan, had given priority to Britain's special relationship with the United States and to the preservation of links with the Commonwealth, the new generation of Conservatives saw their country's future as lying primarily with Europe. Britain should be freed of excessive reliance upon the United States. Only membership in a politically integrated western Europe would enable her to become less dependent on the United States militarily and politically, and in key sectors of advanced technology. An integrated western Europe might join eventually with the United States in the formation of an Atlantic Partnership. But such a Europe, by virtue of political, military, and economic integration, would possess greater strength, and hence bargaining power, and independence.

In some Conservative minds the question of Britain's technological future was closely related to British entry into the European Commu-

---

1965). According to this statement, prepared by the Cambridge University branch of the Monday Club, an organization of Young Conservatives: "With the U.S. herself vulnerable to nuclear annihilation Europe could not be sure that America would risk national suicide for her sake. The feeling has begun to grow that only a deterrent controlled from this continent will provide the ultimate guarantee against attack or nuclear blackmail. Even in Germany the feelings have been voiced that an Anglo-French guarantee might be more credible than America's because France and England are inevitably territorially involved in any attack on Germany." See also *Britain, Europe and the World*, (London: Conservative Political Centre, 1967), pp. 4–5; *Britain and Europe: Notes on Current Politics* (London: Conservative Research Department, 1967), pp. 18–19.

[25] Edward Heath, "West European Integration and East-West Relations," in "Western Europe and Eastern Europe: The Changing Relationship," *Adelphi Papers* (London: Institute for Strategic Studies, No. 33 March 1967), pp. 34–35. For a similar proposal, see Lord Gladwyn, *The European Idea*, 77–78; 103–107. At the time he wrote this book, Lord Gladwyn was Chairman of the European organization, Britain in Europe; Edward Beddington-Behrens, *Is There Any Choice? Britain Must Join Europe*, 103–106. At this time Beddington-Behrens was Chairman of the British Council of the European Movement (formerly The United Kingdom Council of the European Movement).

[26] The term "Gaullist" is used here to mean sentiment favoring the development of a Europe less dependent, especially militarily and technologically, upon the United States than is presently the case. It connotes also a willingness to give greater emphasis to relationships, including economic, military, and political integration, with other West European peoples than to the United States.

nity.[27] Britain could contribute to the building of a European technological base in some respects similar to that of the United States or the
Soviet Union. If advanced technologies could be developed on the U.S.
scale, Europe might build a more credible military capability. But
Britain, according to some Conservatives, should insist on Common
Market membership before agreeing to collaboration between her
technologically advanced industries and those of other West European
countries. By collaborating technologically with other European countries without first achieving EEC entry, she would give away one of
her greatest remaining bargaining advantages.[28]

At the time of the Brussels negotiations the Macmillan government
had committed Britain in principle to the EEC farm policy. However,
Britain and the Six were unable to reach accord on the timetable for
adoption of the EEC system, since Britain sought a longer transitional
period than the Six were willing to grant. After the selection of Heath
as party leader, the Conservatives committed themselves, if returned to
office, to basic changes in Britain's system of agricultural subsidization
and in social services in order to reduce differences between the British
and Continental systems.[29] By taking such action Britain might reduce

---

[27] Regarding Conservative views of the relationship between European technology
and integration see, for example, *Action, Not Words: The New Conservative
Program* (London: Conservative and Unionist Central Office, 1966). Britain must
be part of a wider grouping if she is to exert her full influence in the world.
British industry must have far bigger markets if it is to develop on the scale
required in so many cases by modern technology. "*A Europe of Nations: A
Practical Policy for Britain* (London: Conservative Political Centre, 1965), p. 17;
Ben Patterson, *Britain and Europe* (London: Conservative Central Office, 1967), p.
7, 13; *Britain's Place in Europe* (London: Conservative Political Centre, 1967), pp.
6–7; Sir Anthony Meyer, *A European Technological Community* (London:
Conservative Political Centre, 1966).

[28] See, for example, the April 1965 speech by Duncan Sandys: "In the long run, it
is not satisfactory for us to put the resources of our most technologically
advanced industries into the European pool without having any say in the shaping
of Europe's overall economic policies. We do not want to be investors with
non-voting shares." *Observer* (London), April 11, 1965, p. 3. See also Conservative
Research Department, *Six Point Policy for Europe*. Summary of speech by Mr.
Duncan Sandys, Church House, Westminster, April 28, 1965.

[29] See National Union of Conservative and Unionist Associations, *83rd Annual
Conference* (Brighton, October 13 to 16, 1965), p. 26. See also *Putting Britain
Right Ahead: A Statement of Conservative Aims* (London: Conservative and
Unionist Central Office), 1965; *Action, Not Words: The New Conservative
Program* (London: Conservative and Unionist Central Office, 1966), p. 10. In this
statement, the Conservatives indicated that in addition to making changes in social
and agricultural policy, they would prepare for EEC entry "by relating the
development of our new policies to those of the Common Market, wherever
appropriate."

the obstacles in advance of Common Market membership, and provide evidence of her European orientation.

In both political parties interest in the European Community rose as British interest in extra-European commitments, especially east of Suez, waned. In the Defense White Paper of 1966 the British announced that they would "not undertake major operations of war except in cooperation with allies." [30] Nor would Britain "accept an obligation to provide another country with military assistance unless it is prepared to provide Britain with the facilities British forces needed to make such assistance effective in time." Britain would make no effort to maintain defense facilities in an independent country "against its wishes." Although not without opposition, the Wilson cabinet cut back drastically on the construction of naval craft which would be needed to retain an independent British role east of Suez.[31] Instead, Britain decided to purchase F-111 aircraft from the United States. Conceivably, such aircraft could be used for missions east of Suez, although they were designed primarily to lengthen the life of the British nuclear force and thus to safeguard Britain.[32] Not only was the assumption that Britain should aspire to a major role outside Europe challenged by members of both major parties, as well as the Liberal Party; in the press, it was suggested that successive British governments had striven to maintain expensive commitments especially in Asia; now in reduced circumstances, Britain should no longer act as though she were the leading "policeman of the world." [33] Withdrawal from commitments east of Suez would make it possible to conserve scarce foreign exchange, release resources needed for the modernization of the economy, and enable Britain to assume a position of leadership in an integrated Europe.[34]

This reassessment of Britain's international political position was accompanied by a reconsideration of economic commitments and, in particular, the future of sterling as a reserve currency. Although the

---

[30] *The Defense Review,* Statement on defense issued in London, February 22, 1966. Official text released by British Information Services, New York.

[31] This decision led Christopher Mayhew, Minister for the Navy, to resign in protest from the Wilson government. He declared that the Royal Navy must be provided with an aircraft carrier if Britain intended to retain a military presence east of Suez.

[32] In sweeping defense reductions in January 1968, Wilson announced that the British order for the F-111 would be cancelled.

[33] For a Liberal statement, see Stephen Holt, *New Steps to Europe* (London: Liberal Publications Department for the New Orbits Group, 1967), pp. 11–12.

[34] See, for example, *Observer* (London), August 1, 1965; *Economist,* Vol. CCXIV, No. 6340 February 27, 1965, pp. 862–863.

Wilson government still strove to preserve sterling as one of the world's two major reserve currencies, there was discussion about the extent to which such a role imposed an unacceptable economic burden upon Britain. None of the EEC countries bore such an economic burden, even though they had gold and dollar reserves far in excess of those available to Britain. Unless she strengthened her economic position, Britain would be compelled to abandon her role as banker for the sterling area. It was suggested, however, that Common Market membership might enable her to obtain backing for sterling from the Six with their very considerable gold and dollar reserves.[35]

The first Common Market application was preceded by the rise of support among elite groups. Just after the breakdown of the negotiations, interest in the Common Market declined, although those elites who had favored EEC entry retained a pro-European bias. Among proponents of European integration in the civil service, as well as in British industry, the press, and European groups, the view held sway that Britain was barred only temporarily, and should await another opportunity for joining the EEC.[36]

With the end of the Brussels negotiations, European groups in Britain curtailed their activities. Organizations such as the Labour Committee for Europe, formed from the Labour Common Market Committee after the Brussels negotiations, and the group called Britain in Europe, which Federal Union had spawned, undertook educational programs designed to increase public awareness of the European Community rather than devoting themselves, as they had during the negotiations, to the dissemination of propaganda on behalf of EEC entry. By the end of 1965, however, the leaders of European organizations had decided to shift back to a more activist role. As interest in Common Market entry revived, the major European organizations undertook to build support for another British EEC bid, especially among Members of Parliament and within the constituency political parties and the trade union movement.

---

[35] See, for example, Holt, op. cit., p. 10. "We can no longer afford to act as banker to the sterling area; some solution will have to be found, sooner or later, and the possibility of joining with our European partners in creating a new European reserve currency offers an excellent alternative." See also Britain, Europe and the World (London: Conservative Political Centre, 1967), p. 10.

[36] Prime Minister Macmillan's assessment was characteristic of this view: "While it would be absurd not to recognize with our heads that Britain's entry is not capable of early realization, we should strive to keep the vision in our hearts." Great Britain, Parliamentary Debates (Commons), Vol. 671 (February 11, 1963), col. 961.

For the most part, the activists in these organizations, as had been the case several years earlier, were people under the age of forty with university educations. In educational background, they did not differ, by and large, from members elected to Parliament in 1964 and 1965, especially in the Labour party. In fact, many of those active in European organizations were either Members of Parliament or holders of nonelective positions in political parties. They had varying conceptions of the kind of political integration Europe should achieve. However, there was among them a general consensus that, over the long run, western Europe would evolve a form of political integration especially suited to its needs, but differing profoundly from that of the United States or other extant political systems. Indicative of the growth of British interest in European political integration was the formation of a new European organization, the Campaign for European Political Unity, founded in July 1966, in support of which 150 Members of Parliament from all parties, signed a declaration for European political unity.[37] This organization represented the first effort to form an interest group whose primary objective avowedly was the building of support for British membership in a politically integrated Europe.

Even before the Macmillan government's announcement of the decision to apply for Common Market membership, substantial support had existed within British industry for such a step, and industrialists did not lose interest in the expansion of trade with western Europe when the negotiations failed. Instead, they made plans to establish subsidiaries on the Continent in order to avoid tariff discrimination against imports from outside the European Community. The continued growth of British exports to the Six after the breakdown of the negotiations confirmed those in technologically advanced industries, especially, in the belief that eventually Britain must join the Common Market. Although support for EEC entry was most pronounced among the larger and more competitive sectors of British industry it became

---

[37] The Declaration contained the following statement: "It should indeed be made crystal clear that the Community which Britain would wish to join is one in which economic decisions in carefully defined areas are taken by a Council of Ministers by qualified majority voting on the proposals of an independent Commission, similar techniques being gradually adopted in the political sphere as well. Britain's long and unbroken parliamentary and legal tradition would also contribute to the system of democratic control, supported by a strengthened European Parliament and upheld by the European Court. Finally, Britain should make it clear that each step towards the creation of an economic and political community must be guided by the paramount need to create a united western Europe within the framework of the Atlantic Alliance."

fashionable among industrialists in general to favor Common Market membership. To oppose such a course of action was often tantamount to an admission of industrial inefficiency. This rise of interest in EEC entry may be attributed at least in part to a growing concern about the eventual competitive position of British exports as the EEC progressed toward the completion of the customs union. In 1966, the Confederation of British Industry embarked upon a major study of the implications of entry for various sectors of British industry.[38] This study assessed the implications of EEC entry for costs, markets, competition, and the availability of labor and financial resources in Britain. The results of the study, published in December 1966 and January 1967, given the mood of leading British industrialists, were not unexpected. The report urged Britain's EEC entry as soon as possible.[39]

In the months before and after the Election of 1966, the Wilson government was engaged in a review of its policy toward EEC entry. Although the Common Market was not a major issue in the election campaign, it did spark a debate between Conservative and Labour leaders. Heath accused the Labour government of being "unbelievably smug and complacent about the European situation" and maintained that the Labour party was divided down the middle on the question of Common Market membership. Heath's statements produced several responses from Labour leaders indicative of party differences on this issue. James Callaghan, Chancellor of the Exchequer, accused Heath of being prepared to join the Common Market without any safeguards

---

[38] The Confederation of British Industry (CBI) is the product of a merger in 1965 of the British Employer's Confederation, the Federation of British Industries, and the National Association of British Manufacturers. The chief spokesman for British industry, the CBI membership includes about 13,000 companies and more than 200 trade associations and employers' federations. Like the Trades Union Congress and the National Farmers Union, the CBI enjoys the right to consultation on a regular and continuing basis with the British government on issues of vital interest to its members. At the time of the Brussels negotiations and since, CBI officials have met with cabinet members and civil servants in the ministries concerned with problems of European integration.

[39] According to the CBI study: "(1) there would be a clear and progressive balance of advantage to British industry from membership of an enlarged European Economic Community, (2) the Treaty of Rome and the Community's method of operation are acceptable given reasonable transitional arrangements, and (3) entry should be negotiated as soon as possible." *Britain and Europe: An Industrial Appraisal* (London: Confederation of British Industry, December 1966), Vol. 1, p. 2. Another volume, *Britain and Europe: Supporting Papers*, Vol. 2, was published in January 1967. In the preface to the first volume, the CBI acknowledged the need for further study to assess the potential impact of Common Market entry upon specific sectors of British industry.

"for the position of the British housewife, farmer, Commonwealth, and EFTA." [40] Several other Labour candidates, including Barbara Castle and Douglas Jay, both of whom were noted for their anti-Common Market views, suggested that British entry would undermine the balance of payments, lessen the prospects for strengthening the economy, and render the British government powerless to engage in national economic planning.[41] The Liberal position was critical of both major parties. The leader of the Liberal party, Jo Grimond, described Wilson's attitude toward EEC membership as that of a "man of many faces in different places," while suggesting that in their Common Market policy the Conservatives were "once again ten years late." [42]

During the British election campaign, the Western European Union Council met in London, and on March 16, 1966 issued a vaguely worded statement urging Britain to join the Common Market. Both the French representative, M. de Broglie, and M. Jean Rey, the member of the EEC Commission in charge of external relations of the Community, suggested that the obstacles to British entry, although they still existed, had diminished in importance since the Brussels negotiations.[43] In particular, de Broglie declared, the problems set forth in 1962 in the Labour party's five conditions for Common Market entry were no longer so formidable. He noted that Commonwealth trading problems were of less importance than in 1962 and that a solution for the special case of New Zealand could be found. The interests of other EFTA countries could be accommodated if Britain joined the Common Market. Moreover, Britain, like France, could continue as an EEC member to plan her economy and maintain an independent foreign policy.

Coming as it did in the midst of the election campaign, this statement helped to revive the Common Market issue in domestic politics. In his campaign speech in Bristol, Wilson revealed that the statement had removed one of the major obstacles to another British application, namely, French opposition. He attributed the change in French attitude he perceived to policies his government had followed, especially in technological collaboration, such as the building of the Anglo-French supersonic airliner, the Concorde. Whereas the Conservatives had not been frank with the French at the time of the Nassau agreement, Labour had striven to remove de Gaulle's suspicion of British

---

[40] *Financial Times* (London), March 18, 1966.
[41] *Ibid.*, March 18, 21, 1966.
[42] *Ibid.*, March 18, 1966.
[43] *Ibid.*, March 19, 1966.

motives.[44] Although the Wilson government was "ready for contacts, for informal discussions through the proper channels, for any probings that might be necessary to assess the kind of terms on which Britain might join the Common Market," Labour, unlike the Conservatives, would not surrender unconditionally to the Six. Labour would insist on Britain's freedom "to go on buying food and raw materials as we have done for 100 years in the cheaper markets in Canada, Australia, New Zealand, and other Commonwealth countries, and not have this trade wrecked by the levies the Tories are so keen to impose." [45] Wilson accused the Conservatives of "rushing fences" in responding to the apparent modification of French opposition to another British bid implied in de Broglie's WEU speech.[46]

After the election of 1966, the granting of special responsibility to George Brown for co-ordination of British economic policy toward EFTA and the Common Market, and the designation of George Thomson as Minister of the Foreign Office responsible for Britain's political relations with western Europe were indicative of Wilson's growing interest in the European Community. The subsequent appointment of Brown as Foreign Secretary in August 1966, strengthened the European forces in the Cabinet.[47] With these appointments, the Wilson government made a series of probings designed to gain a greater understanding of the attitudes and the policies of the Six toward an-

---

[44] Wilson suggested: "In 1963, when the present Conservative leader was negotiating for entry, Britain suffered an intolerable humiliation by the curt French refusal to allow Britain to join, even on the unacceptable terms the Conservative government was ready, even willing, to be imposed upon it." According to Wilson, the French veto resulted from the unwillingness of the Conservatives to inform de Gaulle of their proposed defense policy. "They failed to tell him that following the breakdown of the disastrous Tory Skybolt policy, they were about to go to the U.S. for Polaris submarines. It was the Nassau Agreement that slammed the door of the Common Market in Britain's face." *Ibid*

[45] For a more detailed examination of Common Market membership as an issue in the British election of 1966, see D. E. Butler and Anthony King, *The British Election of 1966.* Especially pp. 110–114; 160–162; 165–169.

[46] To the obvious delight of his listeners, Wilson declared: "Now, one encouraging gesture from the French government and the Conservative leader rolls on his back like a spaniel." *Financial Times* (London), March 19, 1966.

[47] Shortly after his appointment as Foreign Secretary, Brown declared: "I have a tremendous sense of the importance of the Commonwealth and the importance of maintaining it. On the other hand, I am absolutely persuaded, *as the government as a whole is*, that we can be of greater use to the world, and to the Commonwealth, if we are among the leaders of the European Community of which we are historically a member." *Observer,* (London), August 14, 1966, p. 3. Emphasis added.

other Common Market application. As a result of these studies, on November 10, 1966 Wilson announced to the Commons that "in the light of this review the government has decided that a new high-level approach must now be made to see whether the conditions exist—or do not exist—for fruitful negotiations, and the basis on which such negotiations should take place." [48]

In public statements at the end of 1966, Wilson adopted much of the substance as well as the terminology of the British Europeans, and thus took from the Conservatives one of their major issues. On November 14, he called for the creation of a European technological community to pool scientific and technological capabilities in order to reduce dependence on outside powers. "I can think of nothing," he declared, "that would make a greater reality of the whole European concept. And in this field of technological cooperation no one has more to contribute." According to government spokesmen, European technological collaboration was closely related to the question of British entry into the Common Market.[49]

After Wilson's apparent conversion to Common Market membership, the theme of U.S. hegemony had come to occupy a place of considerable prominence in his statements. He argued that unless western Europe formed a unit which included Britain and the Common Market Six, Europeans would be hard pressed to meet American technological competition. Only greater unity could prevent western Europe from falling under the technological and economic hegemony of the United States. The effort to reconcile Britain's long-standing friendship with the United States with her new found interest in European integration was apparent when Wilson declared in his address to the Council of Europe Consultative Assembly, on January 23, 1967:

> Let no one here doubt Britain's loyalty to NATO and the Atlantic Alliance. But I have always said that that loyalty must never mean subservience. Still less must it mean an industrial helotry under which we in Europe produce only the conventional apparatus of a modern economy, while becoming dependent on American busi-

---

[48] He declared that the government had held a "deep and searching review" of Britain's relations with the EEC. "Every aspect of the Rome Treaty itself, decisions taken subsequent to its signature, and all the implications and consequences which might be expected to flow from EEC entry, have been examined in depth." Great Britain, *Parliamentary Debates* (Commons), Vol. 735 (November 10, 1966), cols. 1539–1540.

[49] *British Record*. Supplement to No. 18, November 30, 1966.

ness for the sophisticated apparatus which will call the industrial tune in the seventies and eighties.[50]

After this speech in Strasbourg, Wilson went to Paris, where he set forth British policy and sounded out the French on another EEC application. In contrast to the period preceding the first application, when British officials visited the capitals of Commonwealth countries, the chief emphasis this time was on the likely response of EEC countries to another British bid. During the early months of 1967, Wilson and Brown visited the capital of each EEC country for consultations. In four of the Common Market members, they found strong support. In Paris, perhaps because of the French parliamentary elections scheduled to be held in March, de Gaulle was not prepared to state categorically his opposition to another application. Nevertheless, the French expressed concern about British economic problems, and in particular the position of sterling as a reserve currency.[51] Apparently, the British attempted to convince the French that Britain's economy had been strengthened, and that the Wilson government would not resort to devaluation in order to conserve the British competitive position. Moreover, over, the British were intent on converting the French to the idea that sterling should retain a role as an international reserve currency.[52] Although the talks failed to produce agreement, Wilson expressed the view that the French had been "extremely friendly and cordial." [53]

The German economic interest clearly lay in British Common Market membership. Yet Wilson found the German government reluctant to press Britain's case at the risk of jeopardizing the special relationship with France which the Kiesinger government had striven to restore.[54]

---

[50] *Ibid.*, January 24, 1967.

[51] See *Le Monde* (Paris), January 26, 27, 1967.

[52] See *Manchester Guardian Weekly*, January 26, 1967, p. 2.

[53] After returning to London, Wilson described his Paris talks: "No relevant question was overlooked or made light of. Our hosts were impressed by our depth of purpose in everything we said and our desire to join the EEC. We did not ask the French government to answer yes or no, or to put any particular questions to it. This is one of six visits and it was always understood that when our talks were over, the six governments would wish to consult together before taking a final decision." *European Community* (London), February 1967, p. 15.

[54] See the *Times* (London), February 14, 1967. Reportedly, Chancellor Kiesinger received French agreement to support German policies of "developing new political and economic links with communist countries, in eastern Europe, in return for Bonn's acquiescence in French policy on Britain's admission to the Common Market. See the *Observer* (London), February 19, 26, 1967.

The discussions in Bonn were marred by the German reaction to a British statement about Germany's eastern frontier.[55] For another reason, however, the Germans had reservations about British EEC entry. With her accession to the Rome Treaty, Britain might replace Germany as the principal French ally in western Europe. Collaboration in the development of advanced technology, the possibility of creating an Anglo-French nuclear force, and the prospects of agreement on major political issues might lead to a new Franco-British entente, isolating Germany.

The visits to the Common Market capitals completed, Wilson and his cabinet evaluated their findings. Despite the obstacles encountered in Bonn and Paris, the Common Market policy was pressed. After a series of meetings of cabinet members during the last week of April 1967, Wilson announced in the Commons on May 2 that Britain had "decided to make an application under Article 237 of the Treaty of Rome for membership of the European Economic Community and parallel applications for membership of the European Coal and Steel Community, and Euratom." [56]

Studies undertaken in the British government in the spring and summer of 1966 to determine the feasibility and ascertain the cost of Common Market membership, the appointment of Brown as Foreign Secretary, and Wilson's own statements all provide evidence of the gradual shift in his position from of one of non-commitment and even skepticism to support for membership. Certainly by the end of 1966, however, he had become convinced that British entry into the Common Market would contribute to an expansion in both industrial production and investment and thus benefit the British economy. Al-

---

[55] In response to a question put to him just before leaving London for his visit to Bonn, as to whether British policy on German reunification had changed to include recognition of the Oder-Neisse line as the eastern frontier of a reunified Germany, Brown replied: "Yes, in a way." This incident, which received wide coverage in the German press, dampened the atmosphere in which the talks on British Common Market relations were held. See, for example, *Washington Post*, February 15, 1967; *Times* (London), February 16, 1967.

[56] According to Wilson, the British government chose this moment for the application because "our discussions in the capitals of the Six have confirmed the validity of this approach in terms of the practical working of the Community and its institutions." Great Britain, *Parliamentary Debates* (Commons), Vol. 746. (May 2, 1967), col. 310. Undoubtedly, the successful completion of the Kennedy Round negotiations just a few days earlier influenced Wilson's timing of his Common Market announcement. Wilson had not wanted to reopen the Common Market issue at a time when the EEC, Britain, and the United States had reached a critical stage in the trade negotiations.

though in his estimation it was impossible to express in quantifiable terms the impact of EEC entry on the British economy, he believed that the European Community would provide a stimulus to businessmen to expand production, sales, and plant capacity. Common Market membership would make it possible for Britain to exploit whatever advantages she presently possessed in advanced technology. In the absence of a European Community which included Britain, there would be little prospect even of maintaining her existing technological position.

According to Wilson's statements, the political arguments on behalf of membership, however important the economic rationale, were decisive. Politically united, Europe could play a role in international affairs which was no longer open to the individual nation-state of western Europe. The issue was "whether it is going to be possible to build up Europe, as I think most Europeans understand it, with as a major objective the breaking down of tension between East and West." As to the specific institutional form European unity might assume, Wilson saw little prospect for the development, in the foreseeable future, of a federal Europe.[57] Thus, he was convinced that the development of political integration on the basis of the existing nation-states was more in keeping with Europe's mood. To this extent, his conception resembled de Gaulle's ideas about European political unification, as well as those of his Conservative predecessors.

The detailed studies undertaken within the British government had led Wilson to the conclusion that the obstacles to Common Market membership were no longer so formidable as they had seemed in 1962. According to Wilson, the essential British interests included: (1) the operation of the EEC agricultural policy, including its potential effect on the cost of living, the structure of British agriculture and the balance of payments; and (2) Commonwealth trade, including the future of New Zealand's trade and that of the sugar-producing Commonwealth countries.

Much of British farming, it was acknowledged, was competitive

---

[57] He declared: "I still believe that for the immediately foreseeable future this country would not—any more than would most of the Community countries—contemplate a rapid move to a federal Europe. But it is also right to say—as the Foreign Secretary and I have said in Europe—that in all these matters we are prepared to accept the same obligations as our prospective Common Market colleagues—no more, no less." Address by Prime Minister Wilson to the parliamentary Labour party, House of Commons, April 27, 1967. Reprinted in *European Community* (London), May 1967, p. 16.

with that of the Six. If Britain joined the Common Market, some British farmers, especially producers of cereals, might even benefit because of their greater efficiency in comparison with Continental counterparts. However, certain producers of beef cattle and much of Britain's horticultural farming might face severe adjustments, since subsidies accorded under the British system would no longer be available in an enlarged European Community.

The agricultural problems Britain faced were related not so much to the future of British farming as to the potential implications for other sectors of the economy of the change from Britain's farming policy to that of the EEC. It was generally acknowledged that food prices—for dairy products, for example—would rise. In the official British view, after joining the Common Market Britain might be compelled to pay about $600 million per year in foreign exchange for agricultural imports, while retail prices for food could increase between 10 and 14 percent.[58] Such increases might be offset by reductions in the prices of certain other products, including imported consumer goods, and by lowering of taxes after the existing system of subsidy payments had ended. If living costs and outlays of foreign exchange for agricultural imports rose, Britain might face a balance of payments crisis shortly after joining, unless steps were taken in advance to avert such a contingency. Moreover, people with fixed incomes, such as old age pensioners—a group of sizeable proportions in Britain—might face some hardship, since food costs would consume a larger proportion of their budget than previously. Because Britain would be expected to import more foodstuffs from the EEC and less from other Commonwealth countries, EEC entry might precipitate a further decline in Commonwealth trade. In turn, sterling area members might withdraw deposits of funds from London. As a result, the position of sterling as a reserve currency might be weakened, with important consequences for the international monetary system.

For Britain, the financing of the EEC agricultural policy remained a problem of considerable importance. It was feared that the payment of funds from levies on agricultural imports to the European Community would impose a major burden on her balance of payments, and might

---

[58] Great Britain, *The Common Agricultural Policy of the European Economic Community* (London: HMSO, May 1967), Cmnd. 3274, p. 19. See also *New York Times*, November 11, 1966, p. 1. For a similar estimate of the likely effect of EEC membership on British food prices, see Confederation of British Industry, *op. cit.*, Vol. 1, p. 15.

increase the annual payments deficit by as much as £250 million after she had joined the EEC.[59] Of course, this figure might be offset by increases in British exports. Yet it was not possible to gauge the immediate effect of EEC entry on earnings from exports.

Despite the agricultural problems, by 1966 the National Farmers Union (NFU) had modified the position which it held during the Brussels negotiations. It was now prepared to accept the EEC system of agricultural subsidization so long as the interests of British farming were safeguarded to the same extent as those of the Common Market Six. The EEC levy system would not be especially objectionable to the NFU, provided Britain could obtain from the EEC an annual review for agriculture comparable to that which British agriculture enjoyed under Britain's farming legislation.[60]

After 1963, the problems which had preoccupied the negotiators in Brussels declined in importance. The major remaining Commonwealth trading problem was that of New Zealand which, of the Commonwealth countries, was most heavily dependent for her national liveli-

---

[59] According to the British White Paper: "The application of the EEC's agricultural arrangements and financial regulations as they stand would impose an additional charge on the United Kingdom's balance of payments. This would arise in two ways. First, we would be paying full Community prices for imports of food from other members of the Community. Secondly, on the basis of the financial arrangements agreed for the present Community for 1967–1969, we would be a very substantial net contributor to the European Agricultural Guidance and Guarantee Fund." *The Common Agricultural Policy of the European Economic Community, op. cit.,* p. 20.

[60] Under the Agriculture Act of 1947, the NFU presents to the British government each year a detailed study of farming incomes, prices of commodities, and other relevant data on British agriculture. After detailed bargaining, the government and the NFU reach agreement upon the level of subsidization to be given to British farmers. If Britain joined the Common Market, the NFU would favor an annual review to determine the level of levies and pricing of agricultural commodities in the European Community. In a speech on July 26, 1966, Asher Winegarten, Chief Economist of the NFU, declared: "Production patterns would, of course, be affected if the United Kingdom were to become a member of an enlarged European community. Problems would arise from the fact that the present Common Market agricultural policy differs substantially in some respects from our own. These problems would need to be met and resolved before entry. We believe that there are certain features of our system, such as the Annual Review concept and firm price assurances which could well be embodied in an agricultural policy for an enlarged Community. Agriculture will prove a major obstacle to our becoming a member of the EEC only if the Six fail to recognize that we are entitled to seek to safeguard our basic interests as they were to protect their interests when negotiating the Rome Treaty and the subsequent agricultural regulations under the Treaty." Asher Winegarten, *British Agriculture: The Way Ahead,* mimeographed release. (London: National Farmers' Union, 1966).

hood on trade with Britain. Hence the British government felt obliged to assure that New Zealand, and to a lesser extent Canada and Australia, would gain access to alternative markets should they be deprived of existing outlets in Britain for their exports.

The Macmillan cabinet's pledge that Britain would not enter the EEC until satisfactory arrangements could be made for other EFTA members was less important after 1963. British officials no longer held that British entry into the Common Market was contingent upon the achievement of satisfactory arrangements for other EFTA members.[61] At their Ministerial Meeting in May 1966, EFTA members modified their commitment not to work out arrangements separately with the Common Market. Instead, they agreed simply to "keep each other fully informed of their individual efforts and remain in close consultation at all stages." [62] It was acknowledged that even if Britain did not join, other EFTA countries would make their own arrangements with the Six. For example, in 1965 Austria began discussions for association with the EEC. Denmark also expressed an interest in association or membership.

Although Wilson enjoyed greater support for his Common Market bid than had the Macmillan government, he still faced the active opposition of a vociferous minority within the parliamentary Labour party as well as his own cabinet. Opposition remained especially strong among the Labour left in the Commons. Indicative of backbench opposition were the motions anti-Common Market Labour MP's signed in the early months of 1967. In February, an anti-Common Market motion, so worded to attract broad support, received the signatures of more than half the parliamentary Labour party outside the Wilson

---

[61] In a speech to the WEU Assembly on June 13, 1966, George Thomson declared: "Since 1962, neither Britain nor the Community have stood still. Some of the conditions then formulated no longer appear in the same light as difficult problems for negotiations. For example, the position of the EFTA neutrals is a much less formidable problem now than it seemed in 1962. Again, the Commonwealth problem seems likely to present fewer difficulties, since it is clear that the Community is willing to discuss association arrangements for those Commonwealth countries in Africa that wish to have them. However, Canada, Australia, and New Zealand—80 percent of whose exports to the United Kingdom are foodstuffs—still present serious problems." Western European Assembly, *Twelfth Ordinary Session* (First Part) Official Report, June 13, 1966. Document A-WEU (12) GR 1. According to Thomson, another British approach to the EEC "must be in consultation with our EFTA partners." Quoted in *Manchester Guardian Weekly*, April 28, 1966.

[62] Communiqué issued at the end of the EFTA Ministerial Meeting, Bergen, Norway, May 13, 1966. *EFTA Reporter*, May 23, 1966.

government.[63] Moreover, just before Wilson's May 8, 1967 announcement of the second Common Market application, a group of thirty-seven MP's of the Labour left tabled an amendment to the government's motion approving a decision to seek membership in the European Community.[64] Finally, seventy-four Labour MP's had signed an anti-Common Market manifesto published in the left-wing newspaper, *Tribune*, on May 4, 1967.

Membership in the Labour Committee for Europe provides one indication of ministerial opinion on Common Market membership. Of a total of fifty-four ministers, only nineteen held membership in the Labour Committee for Europe.[65] Nevertheless, in addition to backbench opposition, two members of the Wilson Cabinet in particular—Fred Peart, Minister of Agriculture, and Douglas Jay, President of the Board of Trade—remained opponents of EEC entry. In fact, on February 15, 1967, while Wilson and Brown were in Bonn for discussions on Common Market membership, Jay had addressed a group of Labour party backbenchers. He maintained that Britain, if she signed the Rome Treaty as it stood, would face a series of economic crises. Acceptance of the EEC agricultural policy would place great strain on the balance of payments; the freeing of capital movement would result in a net loss for Britain; increases in the cost of living, particularly food prices, and higher wages would raise the cost of exports and make

---

[63] The motion read: "This House takes note of the exploratory nature of the visits to West European capitals by the Prime Minister and Foreign Secretary; regrets the activities of those who have seized this occasion to intensify their demand that Her Majesty's government should apply unconditionally for entry into the EEC; deplores, in particular, the speeches in which the leader of the Opposition has invited Her Majesty's government to break its pledged word to the electorate and to other peoples of the Commonwealth; and declares that Britain, in consultation with her EFTA partners, should be ready to enter the EEC only if essential British and Commonwealth interests can be safeguarded." *Times* (London), February 23, 1967, p. 12.

[64] This faction had as its chief supporters Emmanuel Shinwell, Michael Foot, and Ian Mikardo. Until the spring of 1967 Shinwell had been chairman of the parliamentary Labour party. Mikardo was a member of the party's National Executive Committee. Their motion read as follows: "This House refuses to give its approval to Command Paper No. 3269 [setting out the government's decision to apply for Common Market membership] because it fails to affirm in explicit terms Her Majesty's government's adherence to the conditions laid down by the Labour party and reaffirmed in Labour's election manifesto, on which the United Kingdom should decide whether to apply to enter the European Economic Community." *Ibid.*, May 9, 1967.

[65] See *Labour Left*, January, February 1967. Ninety-six Labour MP's and Labour Peers were listed as members of the Labour Committee for Europe. *Times* (London), January 24, 1967; February 23, 1967.

British goods less competitive.[66] Opposition within the Labour party to Wilson's Common Market policy, his support for the United States in Vietnam, the prices-incomes policy, and cuts in defense spending, led the Prime Minister, in early 1967, to admonish his ministerial colleagues and to threaten punishment of recalcitrant backbenchers.[67]

Although by 1967 the Conservative party was far more united than had been the case in 1961, there remained a small anti-Common Market faction led by Sir Derek Walker-Smith and Robin Turton. Just before Wilson's announcement of May 8, a Conservative anti-Common Market amendment to the government's motion calling for another EEC application attracted the signatures of twenty-two dissident Tories.[68] The arguments of Walker-Smith and his followers had not changed greatly, but their base of support within the parliamentary party had dwindled from about eighty Conservative backbenchers at the time of the Brussels negotiations.

The voting that followed the Commons debate of May 8–10 furnished further evidence of the broadened parliamentary consensus on Common Market membership. The Wilson cabinet's decision received 426 votes, with 62 votes against entry and more than 60 abstentions. Of those voting against the government, 36 came from the Labour side, with 51 Labour MP's abstaining. Among the Labour votes against entry were those of seven parliamentary private secretaries, whom Wilson ordered dismissed from their jobs.

---

[66] *Ibid.*, February 16, 1967.

[67] In response to Jay, Wilson repeated what he termed "two long-standing principles governing ministerial conduct. The first is that Ministers must so order their affairs that no conflict arises, or appears to rise, between their private interests and their public duties. The second is that Ministers speaking on public occasions on matters of political controversy expound the views of the government as a whole. I do not think that any further instructions are needed." For dissident backbenchers he reportedly had a harsher message: "All I say is 'watch it.' Every dog is allowed one bite, but a different view is taken of a dog that goes on biting all the time. If there are doubts that the dog is biting not because of the dictates of conscience but because he is considered vicious, then things happen to that dog. He may not get his license renewed when it falls due." *Ibid.*, February 21; March 3, 1967.

[68] Their Amendment read as follows: "This government regrets that Her Majesty's government, having failed to inform the country of the estimated results of Britain's entry into the EEC, have nevertheless declared their intention of applying for entry, leaving substantial matters to be negotiated thereafter, and thereby causing anxiety to our partners in the Commonwealth and EFTA and creating the probability of injurious repercussions on British sovereignty and the rule of law, on the price of food, on the balance of payments and on the role of sterling in the world." *Ibid.*, May 5, 1967.

Especially in the period between 1964 and 1966, public support for Common Market membership had increased. In the months after the Wilson government embraced the European cause, however, opinion appeared to have become divided once again, as at the time of the Brussels negotiations.[69] According to opinion polls, the decline in support was sharpest among Conservative voters. Seizure of the Common Market issue by Labour may have alienated Conservative voters, even though the Conservative parliamentary party remained more solidly in support of Wilson's Common Market bid than did the parliamentary Labour party.

As in the period following the July 1961 announcement by Prime Minister Macmillan after the Wilson cabinet undertook its Common Market initiative, there was a polarization of opinion. Organizations in favor of entry increased their activities.[70] At the same time organizations opposed to the Common Market bid, such as the Anti-Common Market League and the Keep Britain Out Campaign, reconstituted themselves and began to disseminate propaganda in support of their cause. Conceivably, the activities of such organizations, together with a greater understanding of the potential cost of Common Market membership, contributed to a growth of domestic opposition. As in the period 1961–63, Englishmen, although often prepared in principle to join the European Community, had second thoughts when they faced the need to reconcile the cost of membership with other interests and commitments.

The case against membership had essentially the same points put forward in the 1961–1963 period: that British sovereignty would be impaired; that Commonwealth and EFTA trade would suffer; that food prices to the British consumer would increase; that a rapproche-

---

[69] According to polls conducted by National Opinion Polls Ltd., there was a sharp decline in popular support for Common Market membership between July 1966 and May, 1967. In July 1967, when asked, "Do you think Britain should now try to enter the Common Market or not?" 62 percent of the electorate favored such an attempt, 18 percent were opposed, and 20 percent registered "don't know." By April 1967, however, public support for the British government's Common Market policy had declined dramatically. In response to the question "Do you approve or disapprove of the government's decision to try and join the Common Market?" 37 percent expressed approval, 41 percent were opposed, and 22 percent responded "don't know." This compares with surveys conducted by the same organization in October 1961 and September 1962, when respectively 45.9 and 40.8 percent favored Common Market membership. National Opinion Polls *Political Bulletin*, November 1961, October 1962, July 1966, November 1966, January 1967, May 1967.
[70] See, for example (London), February 23, 1967.

ment between communist and non-communist states would be rendered more difficult. But greater stress was now placed on the adverse impact of entry on the British balance of payments. It was recognized that both France and Germany had begun to establish new relationships, or to re-establish old ones, with East European countries. Whereas between 1961 and 1963 the "rigid" foreign policies of France and the Federal Republic, for example, on the Berlin issue, were deemed antithetical to closer ties with East European countries, especially by the Labour left, by 1967 the EEC itself came to be viewed as a barrier. By the end of the third stage of its transitional period, the European Community would have a common commercial policy and external tariff which would not be any more conducive to trade agreements with East European countries than with Commonwealth countries. According to William Pickles, who remained one of the most articulate opponents of Common Market membership, de Gaulle's alleged dislike for the Common Market was "not based solely on his contempt for supranational institutions—which is unbounded—nor only on his hostility to the pro-Americanism of his EEC allies. It is due in part to his mistrust of the EEC as an obstacle to a possible East-West détente." [71]

As at the time of the first British application, de Gaulle's critique of Britain's qualifications resembled to a considerable extent the misgivings about EEC entry voiced by Englishmen themselves. Although French officials insisted that there had not been, nor would there be, a political veto of the British application,[72] the primary concern was that before joining the Common Market Britain must solve her major economic problems, including domestic inflation and balance of payments deficits, and must remove restrictions on the international flow

---

[71] William Pickles, *Britain and Europe: How Much Has Changed?* (Oxford: Basil Blackwell, 1967), p. 91. Restating the position which he held in 1961–63, Pickles wrote: "The important thing, surely, is that Britain should not at this stage of history be committed to a structure like the Treaty of Rome, still stiff with rigidities in spite of changes; still having as its only certainty for us the enormous political and economic price we should have to pay to get in; still (quoting Nora Beloff of *The Observer*) 'always on the brink of rupture . . . a strange coupling of commercial horse trading with ideological self-righteousness,' still run by and for peoples brought up in the tradition of written constitutions and multi-party systems, with all the consequences those things have on modes of thought and behavior and still, therefore—again in Miss Beloff's words—'so difficult for the British onlooker to grasp.' " *Ibid.*, p. 118.

[72] See, for example, de Gaulle's press conference of May 16, 1967. Ambassade de France, *Speeches and Press Conferences*, No. 26 OA (May 16, 1967), p. 8.

of capital. The position of sterling as a reserve currency posed problems. According to de Gaulle, British entry into the Common Market was not compatible "with the state of the pound sterling as it has once again been brought to light by the devaluation [of November 1967]."[73] By placing immediate economic strains on Britain, Common Market membership might jeopardize the position of sterling as a reserve currency. Although the Six had the resources to underwrite the reserve position of sterling, the French opposed the assumption of such a burden either by France or the European Community.[74]

Aside from the future of sterling as a reserve currency, the French economic objections to British Common Market membership remained essentially unchanged. In his press conferences of May 16, and November 27, 1967, de Gaulle based his case on arguments similar to those voiced in his press conference of January 14, 1963, except that he gave greater emphasis to Britain's economic problems. He was not yet convinced that Britain could accept the EEC agricultural policy without "exceptional and prolonged delays" and "upsetting the equilibrium of the Common Market." Even if Britain were to "submit to the rules of the Six, then her balance of payments will be crushed by levies and, on the other hand, she would be forced to raise the price of her food to the price level adopted by the Continental countries, consequently to increase the wages of her workers and, thereby, to sell her goods all the more at a higher price and with more difficulty." For British officials this was an economic problem to which Britain and the Six must find a solution. To de Gaulle, the burden was upon Britain, before joining the Common Market, to solve this and other major economic problems, even though France had taken major steps toward economic reform after, not before, joining the European Community.

---

[73] De Gaulle added: "In fact, parity and monetary solidarity are essential rules, essential conditions of the Common Market. They cannot be extended to our neighbors across the Channel unless some day the pound sterling appears in a completely new position so that its future value appears assured, it is freed from its character as a reserve currency, and the mortgage of Britain's sterling balance within the sterling area disappears." *Ibid.*

[74] According to Article 108 of the Rome Treaty, any member of the EEC can call upon other signatories of the treaty for cooperative action in case of currency problems. France and other EEC members have expressed concern that they might be asked to provide major assistance to Britain because of the weakness of pound sterling. During his visit to Luxembourg on March 8, Wilson announced that Britain, as a member of the Common Market, would not request aid from other EEC countries in the event she faced a new sterling crisis arising from some external problem. Great Britain, *Parliamentary Debates* (Commons), Vol. 742 (March 9, 1967), cols. 1754–1761, *New York Times*, March 10, 1967, p. 13.

In addition to economic changes, Gaullist criteria for British Common Market membership included the development of a European outlook on issues of major international importance. According to de Gaulle: "The idea, the hope which, from the beginning, led the Six Continental countries to unite tended without any doubt toward the formation of a unit which would be European in all respects, and because of this would become capable not only of carrying its own weight in production and trade but also of acting one day politically by itself and for itself toward anyone." In his estimation, Britain did not yet place primary emphasis on European interests,[75] since the British retained a special relationship with the United States, as well as special commitments in various parts of the world, which "distinguishes them from the continentals."

Undoubtedly, British opposition to the EEC policy at the time of the Kennedy Round trade negotiations in Geneva, the continued British presence east of Suez, London's support for U.S. policy in Vietnam, the eagerness of the British government for a nonproliferation treaty, and the similarity between British and U.S. policies, in contrast to French policy, during the 1967 Arab-Israeli conflict, did not enhance Britain's prospect for fulfilling Gaullist European criteria. In the case of the Nonproliferation Treaty, Britain faced once again a choice between Europe and her other interests, including the special relationship with the United States. By signing the treaty, she would reduce drastically her ability to collaborate with other European powers in the development of advanced weapons systems, and thus would forfeit one of her few bargaining advantages. Moreover, in adopting a policy similar to the United States, and at odds with French policy as well as sentiment in the German Federal Republic, Britain would stiffen opposition to her Common Market candidacy.

Since 1963 Britain had not sufficiently transformed herself as to make possible Common Market membership without profoundly altering the European Community. British participation would have a major effect

---

[75] In his Press Conference of October 28, 1966, de Gaulle again alluded to the question of Britain as a European power. He declared: "Thus, in 1963, we were led to put an end to the negotiations that Britain opened in Brussels with a view to entering the organization; not, to be sure, that we despaired of ever seeing that great island people truly wed its destiny to that of the Continent, but the fact is that it was not then in a position to apply the common rules and that it had just, in Nassau, sworn an allegiance outside of a Europe that would be a real Europe. But, by continuing fruitlessly, these negotiations were actually preventing the Six from building their Community." Ambassade de France, *Speeches and Press Conferences*, No. 253 A (October 28, 1966).

on the institutions of the Community.[76] Another Gaullist argument was that British Common Market membership would so strengthen the West European bloc as to force the East European communist states to revert to closer ties with the Soviet Union. This, in turn, would dampen the prospects for the attainment of the Gaullist objective of a European association of states embracing eastern and western Europe. Whatever the likely impact of British EEC entry on the cohesion of communist states, this contention was not fully consistent with the French argument that British admission would transform the European Community to an association with little cohesiveness.

If Britain was not yet sufficiently European to enter the Common Market without the "building of an entirely new edifice, scrapping nearly all of that which has just been built," she had essentially two alternatives. As he had in January 1963, de Gaulle offered Britain a form of associate membership. The other alternative was for Britain to "wait until a certain internal and external evolution, of which Britain seems already to be showing signs, is eventually completed." [77]

Since the breakdown of the Brussels negotiations, Britain had undergone important internal and external change. Many of the problems then of importance no longer occupied either the framers of British Common Market policy or the staffs of the EEC Council and Commission in Brussels—yet a series of new problems had arisen. In the 1961–1963 period little thought was given to the implications of Common Market membership for the British economy, the balance of payments, and the position of sterling as a reserve currency. Moreover, except in the field of defense, the question of a European outlook on issues of major international importance played a less prominent part in the French critique of Britain's qualifications for membership. Presumably, Britain's commitments east of Suez, her support for U.S. policy in Southeast Asia, British policy on the Nonproliferation Treaty, and disagreement between Britain and the EEC during the Kennedy Round trade negotiations, were indicative of the inability of the British to adopt a European outlook.

---

[76] According to de Gaulle: Britain's delegates would "represent the very substantial and very special mass of interests and of economic and political authorities of their own country," and "would be joined there immediately by the delegations of several of the states which now constitute with them the Free Trade Area (EFTA); it is obvious that the inspirations, dimensions and decisions of what is today the organization of the Six would give way to an inspiration, dimensions, and decisions that would be entirely different." Ibid., p. 11.
[77] Ibid.

Yet in accepting a European position on such issues, Britain would have altered her policies to an extent not even demanded of the existing members of the European Community. In foreign policy and strategic doctrine, the European position of which de Gaulle spoke was essentially the French position, for by 1967 the Six had not evolved a consensus on these issues. Only in sectors falling within the purview of the EEC had the Six developed a common policy. The fact that in tariff negotiations with Britain and the United States they spoke with one voice was attributable to the existence of the European Community, within which they had developed a consensus on major commercial issues, as well as an interest in the preservation of the Community itself. As a member of the Common Market, Britain would participate in the so-called Community method of evolving a European position on economic issues. Although with her admission the development of a common European policy might be more difficult and cumbersome because of the need to reconcile additional interests, the obstacles would not be insurmountable. Implicit in the Gaullist argument was the assumption that once Britain had joined the Common Market, she would discontinue her effort to transform herself from a power with global interests, perspectives, and commitments to a Europe-oriented nation. It may be argued that membership in the European Community would actually hasten the evolutionary process in which Britain had been engaged for at least the past decade.[78]

In response to French policy, the strategy of the Wilson government was to present Common Market membership as inevitable, to suggest that although Britain's entry could be delayed, the British could not be permanently excluded.[79] Britain would attempt to meet French objections and, in doing so, strengthen support for British membership among France's EEC partners and thereby isolate the French. The British were determined to make a success of negotiations and, according to Wilson, to "carry them forward as quickly as lies within our power."

In its second bid for EEC membership, the British government enjoyed greater flexibility than at the time of the first application. To a far greater extent, Britain was prepared, politically and psychologi-

---

[78] For a similar argument against British Common Market membership because of its potentially adverse effect on Anglo-American relations, see Lionel Gelber, *The Alliance of Necessity: Britain's Crisis, the New Europe, and American Interests.*
[79] See Wilson's speech in the Commons on May 8, 1967. Great Britain, *Parliamentary Debates* (Commons), Vol. 746 (May 8, 1967), cols. 1061–1097.

cally, if not economically, to meet French objections to her candidacy. By 1967 Common Market membership had widespread support within both major parties, as well as among British elites. Large numbers of Englishmen concluded that EEC entry offered the major remaining option if Britain was to modernize her economic system, develop new markets, assure for herself a position of importance in the discovery and development of advanced technologies, and find a new role in world politics. The challenge facing Britain was to convince the Six, and France in particular, that British Common Market membership was as much to their interest as the British government thought it was to Britain's interest.

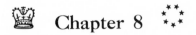

Chapter 8

BRITAIN, THE COMMON MARKET, AND INTERNATIONAL INTEGRATION

Although it is impossible to develop generalizations about political behavior from one study, the British Common Market bid is instructive for several reasons: (1) It represents an effort by an important national unit to respond to perceived changes in its international position from a power with worldwide interests to an essentially regional foreign policy focus. (2) It illustrates the problems facing a nation in the reconciliation of diverse, and often divergent, domestic and international interests and commitments; (3) It provides an indication of the process by which Britain embraced Common Market membership. Despite the limitations of a study focused on one case, several conclusions relevant to the study of integration at the international level emerge from an examination of British policy and attitudes toward the European Community.

In the period under consideration, Britain was engaged in a reassessment of existing international commitments, as well as her future role in international politics. From an abiding faith in the Commonwealth and the Anglo-American special relationship as the cornerstones of British foreign policy, Englishmen shifted their focus toward the European Community. Their ability to make such a change, however, was limited by residual loyalties to the Commonwealth and, to a lesser extent, the United States, and by fears about the potential loss of national decision-making authority to the European Community. Successive British governments strove, not always with success, to reconcile commitments and interests in the Commonwealth, the special relationship, and western Europe.

For Britain, the problem of obtaining Common Market membership was complicated by several factors. To a greater extent than any of the Six, the British, because they saw themselves as a world power, found it difficult to accept the limitations on their independence they believed would result from joining the European Community. Far more than the Six, Britain retained commitments and interests outside Europe which British decision-makers and other elites sought to preserve. In its ability to reconcile such commitments and interests with membership in the European Community, the British government faced important limitations. The Macmillan cabinet was not prepared to sacrifice what were deemed to be vital Commonwealth trading interests, especially those of the older dominions. Domestic opinion provided yet another important constraint. The impetus for Common Market membership had come from the British government, with the support of much of the press, industry, and European groups. However, the British government, especially from 1961 to 1963, did not enjoy a broadly based consensus in favor of Common Market membership.

In supporting or opposing Common Market membership, domestic groups sought to enhance, defend, or preserve certain cherished interests and values. In pursuit of their objectives, such groups used a variety of means: distribution of propaganda, gatherings of potentially influential persons, public meetings designed to reach a mass audience, and systematic consultation with government officials. In addition to such domestic pressures, the British government was beset with a variety of demands from the Commonwealth and to a lesser extent, EFTA. Given the need to reconcile such interests, domestic and Commonwealth, the government was unable to move with great haste to join the Common Market.

The study of the rise of domestic interest in Common Market membership reveals that the vast majority of Englishmen had little knowledge of, or preoccupation with, the European Community. Especially before 1961, the idea of Common Market membership was not a topic of widespread concern or discussion. In applying for Common Market membership, the Macmillan cabinet was in advance of British public opinion. The study of British Common Market attitudes reveals the absence of mass involvement or interest in the re-evaluation of Britain's international position. If such discussion was confined to a small segment of the population, the British government was limited in its maneuverability as a result of domestic and international constraints. As the Brussels negotiations progressed, popular support for Common Market membership declined as public awareness of the ratio between potential gains and losses increased. Although prepared in many cases to support in principle a bid for Common Market membership, Englishmen found it difficult, and often impossible, to maintain such support after they became aware of the likely cost of entering the

European Community. As the British pondered Common Market membership, the problems of reconciling such a European commitment with other interests, especially with the Commonwealth, haunted them.

Despite the relatively small segment of the British public actively concerned with the question of Common Market membership, in a political system such as that of Britain, widespread acceptance, or a political leadership capable of building a broadly based consensus, may be essential. In 1961 and 1966, the announcement of the British Common Market decision was followed by a marked increase in public awareness of, and interest in, the European Community. This in turn contributed to a division of opinion for or against Common Market membership, especially as the terms of entry became clearer. If the Common Market case is instructive, in the British political system at least, integrative efforts may not succeed: (a) if politically important strata are divided, as they were in Britain, especially between 1961 and 1963; (b) if widespread apathy or opposition exist among the public at large or (c) if many diverse or divergent interests cannot be accommodated.

The Six also faced the need to reconcile a series of interests before negotiating with Britain. Because the EEC was the product of an upgrading of the national interests of its members—a series of delicate compromises worked out only after long and detailed negotiations—the Six were not prepared to make major changes in the European Community in order to accommodate Britain. If she had joined at the time of its formation, Britain would have had a major voice in framing the Rome Treaty and in the evolution of the EEC. The inability of Britain to obtain major concessions from the Six illustrates the rigidity which the process of consensus formation within the EEC imposed upon the European Community in dealings with non-member countries. Conceivably, the latitude available to the European Community in accommodating its interests to those of outside powers is less than that possessed by each of its members.

In the case of Common Market membership Englishmen, by and large, made up their minds on the basis of a calculus of potential gain or loss. Before Macmillan's announcement of July 31, 1961, Englishmen developed a variety of expectations of gain—first from participation in a free trade area, and later, the Common Market. In the government as well as among interest groups representative of industry and labor, and in the press, the decision to seek Common Market membership was preceded by the rise of expectations of gain. In general, those who espoused Common Market membership did so not for altruistic motives but because they saw in such a policy specific gains: greater markets for industry, higher living standards for workers, opportunities for Britain to gain a new international political role, and the prospect of narrowing the Atlantic technological imbalance.[1] Similarly, the opponents of Common Market membership stated their case in terms of potential losses from Common Market membership: the reduction of Commonwealth trade, the weakening of the Commonwealth, increased prices for British consumers, an adverse impact upon Britain's political institutions, and restrictions on British independence in political and economic affairs.

In the case of one expectation of gain in particular, namely greater markets in western Europe, there was an interactive process in which expectations apparently affected trade, and trade, in turn, affected expectations. Having first developed expectations of gain from a free trade area, and later the Common Market, businessmen placed greater emphasis on increasing sales in western Europe. As Englishmen focused attention on European markets, trade with the Six increased. Almost like a self-fulfilling prophecy, trade rose in response to British expectations which, in turn, generated even greater expectations and a drive for increased markets. Exporters made an effort to boost sales in the Six in order to be in an advantageous position for further increases if Britain joined the Common Market. The fact that British trade with the EEC, as a percentage of total exports, increased even after Britain was excluded from the Common Market, contributed to a rise in British interest in the European Community.

Not a few Englishmen found Common Market membership attractive because Britain might increase its laggard economic growth rates. The European Community might become a new center of economic strength, if not eventually even a new world power. The demonstrated durability of the EEC, together with its success in attaining at least some of the major goals set forth in the Rome Treaty, contributed to the rise in British support for Common Market membership. Because of its strength, the European Community would supersede Britain as the principal ally of the United States. In short, the EEC formed a "core area" which, because of its superior economic growth and other indica-

---

[1] This substantiates propositions stated by at least two students of integration. See Karl W. Deutsch *et al. Political Community and the North Atlantic Area*, 46–50. Ernst B. Haas, *The Uniting of Europe*, 13.

tions of strength, exerted a pull upon such outside countries as Britain and other EFTA members.[2]

Since World War II, the impetus toward integration has been greater among units having geographic proximity than among more widely separated territories. If the Channel had not separated Britain from the Six, the problem of Common Market membership, as de Gaulle suggested in his Press Conference of January 14, 1963, might not have been so formidable.[3] Unlike Britain and the Six, or Britain and other Commonwealth members, the EEC members were geographically contiguous. The British Common Market experience lends credence to the contention stated in integration literature that there is a relationship between geographic proximity and integration.[4]

To what extent may previous integrative experience increase the likelihood that a people will look favorably on new schemes for integration? Although the British had no integrative experience directly relevant to Common Market membership, between 1957 and 1967 support for the European Community increased despite the failure of British initiatives. In fact, the failure of the effort first to form a free trade area and then to join the Common Market strengthened support for membership in the European Community. The collapse of the free trade area negotiations in 1958 contributed to a reassessment of British attitudes toward European integration. Conceivably, a large number of those who eventually became advocates of Common Market

---

[2] See Deutsch *et al.*, *op. cit.*, 37–38. According to the authors, integration occurs around core areas, i.e., units with relatively advanced political and economic capabilities.

[3] According to de Gaulle: "The Treaty of Rome was concluded between six continental states. States which are, in short, economically of the same nature. Whether in terms of their industrial or agricultural production, of their foreign trade, of their commercial customs and clients, or of their living and working conditions, there are many more similarities than differences between them. Moreover, they are adjacent, they interpenetrate, they are extensions of each other through their communications. The very fact of grouping them and linking them together in such a way that what they produce, buy, sell, and consume, they produce, buy, sell, and consume by preference within their own grouping thus conforms to reality." In contrast, de Gaulle suggested: "England is, in effect, insular, maritime, linked through its trade, markets and food supply to very diverse and often very distant countries. . . . In short, the nature, structure, and economic context of England differs profoundly from those of the other states of the Continent." Ambassade de France, Service de Presse et d'Information, New York. *Major Addresses and Press Conferences of General Charles de Gaulle*, pp. 212–213.

[4] See Philip E. Jacob and James V. Toscano (Eds.), *The Integration of Political Communities*, 50–51.

membership would have been satisfied if the free trade area proposal had borne fruit. As a member of the projected free trade area, Britain would have experienced many of the gains which Common Market proponents expected from the European Community.

If the failure of the free trade area talks contributed to a rise in support for Common Market membership, the collapse of the Brussels negotiations led EEC proponents not only to call again for Common Market membership, but often to broaden their appeal to include formation of a European defense, technological, and political community. In fact, Wilson emphasized the need to achieve greater technological collaboration within western Europe. Heath placed even greater stress upon the potential gains from European technological, political, and military integration. For the leaders of both major British parties, membership in the EEC was the key to the broadening of European integration to non-economic sectors. Between 1957 and 1967, there was a movement of elite opinion and official policy from interest in economic cooperation, as embodied in the free trade area proposals of 1957, to acceptance of economic integration provided in the European Community, and discussion about the formation of European political and technological communities.

The evolution of British opinion toward European integration had at least two dimensions. The decisions Macmillan and Wilson, respectively, announced in 1961 and 1966, were preceded by increasing domestic support for Common Market membership. In both cases, however, domestic opposition increased as Englishmen in accord in principle with Common Market membership weighed the potential gains and losses and concluded that Britain could not join the European Community without sacrificing other important interests. But superimposed on these shifts in opinion was a longer range British evolution, over the decade, toward a primarily European orientation. This shift in sentiment was more noticeable in the Conservative party, where the Europeans displaced those who gave greatest emphasis to the Commonwealth and the special relationship. The one-time party of Empire and Commonwealth rejected commitments east of Suez and took on a European orientation. Although to a lesser extent and somewhat later, the Labour party experienced a similar shift in outlook. It was a Labour government which made the decision to withdraw by 1971 from the major remaining British military commitments east of Suez.

Having thought favorably of one scheme for European integration, Englishmen became receptive to another, even though the second would have made necessary greater economic adaptation and transfer of authority from London to Continental Europe. Although the gains the British anticipated from the free trade area, and initially the Common Market, were almost exclusively economic, Englishmen later gave increasing emphasis to expectations of political gain from European integration. Thus by 1961 the Conservative government was prepared to join the Common Market. By 1967 the Conservative party gave active support not only to the European Community, but stressed to an even greater extent the need for British participation in a European political community. The Labour party, reluctant in 1961 to support EEC entry, had adopted by 1967 a policy which emphasized the potential economic and technological gains from membership in the European Community—using arguments which bore some resemblance to the earlier Conservative position. The respective experiences of the two major British parties suggest an evolution in thought toward integration at the international level.

This increase in support stemmed from the growth of a consensus that Britain could no longer play an important role as leader of the Commonwealth, as a participant in an Anglo-American special relationship, and a power in, but not of, western Europe. As the realization that the first and second roles were no longer possible, British interest in the third role increased. As a result, Britain was prepared to accept institutional links in economic, political, and even military affairs which once would have been considered unthinkable. The British concluded that membership in the European Community was essential to their future in a world in which Britain was dwarfed by larger political, economic, and technological units.

An examination of the British Common Market case reveals a process which may be characterized as follows:

(1) Stage 1: 1956–1959. The focusing of attention within the government and in industry, the press, the leadership of the trade union movement, and the political parties upon the alleged benefits of a European free trade area embracing West European countries, including Britain itself; the development of expectations of gain, both in the governmental and private sectors, from an organization which would impose relatively few burdens on Britain; a rise both in expectations of gain and transactions, especially trade, with western Europe.

(2) Stage 2: 1959–1961. With the failure of the free trade negotiations, a shift in focus to EFTA as a device for enabling Britain to gain access to growing European markets and to build a bridge to the EEC;

i.e., to strengthen the British negotiating position vis-à-vis the Common Market. In this stage the British, both in the governmental and private sectors, developed expectations of gain from Common Market membership and increasingly questioned the importance of the Commonwealth and special relationship as priorities which had guided British foreign policy. With the encouragement of much of the press, industry, and European organizations, the government applied for Common Market membership. In the aftermath of failure of an attempt to frame an organization which would have placed relatively few burdens on Britain, there was an increased willingness to contemplate membership in an organization in which obligations and costs would have been greater. The willingness to consider such membership increased as expectations of gain rose both within the governmental and private sectors.

Stage 3: 1961–1963. An attempt, in the Brussels negotiations, to reconcile diverse British goals in order to obtain Common Market membership while leaving intact to the greatest extent possible trading links with the Commonwealth, safeguarding the interests of the other EFTA countries, and protecting British farmers and consumers from drastic and unacceptable changes as a result of the agricultural policy of the European Community. This was a period of intensive activity by pro-Common Market forces, as well as the rise of anti-Common Market groups in Britain. The Common Market debate produced cleavages which cut across party lines. Opposition increased as the potential cost of EEC entry became known as a result of the Brussels negotiations.

Stage 4: 1963–1964. A period of markedly reduced interest in immediate Common Market membership as a result of the failure of the Brussels negotiations. Both the proponents and opponents of EEC entry curtailed their activities. Although discussion focused on alternatives, those who had favored Common Market membership retained a pro-European bias in the expectation that at some future time Britain could once again apply for entry.

Stage 5: 1965–1966. A revival of interest, first in the strengthening of trading links and subsequently in Common Market membership, with a reactivation of groups favoring EEC entry. This was a period of intensive examination of the problems associated with EEC entry and the exploration of the prospects for membership in official probings with the Six.

Stage 6: 1967. A period of intensive discussions with the EEC countries, capped by a decision to apply once again for membership.

In sum, the acceptance and advocacy of participation in one proposed European organization, a broad free trade area (1957–1959) led, despite and perhaps even as a result of its failure, to willingness to take a bolder step toward integration, in the form of membership in the EEC. The failure of one bid contributed to the growth of sentiment in favor of bolder initiatives and a willingness to join the European Community at a cost which a few years earlier had seemed prohibitive. Such a change in outlook can be attributed to altered conceptions of the other options open. But it may also result from the continuing examination of the European Community in which Englishmen were engaged.

In the final analysis, if the British Common Market bid is instructive, the outcome of an attempt to join an institution such as the European Community is dependent upon a combination of factors: elite and popular support, rising levels of expectations of reward, and the ability of decision-makers to restructure their assumptions and thought patterns toward integration. Of crucial importance, however, are the leadership capabilities of the decision-makers of units to be integrated. Britain lacked a leadership capable of molding a broadly based consensus in favor of Common Market membership. Undoubtedly this reflected the magnitude of the task facing successive British governments as much as it did the leadership abilities of Macmillan and Wilson. Conceivably, the inability of British governments, before 1966 at least, to build and sustain a broadly based Common Market consensus reflected the limitations of a European commitment based upon essentially pragmatic considerations—expectations of gain—rather than an emotional, philosophical commitment to Europe. If British political leaders were unable to evoke such a commitment among large numbers of Englishmen, they themselves had not clearly formulated a conception of Europe which might attract widespread popular support.

Although de Gaulle expressed his own expectations of gain from an integrated Europe, his conception of Britain's place in Europe differed from that of British decision-makers. French policy toward British Common Market membership was designed either to restrict EEC membership to the Six or to admit Britain at a price which, especially in the period 1961–63, few Englishmen were prepared to pay. Whatever the calculus of potential gains and losses to France in the form of greater markets for her agriculture and the prospects for greater technological collaboration, they were outweighed by such potential losses as greater competition from Britain for French industry and the threat Britain might pose to French leadership in western Europe. But even greater than such pragmatic considerations may have been de Gaulle's suspicions about the motives of the "Anglo-Saxons" and his conviction that continental western Europe must oppose Anglo-American hegemony. However important the place of elites, expectations of gain, and patterns of interaction between decision-makers and their publics, the British Common Market case stands as a reminder of the importance of the political leader, his personality and philosophical commitment, in an age when the nation-state, for better or worse, remains the dominant political unit.

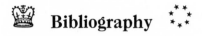 Bibliography

PUBLIC DOCUMENTS

Ambassade de France. *Arrangements Made in Luxembourg between the Foreign Affairs Ministers of the Six on January 31, 1966.* (French Affairs, No. 188).

———. *Speeches and Press Conferences.* No. 260 A. (May 16, 1967).

———. *Speeches and Press Conferences* No. 253 A. (October 28, 1966).

———. *Texts of the Common French-German Declaration and of the Treaty between the French Republic and the Federal Republic of Germany of January 22, 1963.*

British Information Services. *British Record.*

———. *Towards European Integration* I. D. 1393 (November 1961).

———. *Towards European Integration* I. D. 1393/2 (September 1962).

EFTA *Bulletin.*

EFTA *Reporter.*

Council of Europe, Consultative Assembly, *Official Report.*

European Community Information Service, *European Community* (London).

———. *European Community* (Washington, D.C.).

European Economic Community. *Avis de la Commission au Conseil concernant les Démandes d'Adhesion des Royaume Unie, du Ireland, Denmark, et de la Norwége.* Brussels, 1967.

———. *Background Documents on British, Danish and Irish Applications for Membership of the European Economic Community.* Brussels, 1961.

———. *Report to the European Parliament on the State of Negotiations with the United Kingdom.* Brussels, 1963.

French Embassy Press and Information Division, *Major Addresses, Statements, and Press Conferences of General Charles de Gaulle,* May 19, 1958—January 31, 1964. New York, 1964.

Great Britain. *Amendments to the Convention Establishing the European Free Trade Association, signed at Stockholm on January 4, 1960.* Cmnd. 1668 London: HMSO, 1962.

———. *Background to the Negotiations: Britain and the European Communities.* London: HMSO, 1961.

———. *Bulletin for Industry: A Monthly Review of the Economic Situation.* Prepared by the Information Division of the Treasury. No. 150, (March 1962).

Great Britain. Central Statistical Office. *Annual Abstract of Statistics.* London: HMSO, 1952–1966.

———. *Monthly Digest of Statistics.* London: HMSO, 1954–67.

———. *Commonwealth Consultations on Britain's Relations with the European Economic Community.* London: HMSO, Cmnd. 1339, July 1961.

———. *Convention Establishing the European Free Trade Association.* London: HMSO, Cmnd. 1026, 1960.

———. *A European Free Trade Area: The United Kingdom Memorandum to the Organization for European Economic Cooperation.* London: HMSO, Cmnd. 72, February 1957.

———. *European Political Union.* London: HMSO, Cmnd. 1770, April 10, 1962.

———. *Legal and Constitutional Implications of United Kingdom Membership of the European Communities.* London: HMSO, Cmnd. 3301, 1967.

———. *Negotiations for a European Free Trade Area: Documents Relating to the Negotiations from July 1956, to December 1958.* London: HMSO, Cmnd. 64, 1959.

———. *Parliamentary Debates* (Commons).

———. *Parliamentary Debates* (Lords).

———. *The Common Agricultural Policy of the European Economic Community.* London: HMSO, May 1967, Cmnd. 3274.

———. *The Defense Review.* Statement on Defense issued in London, February 22, 1966. Official Text released by British Information Services, New York.

———. *The United Kingdom and the European Economic Community.* London: HMSO, Cmnd. 1565, November 1961.

———. *The United Kingdom and the European Economic Community: Report by the Lord Privy Seal on the Meeting with Ministers of Member States of the European Economic Community from August 1–5, 1962.* London: HMSO, Cmnd. 1805.

Organization for European Cooperation and Development (OECD), *General Statistics.*

Western European Union. *Britain, EFTA, and the EEC.* Assembly of Western European Union, Eleventh Ordinary Session (First Part), Document 341, 1965.

Western European Union Assembly. *Proceedings.*

BOOKS

Beddington-Behrens, Edward. *Is There any Choice? Britain Must Join Europe.* Baltimore: Penguin Books, 1966.

Beer, Samuel H. *British Politics in the Collectivist Age.* New York: Alfred A. Knopf, 1966.

Beever, R. Colin. *European Unity and the Trade Union Movements.* Leyden: Sythoff, 1960.

Bell, Coral (ed.). *Europe without Britain.* Melbourne: F. W. Cheshire for the Australian Institute of International Affairs, 1963.

———. *The Debatable Alliance: An Essay in Anglo-American Relations.* London: Oxford University Press for the Royal Institute of World Affairs, 1964.

Beloff, Nora. *The General Says No: Britain's Exclusion from Europe.* Baltimore: Penguin Books, 1963.

Benoit, Emile. *Europe at Sixes and Sevens.* New York: Columbia University Press, 1961.

Bryant, Arthur. *A Choice for Destiny: Commonwealth and Common Market.* London: Collins, 1962.

Butler, D. E. and Rose, Richard. *The British General Election of 1959.* London: Macmillan and Co., Ltd., 1960.

———, and Anthony King. *The British General Election of 1966.* New York: St. Martin's Press, 1966.

Camps, Miriam. *Britain and the European Community, 1955–63.* Princeton: Princeton University Press, 1964.

———. *European Unification in the Sixties: From the Veto to the Crisis.* New York: McGraw-Hill Book Company, for the Council on Foreign Relations, 1966.

———. *What Kind of Europe? The Community since De Gaulle's Veto.* London: Oxford University Press, 1965.

Carter, W. Horsfall. *Speaking European.* London: Allen and Unwin, 1966.

Churchill, Winston S. *Europe Unite: Speeches, 1947 and 1948.* London: Cassel and Company Limited, 1950.

Clark, Colin. *British Trade in the Common Market.* London: Stevens and Sons Limited, 1962.

De Gaulle, Charles. *War Memoirs.* (3 Vols.) London: Weidenfeld and Nicolson, 1959.

Deutsch, Karl W., et. al. *Political Community and the North Atlantic Area.* Princeton: Princeton University Press, 1957.

Eckstein, Harry. *Pressure Group Politics: The Case of the British Medical Association.* Stanford: Stanford University Press, 1960.

Gelber, H. G. *Australia, Britain and the EEC, 1961 to 1963.* London: Oxford University Press, 1966.

Gelber, Lionel. *The Alliance of Necessity.* New York: Stein and Day, 1966.

———. *Beyond the New Europe: Where Britain Must Look.* London: Ludgate Press, 1963.

Gladwyn, Lord. *The European Idea.* New York: Praeger, 1966.

Haas, Ernst. *Beyond the Nation State.* Stanford: Stanford University Press, 1965.

———. *The Uniting of Europe.* Stanford: Stanford University Press, 1957.

Hartley, Anthony. *A State of England*. London: Hutchinson and Company, Ltd., 1963.

Heiser, Hans Joachim. *British Policy with Regard to the Unification Efforts on the European Continent*. Leyden: Sythoff, 1959.

Jacob, Philip E. and Toscano, James V. (eds.). *The Integration of Political Communities*. Philadelphia: Lippincott, 1964.

Kaiser, Karl. *EWG und Freihandelzone. England und der Kontinent in der europaischen Integration*. Leyden: Sythoff, 1963.

Kitzinger, V. W. *The Politics and Economics of European Integration*. New York: Praeger, 1963.

Kleiman, Robert. *Atlantic Crisis: American Diplomacy Confronts a Resurgent Europe*. New York: W. W. Norton and Company, Inc., 1964.

Koestler, Arthur (ed.). *Suicide of a Nation?* New York: Macmillan, 1964.

Kraft, Joeseph. *The Grand Design: From Common Market to Atlantic Partnership*. New York: Harper and Brothers, 1962.

Kulski, W. W. *De Gaulle and the World: The Foreign Policy of the Fifth French Republic*. Syracuse: Syracuse University Press, 1966.

Lamfalussy, A. *The United Kingdom and the Six: An Essay on Economic Growth in Western Europe*. London: Macmillan, 1963.

Lichtheim, George. *The New Europe*. New York: Praeger, 1963.

Lippmann, Walter. *Western Unity and the Common Market*. Boston: Little, Brown and Company, 1962.

Mackay, R. W. G. *Towards A United States of Europe: An Analysis of Britain's Role in European Union*. London: Hutchinson and Company, Ltd., 1961.

Mally, Gerhard. *Britain and European Unity*. London: Hansard Society for Parliamentary Government, 1966.

Mander, John. *Great Britain or Little England?* Boston: Houghton Mifflin, 1964.

Mayne, Richard. *The Community of Europe*. London: Victor Gollancz Ltd., 1962.

Middleton, Drew. *The Supreme Choice: Britain and the European Community*. London: Secker and Warburg, 1963.

Moncrieff, Anthony (ed.). *Britain and the Common Market 1967*. Chatham: W. & J. Mackay and Company Limited for the British Broadcasting Corporation, 1967.

Nutting, Anthony. *Europe Will Not Wait: A Warning and a Way Out*. New York: Praeger, 1960.

Pickles, William. *Britain and Europe: How Much Has Changed?* Oxford: Basil Blackwell, 1967.

———. *Not with Europe: The Political Case for Staying Out*. London: Fabian International Bureau, 1962.

Pinder, John. *Britain and the Common Market*. London: The Cresset Press, 1961.

———. *Europe Against De Gaulle*. London: Pall Mall Press, 1963.

Potter, Allen. *Organized Groups in British Politics*. London: Faber and Faber, 1961.

Pryce, Roy. *The Political Future of the European Community*. London: John Marshbank Limited in association with The Federal Trust for Education and Research.

Rosecrance, R. N. *Defense of the Realm: British Strategy in the Nuclear Epoch*. New York and London: Columbia University Press, 1968.

Sampson, Anthony. *Anatomy of Britain Today*. London: Hodder and Stoughton, 1965.

———. *Anatomy of Europe*. New York: Harper and Row, 1969

Self, Peter and H. Storing. *The State and the Farmer*. London: George Allen and Unwin, Limited, 1962.

Shanks, Michael and Lambert, John. *Britain and the New Europe: The Future of the Common Market*. London: Chatto and Windus, 1962.

Stewart, J. D. *British Pressure Groups: Their Role in Relation to the House of Commons*. London: Oxford University Press, 1958.

Strausz-Hupé, Robert, Dougherty, James E., and Kintner, William R. *Building the Atlantic World*. New York: Harper and Row, 1963.

Waltz, Kenneth N. *Foreign Policy and Democratic Politics: The American and British Experience*. Boston: Little, Brown and Company, 1967.

Wilson, Harold. *Purpose in Politics: Britain's Role in the Post-Colonial World*. Boston: Houghton Mifflin Company, 1964.

Woodhouse, C. M. *British Foreign Policy since the Second World War*. New York: Praeger, 1962.

Zaring, J. L. *Decision For Europe: The Necessity of Britain's Engagement*. Baltimore: Johns Hopkins Press, 1969.

NEWSPAPERS AND NEWS JOURNALS

The *Banker*

Board of Trade Journal

The *Christian Science Monitor* (Boston)

The *Daily Express* (London)

The *Daily Herald* (London)

The *Daily Mail* (London)

The *Daily Telegraph* (London)

The *Economist*

The *Guardian* (Manchester and London)

The *Financial Times* (London)

Le Monde (Paris)

The *Manchester Guardian Weekly*

The *New Statesman and Nation*

The *New York Herald Tribune* (European Edition)

The *New York Times*
The *New York Times* (European Edition)
The *Observer* (London)
Reynold News (London)
The *Scotsman* (Edinburgh)
The *Spectator*
The *Statist*
The *Stock Exchange Gazette*
The *Sunday Times* (London)
Time and Tide
The *Times* (London)
The *Tribune* (London)
The *Yorkshire Post* (Leeds)
The *Washington Post*

ARTICLES, REPORTS, AND PAMPHLETS

Abrams, Mark. "British Elite Attitudes and the European Common Market," *Public Opinion Quarterly*, Vol. XXIX, No. 2 (Summer 1965).
Associated Rediffusion. *London Profiles*. London, 1962.
Associated Rediffusion. *The Common Market and You*. (London, 1961).
Association of British Chambers of Commerce, Federation of British Industries and National Union of Manufacturers. *A Joint Report on the European Free Trade Area*. London, 1957.
Beaton, Leonard. "Britain's Relations with Europe—A Reply," *Journal of Common Market Studies*, Vol. IV, No. 3 (May 1966).
Beer, Samuel M. "Pressure Groups and Parties in Britain," *American Political Science Review*, Vol. L, No. 1 (March 1956), pp. 1–23.
Beever, R. Colin. "Trade Union Rethinking," *Journal of Common Market Studies*, Vol. II, No. 2 (November 1963).
———. "When Britain Joins: The Consequence for Labour and Social Policy," *The Political Quarterly*, Vol. 34, No. 1 (January–March 1963).
Beloff, Nora. *What Happened in Britain after the General Said No*. London, 1966. (Mimeograph)
Briginshaw, R. W., *et. al. Britain Should Stay Out*. London: Forward Britain Movement, 1962.
Britain in Europe. *Monthly Newsletter*.
Britain in Europe. Published by Britain in Europe Limited.
Britain in Europe. *Report of Activities*. London, 1962.
British Iron and Steel Federation. *Into Europe?* London, 1961.
British Iron and Steel Federation. *Steel and the Free Trade Area*, London, 1957.
Bryant, Sir Arthur. *A Choice for Destiny: Commonwealth and Common Market*. London: Collins, 1962.

Caine, Sir Sydney. "When Britain Joins: The Consequences for the Commonwealth and the Underdeveloped World," *The Political Quarterly* Vol. 34, No. 1, January–March 1963.

Camps, Miriam. *Division in Europe.* Center of International Studies, Princeton University, 1960.

———. *The European Common Market and the Free Trade Area.* Center of International Studies, Princeton University, 1956.

———. *The European Free Trade Area: A Preliminary Appraisal.* Political and Economic Planning, Occasional Paper No. 4 (September 7, 1959).

———. *The Free Trade Area Negotiations*, Center of International Studies, Princeton University, 1958.

The Common Market: A Survey by The Times (London). London: The Times Publishing Company Limited, 1962.

Common Market and Commonwealth. A New Survey by The *Times* (London). London: The Times Publishing Company, 1962.

Common Market Campaign. *Common Market Broadsheet.*

———. *Forward Britain into Europe: The Case for Joining the Common Market.* London, 1961.

———, Preparatory Committee. *Letter to Rt. Hon. Edward Heath, June 7, 1961.*

———. *Report.* London, 1962.

———. *Statement on Europe.* (Mimeographed) London, 1961.

"Common Market: Economists' Blunder," *City Press* (London), December 1, 1961.

"Commonwealth and Common Market," The *Banker*, Vol. CXV, No. 426, (July 1961).

Confederation of British Industry. *Britain and Europe: An Industrial Appraisal.* London, 1966.

———. *Britain and Europe: Supporting Papers.* London, 1967.

Conservative and Unionist Central Office. *Action, Not Words: The New Conservative Program.* London, 1966.

———. *Challenge Accepted.* London, 1963.

———. *Commonwealth and Common Market.* London, 1962.

———. *Putting Britain Right Ahead: A Statement of Conservative Aims.* London, 1965.

Conservative Political Centre. *A Europe of Nations: A Practical Policy for Britain.* London, 1965.

———. *Britain, Europe and the World.* (London, 1967).

Conservative Political Centre for the Bow Group. *Britain in Europe.* London, 1962.

Conservative Political Centre. *Britain's Place in Europe.* London: Conservative Political Centre, 1967.

Conservative Political Centre. *What Joining Would Mean.* (London, 1967)

Conservative Political Centre for the Bow Group, *Challenge from Europe.* London, 1967.

Conservative Political Centre. *The New Europe.* London, 1962.

———. *Towards a Free Trade Area.* Two Way Topics, No. 28 (August–September 1959).

Conservative and Unionist Central Office. *Weekend Talking Point,* No. 349 (Week ending June 10, 1961).

Conservative Research Department. *Britain and Europe: Notes on Current Politics.* London, 1967.

———. *Conservative Election Manifesto and Statements by Leading Conservatives on the Common Market since January 1965.* London, 1965.

———. *Britain and the Common Market.* Notes on Current Politics, No. 16 (28th August 1961).

———. *Debate on the Common Market.* Notes on Current Politics, No. 13 (25th June 1962).

———. *Six Point Policy for Europe.* Summary of speech by Duncan Sandys, April 28, 1965.

———. *The U.K. and the European Economic Community.* Notes on Current Politics, No. 3 (5th February 1962).

Corbet, R. Hugh, (ed.). *Britain, Not Europe: Commonwealth before Common Market.* London, Anti-Common Market League, 1962.

Crossman, R. H. S. "British Labor Looks at Europe," *Foreign Affairs* Vol. 41, No. 4, July 1963.

Daily Express (London). *You and the Common Market.* London, 1962.

Day, A. C. L. "When Britain Joins: The Consequences for Economic Planning," *The Political Quarterly* Vol. 34, No. 1 (January–March 1963).

Economist Intelligence Unit. *Britain, the Commonwealth and European Free Trade.* London: Edgar G. Dunstan L. Company, 1958.

Economist Intelligence Unit. *Britain and Europe.* London: The Shenval Press, 1957.

Economist Intelligence Unit. *The Commonwealth and Europe.* London: The Shenval Press, 1960.

"Edging Towards Europe," *Socialist Commentary,* June 1966.

Edwards, Robert. "The Outlook for Labour," *European-Atlantic Review,* Vol. XI, No. 4 (September–October 1961).

"Europe after Britain Joins," *New Directions 62.* London: Liberal Publications Department, 1962.

European Review. Published by European Atlantic Group, British Council of the European Movement.

Europe Left. Review of the Labour Committee for Europe.

Export Council for Europe. *Report by the Chairman on the First Two Years and the Future: Achievement and Challenge.* London, 1961.

Export Council for Europe. *Report of the National Convention East-bourne, 1961.*

———. *Trading Opportunities in Europe,* Part I. London, 1961.

Federal Trust for Education and Research. *Finance and Investment in the Common Market*. London, 1962.

——. *The Common Market and Agriculture*, London, 1962.

——. *The Common Market: The Second Stage*. London, 1962.

Federation of British Industries. *FBI: What It Is and What It Does?* (Revised Edition). London, 1962.

——. *British Industry and Europe*. London, 1961.

Federal Union. *A Survey of Commonwealth Parliamentary Opinion on British Participation in a Free Trade Area*, London, 1958.

Federal Union. "Policy Statement," *World Affairs*, No. 237 (January–February 1957).

Forward Britain Movement. *Bulletin and News Digest*.

——. *The Case Now against Britain's Entry into the Common Market*. London, 1962.

Freg, Cynthia W., "Meaning Business: The British Application to Join the Common Market, November 1966–October 1967," *Journal of Common Market Studies*, Vol. VI, No. 3 (March 1968).

Geddes, Charles. "Wages and the Common Market." The *Listener*, Vol. LVII, No. 1462, April 4, 1957.

"Going into Europe: A Symposium," *Encounter* Vol. XIX, No. 6 (December 1962); Vol. XX, No. 1 (January 1963); Vol. XX, No. 2 (February 1963); Vol. XX, No. 3 (March 1963).

Griesing, Peter. "Macmillans Weg in das Europa der Vaterlander," *Aussenpolitik* 9/61 (September 1961).

Haas, Ernst. "The Challenge of Regionalism." *International Organization*, Vol. XII, No. 4 (Autumn, 1958), p. 445.

Hallett, Graham. "British Agriculture and Europe," *Crossbow* (Supplement No. 1/1), Spring 1961.

Healey, Denis. "Commonwealth or Common Market?" The *New Leader* Vol. XLV, No. 11 (May 28, 1962).

Heath, Edward. "West European Integration and East-West Relations." In "Western Europe and Eastern Europe: The Changing Relationship." *Adelphi Papers* London: Institute for Strategic Studies, No. 33 March 1967.

Henig, Stanley, M.P., "Britain and Europe: The Middle Way." *Journal of Common Market Studies*, Vol. VI, No. 2 (December 1967).

Holt, Stephen. *New Steps to Europe*. London: Liberal Publications Department for the New Orbits Group, 1967.

Jay, Douglas. *The Truth about the Common Market*. London: Forward Britain Movement, 1962.

Kitzinger, Uwe, "Britain's Crisis of Identity," *Journal of Common Market Studies*, Vol. VI, No. 4 (June 1968).

Labour Common Market Committee. *Common Sense about the Common Market*. London, 1962.

Labour Left: Journal of the Labour Committee for Europe.

Labour Party Overseas Department. *The Labour Government and Europe.* London, 1965.

The Labour Party, Annual Conference *Report,* 1957–1967.

Labour Party. *European Unity: A Statement by the Executive Committee of the Labour Party.* London, 1950.

———. *Talking Points.*

Layton, Christopher, "Labour and Europe," The *Political Quarterly* Vol. 33, No. 1 (January–March 1962).

Leech, John, *Europe and the Commonwealth.* London: Federal Union, 1961.

Lerner, Daniel. *As Britain Faces the Continent.* Center for International Studies, Massachusetts Institute of Technology, 1961.

Liberal Party Organization. *Liberal Assembly* 1956–1967.

Liberal Party Research and Information Department. *Current Topics,* Vol. 1, No. 2 (June 1961).

———. *Current Topics,* Vol. 1, No. 4 (August 1961).

Luard, Evan. *Britain and Europe.* London: Fabian International Bureau, 1961.

Macmillan, Harold. *Britain, the Commonwealth and Europe.* London, Conservative and Unionist Central Office, 1962.

———. *Commonwealth and Common Market.* London: Conservative and Unionist Central Office, 1962.

Meade, James E., *The Common Market: Is There an Alternative?* Hobart Paper 17 Supplement. London: Institute of Economic Affairs, 1962.

———. *U. K., Commonwealth and Common Market.* Hobart Paper No. 17. London: Institute of Economic Affairs, 1962.

Meyer, Sir Anthony. *A European Technological Community.* London: Conservative Political Centre, 1966.

Millet, John H. "British Interest Group Tactics: A Case Study." *Political Science Quarterly,* Vol. LXII, No. 1 (March 1957), pp. 71–82.

National Farmers' Union. *A Farm and Food Plan.* London, NFU, 1962.

———. *Agriculture in the Community.* London, 1961.

———. *Annual Review 1966* Vol. 21, No. 1, London, 1966.

———. *British Agriculture and the Common Market.* London, 1962.

———. *Horticulture in the Sixties.* London, 1962.

———. *NFU. News.*

National Opinion Polls, *Political Bulletin* (London) November 1961, October 1962, July 1966, November 1966, January 1967, May 1967.

National Union of Conservative and Unionist Associations, *Annual Conference Reports, 1956–1967.*

Nettl, Peter and David Shapiro, "Institutions versus Realities—A British Approach." *Journal of Common Market Studies.* Vol. II, No. 1.

Newsbrief of the Labour Common Market Committee.

One Europe. Is it Possible? London, BBC Publications, 1966.

Patterson, Ben. *Britain and Europe*. London: Conservative Central Office, 1967.

Pinder, John. "When Britain Joins: The Consequences for Economic Structure." The *Political Quarterly*, Vol. 34, No. 1 (January–March 1963).

Political and Economic Planning. "Agricultural Integration in Western Europe," *Planning*, Vol. XXIX, No. 470 (April 8, 1963).

———. *Aspects of European Integration: An Anglo-French Symposium.* London: PEP, 1962.

———. *Commonwealth Preference in the United Kingdom.* London: George Allen and Unwin Ltd., for PEP, 1960.

———. *Food Prices and the Common Market,* Occasional Paper No. 13 (May 29, 1961).

———. "The Growing Economy—Britain, Western Germany and France," *Planning* Vol. XXVI, No. 445 (October 17, 1960).

———. "The Negotiations on Political Union," *Planning* Vol. XXVIII, No. 465 (October 1962).

———. *Trade Diversion in Western Europe.* Occasional Paper No. 9. October 5, 1960.

———. "Trade Unions and the Common Market." *Planning*, Vol. XXVIII, No. 461 (May 1, 1962).

Pryce, Roy. "Britain out of Europe?" *Journal of Common Market Studies*, Vol. II, No. 1.

Raisman, Sir Jeremy. "The Open Secret Weapon of the Banking World." *European-Atlantic Review*, Vol. XI, No. 3 (July–August 1961), pp. 15–18.

Robinson, Geoffrey, *Europe: Problems of Negotiation.* Fabian Society Research Series 263 (London, 1967).

The Rosseau Group. "Canada, Britain and Europe," *Crossbow*, Supplement No. 2, Autumn 1961.

Schneider, Herbert. "E. W. G. Diskussionen in England und im Commonwealth," *Aussenpolitik* 1/62 (January 1962).

Shonfield, Andrew. "After Brussels," *Foreign Affairs* Vol. 41, No. 4, July 1963.

Schur, Val. *Labour in Britain and the Six.* London: The Economist Intelligence Unit, 1962.

Self, Peter. "When Britain Joins: The Consequences for Farming and Food," The *Political Quarterly* Vol. 34, No. 1 (January–March 1963).

Shanks, Michael. "Britain and the Common Market: Who Will Lose?" *FBI Review*, No. 141, February 1962, pp. 31–33.

Silkin, Sam, M. P. "From Westminster to Europe." *Socialist Commentary*, September 1966, pp. 5–7.

Social Surveys (Gallup Poll) Ltd. *Britain and the Common Market.* London, 1961.

Soper, J. P. *Europe and the Commonwealth: A Symposium.* London: Friends of Atlantic Union, 1960.

Spaak, Paul-Henri, *Face to Face with Europe.* London: Conservative Political Centre, 1967.

"The Future of Britain's Relations with Europe: A Symposium," *Journal of Common Market Studies,* Vol. III, No. 3 (July 1965).

Trade on the Ebb Tide: The Annual Report of the Manchester Guardian Staff on Industrial Conditions, Problems and Views. Manchester, 1958.

Trades Union Congress. *ABC of the TUC.* London, 1962.

———. *Economic Association with Europe.* London, 1956.

———. *Report,* London, 1957–1966. Supplementary Report No. 3, 1962.

United Kingdom Council of the European Movement. *Britain's Food and the Common Market.* London, 1961.

———. *The Cost of Labour in the United Kingdom and the Six.* London, 1962.

———. *The United Kingdom Economy and the Common Market.* London, 1961.

Valentine, D. G. "When Britain Joins: The Legal Consequences," The *Political Quarterly.* Vol. 34, No. 1 (January–March 1963).

Walston, Lord. *The Farmer and Europe.* London: Fabian Society and International Bureau, 1962.

Warley, T. K. *The Impact of European Economic Integration on British Agriculture and the Commonwealth.* University of Nottingham, Department of Agricultural Economics, June 1961. (Mimeograph).

Winegarten, Asher. "Agriculture—In or Out?" The *Statist,* December 14, 1962.

———. *British Agriculture: The Way Ahead.* (Mimeograph) Release. London: National Farmers' Union, 1966.

United Kingdom Council of the European Movement. *Chairman's Report, 1961–62.*

———. *Our Social Services and the Common Market.* London, 1962.

Williams, Shirley. *Britain and the Free Trade Area.* London: Fabian International Bureau, 1958.

———. "When Britain Joins: The Consequences for Internal Politics," The *Political Quarterly,* Vol. 34, No. 1 (January–March 1963).

Woodcock, George. "The TUC and Europe." The *Spectator,* No. 6765 (February 21, 1958).

Walker-Smith, Sir Derek and Walker, Peter. *A Call to the Commonwealth.* London, 1962.

Westminster Review

Woodburn, Arthur, M. P. *A Common Sense View of the Common Market.* London: United Kingdom Council of the European Movement, 1961.

World Affairs (Published by Federal Union).

Younger, Kenneth. "Britain and the European Community." *The World Today*, January 1967.

――――. "When Britain Joins: The Consequences for External Policy," The *Political Quarterly*, Vol. 34, No. 1 (January–March 1963).

Zebel, Sydney H. "Britain and West European Integration." *Current History*, Vol. 40, No. 233 (January 1961).

INDEX